FREEZE DRYING
FOOD AT HOME FOR
BACKPACKING TRIPS

OTHER SELECTIONS

The Only Beginner Freeze Drying Book You'll Ever Need
*Learn the Simple Process to Create Food Storage for Your Survival
Pantry and Discover Easy Recipes Your Family Will Love*

Workbooks of Batch Logs

* For ANY Brand Freeze-Dryer - Select Number of Trays (5 options)
BATCH LOGS & TIPS WORKBOOKS for 3, 4, 5, 6, or 7 - Trays

* For Harvest Right Brand Freeze-Dryer - Select Model & Select Size (8 options)
COMPANION WORKBOOKS Original or PRO for Sizes X-L, L, M & S

Coming Soon

Making Freeze Dried Candy for Selling and Fun
*Learn the Various Techniques & Recipes to Turn Store-bought Candies
into a Holiday Treat or Wildly Sellable Product*

GO.2MHE.COM

FREEZE DRYING
FOOD AT HOME
FOR
BACKPACKING TRIPS

PREPARE YOURSELF FOR THE TRAIL WITH
BEGINNER HIKING INSTRUCTIONS, DIRECTIONS, AND RECIPES
TO CREATE TASTY, LIGHTWEIGHT, CALORIE DENSE CAMPING MEALS

MICRO-HOMESTEADING EDUCATION

For our adventurous food-loving families!

CONTENTS

INTRODUCTION

Nothing is more liberating than escaping the hustle and bustle of daily life and connecting with the natural world around us. The fresh air alone is enough to cleanse our minds of stress and bring us some momentary peace. Yet, these moments never seem to last, and before we know it, we are back at the desk wishing for more. What better way to prolong this feeling and experience it to the maximum than backpacking through untamed landscapes?

Backpacking is not just a sport or a fun trip; it is a profound and immersive experience that transcends physical activity. It's a transformative journey that challenges us physically, mentally, and spiritually. Beyond the scenic vistas and challenging trails, backpacking offers a gateway to self-discovery and personal growth.

As we traverse rugged landscapes and navigate the wilderness, we strip away the layers of societal expectations and reconnect with our true selves. In the solitude of nature's embrace, we confront our fears, insecurities, and limitations, ultimately emerging stronger, more resilient, and deeply in tune with ourselves and the world around us. Within the whispering winds, the rustling leaves, and the boundless expanse of the night sky, we find solace, clarity, and a profound sense of belonging.

Through the simplicity of life on the trail, we discover the richness of our inner landscape, unearthing hidden talents, passions, and perspectives that were obscured by the noise of modern life. Each step forward becomes a metaphor for personal progress, and every encounter with the natural world serves as a gentle reminder of our interconnectedness with all living beings. In the wilderness, amidst the untamed beauty of the earth, we find not only ourselves but also a renewed sense of purpose, wonder, and gratitude for our existence.

On a backpacking trip with friends, we embarked on an adventure into the wild, feeling fully prepared with all the essentials. However, the challenges of carrying enough food for our journey without overloading our backpacks loomed ahead. It was during this trip that we discovered the convenience of freeze-dried meals. Not everyone had selected lightweight options, and we could see firsthand the vast difference in weight, convenience, and trash. Those few who had freeze-dried meal options benefited greatly.

Incorporating freeze-dried meals into our eating methods significantly improved the experience in the wilderness. These lightweight and compact meals allowed us to enjoy delicious, nourishing food without carrying heavy cans or bulky cookware. Freeze-drying transformed our backpacking experience, making it more convenient and enjoyable.

However, nature is only sometimes peaceful, and traversing through wild landscapes and changing climates can become just the challenge you need. You will navigate dangerous terrain, overcome obstacles, and learn to adapt to unfamiliar environments. This tremendous push out of your comfort zone is liberating, and you will soon discover that you are capable of much more than you ever thought possible.

The journey sounds phenomenal, and it surely can't be that difficult to do, can it? The idea is simple enough: You only need clothes, food, and camping gear. Yet, before you know it, the car is filled with bulky equipment, cookware, toiletries, first aid kits, and every other item you suddenly realize you can't live without. The spontaneous, free-spirited adventure you had in mind is suddenly a weight-laden challenge, and you still need to pack in the groceries. Speaking of groceries, how are you supposed to carry cans of beans, tuna, and spaghetti on your back when carrying them in from the store is heavy enough?

The list of questions without answers grows longer and longer, and your excitement slowly sizzles until you push your new backpack to the back of the closet and give up on the whole idea. The challenge of preparation is not nearly as exciting as the challenge of the hike. Don't give up just yet; where there is a will, there is always a way. If you're an aspiring backpacker eager to learn, you're in luck.

We at Micro-Homesteading Education are passionate advocates of self-sustainability. With over 35 years of experience, our holistic, nature-loving approach to food growth, preservation, and exploration has never failed us. Our love extends far beyond the reach of our homestead and into the remarkable, wild world around us, in which we spend every free second. Through trial and error, long hikes and short walks, delicious meals, and failed experiments, we have developed a foolproof guide to lightweight backpacking.

Lightweight food is the best; no, it's the only real option for backpacking. Commercially dehydrated and freeze-dried food has long held the monopoly regarding backpacking meals. While convenient, they can become incredibly expensive, especially when planning lengthy trips. Dehydrated foods take a long time to rehydrate and become too hard to eat without rehydration. Freeze-drying is not a new preservation method, but it wasn't until recently that you could buy a freeze-dryer and prepare your food in the comfort of your home.

This revolutionary process gives you the opportunity to choose a variety of your favorite ingredients and incorporate them into delicious meals. Gone are the days of picking between meals you don't truly enjoy. A freeze-dryer allows you to prepare your food in bulk, significantly decreasing overall costs.

The cost and taste benefits should motivate your move to freeze-drying, but if not, let's look at the nutritional factor. The most significant difference between freeze-drying and other preservation methods is that freeze-dried food can retain up to 97% of its original nutritional content. This is outstanding compared to other methods, such as freezing, canning, or dehydrating, which can cause the food to lose around 30% or more of its nutritional value.

Backpacking is not for the fainthearted, but it is well worth it, and with this book as your guide, your preparations will be easy. I will guide you through choosing the best equipment for your trip and proper packing techniques to even out your weight load. Get ready to delve into the depths of the wild and learn how to live with nature, allowing you to navigate dangerous terrain and source water while keeping yourself and the environment around you safe.

I will teach you which foods are best to use and the freeze-drying techniques you need to know to prepare your food for the trail correctly. The freeze-drying world can seem daunting, but armed with the knowledge in this book, you will be ready to make your meals, freeze-dry and package them, and take them with you to enjoy on the trail.

Most importantly, I will walk you through the vital world of backpacking nutrition. There is no point in buying the best gear and having the best packing system if your body cannot carry the load. Using lightweight and nutritious food is the way to go. The longer the trip, the more your body can suffer if you aren't prepared. Meal planning and preparation will be the key to keeping your body and mind healthy and capable.

Let's get started.

1

PREPARING FOR YOUR ADVENTURE

The success of an adventure relies solely on your ability to plan it. While this seems exhausting and takes away the spontaneity of the trip, it is well worth it. While it is evident that the right gear, food, and safety equipment are needed, many people forget the importance of scheduling and mapping out your terrain beforehand. It's always best to prepare for the worst and be pleasantly surprised!

Understanding Your Environment

First, you need to understand the environment you're walking into. This is especially important for long trips with little to no cell signal. While the thought of adventuring into the big wild world is exhilarating, consider the challenges you will face. Numerous dangers are lurking, and I am not just talking about the wildlife you will encounter. Weather changes, terrain, and a lack of water can quickly cut your trip short or worse.

Potential Dangers

There is only one way to prepare yourself for danger: RESEARCH. Please choose your location wisely and ensure that it suits your experience level. If you're a first-time backpacker, it's best to avoid underexplored locations for long periods. Pick a relatively familiar place for you, and then start reading.

Wildlife

During your trip, you're going to encounter wildlife. There are no two ways about it! Understanding the species in the area, how to avoid them, and how to deal with confrontation is the only way to take on this challenge. Not all areas will host the same species or population size. Research your chosen location and find out all you can about the wildlife it holds and its habits. Venomous snakes, bears, and mountain lions are generally severe concerns, but don't underestimate the creepy crawlies! Centipedes, scorpions, and ticks can pose just as significant a threat.

Remember, wild animals cannot be spiteful; they do not target humans purposefully and harm them without reason. Humans are viewed as a threat, and the majority of harmful wildlife encounters are due to the animal's need to protect itself. If you want to experience nature, you need to do your part. Keep your camp clean to limit your chances of experiencing a predator encounter. The smell of food, especially meat, can draw them in for a free meal. In times of drought, these encounters are more likely as animals search for food and water.

Encountering a venomous snake is just bad luck. Many species are ambush predators who lie quietly and wait for hours or days until their prey runs past. Most bites occur when the snake is threatened by being picked up or accidentally stepped on. The best method is to avoid the snake by being aware of your surroundings and watching where you step. A happy snake is one that is left alone; if you see one, keep walking.

Creepy crawlies are easily avoided by securing your campsite. Keep your tent netting zipped up and your gear inside, and always double-check your shoes before putting them on in the morning. Ticks pose a different sort of threat. There are hundreds of species, some harmless and some of which transmit some nasty viruses. Walking through tall grasses can increase your chances of finding ticks. Wearing long, loose pants and thick socks while regularly checking your body is the best way to avoid bites. When a tick bites, it will attach itself to you. While this is a scary thought, at least you can be sure it was a tick that bit you. It's best to research your area and find out which ticks occur there so that you can take the necessary precautions if you do get bitten.

The Elements

The Weather

The scariest part of Mother Nature is how quickly her mood can change. Picking the right season is vital. Hiking through snow is not for the fainthearted; only experienced backpackers and climbers should undertake such an adventure. Even our summer, spring, and autumn months can pose unique challenges.

For first-time backpackers, choose a location that has a relatively stable climate. Each area has a unique range of weather patterns and difficulties. Some areas may be more prone to flash floods in summer, while others are more prone to droughts. Numerous online resources track weather patterns and warn hikers of potential storms.

Difficult Terrain

This is where your fitness comes in. Being a runner doesn't mean you can hike Mt Everest. Again, do your research! Pull up some topographical maps of the area you are looking to explore and take note of the spots that are most likely to cause trouble. Large, fast rivers, steep rocky cliffs, and swampy areas can be highly dangerous for inexperienced hikers with no safety gear. Pre-planning is vital; map your route beforehand and ensure you have the right equipment.

Water Sources

Clean, drinkable water is a fundamental necessity whether at home, camping, traveling, or backpacking. Typically half your weight in ounces is an adequate daily amount, but for hiking it's good to double that and have 1 oz per pound of body weight of water to drink.

The Institute of Medicine of the National Academies recommends that women drink 2.7 liters (91 ounces or 11 cups) and men drink 3.7 liters (125 ounces or 15 cups). This estimation is based on an average amount of activity, so imagine how much you should drink when participating in a strenuous outdoor activity.

You will need to consider the climate and terrain further. Walking in direct sunlight for hours on end will severely deplete your hydration levels, and you will need almost double the amount of water per day compared to walking through a forest. It is vital to have the necessary knowledge to find water sources, carry it efficiently, and purify water for consumption.

Finding Water

Carrying a sufficient amount of water for your trip is impossible. This is where pre-planning comes into play. When mapping out your route, use a topographic map, as it allows you to study the terrain in depth. Mark out the most reliable water sources. These should include rivers, lakes, and dams, which are not prone to drying out in the warmer seasons. If you cannot mark definitive water sources, make note of potential water-bearing sites such as valleys and depressions.

However, even extensive planning can only sometimes be truly relied on. You should collect and purify water as often as possible to keep a reliable backup in your pack. Rain is a valuable resource. If you have a water catcher, use it! If not, seek the areas where it is most likely to collect. Tree hollows, puddles, and even dew on plants can be a lifesaver. In more desperate times, you can dig through dry areas near riverbeds or vegetation and see how much water the ground has.

Carrying Water

You want to carry adequate water for drinking without weighing yourself down too much. Water is heavy, weighing just over 2 lbs per liter/quart, and in general, you will need to carry 2–3 liters of drinking water a day. However, remember that you will need more if you are trekking through rugged, hot terrain. While you can't lighten this load, you can use lightweight, durable water bottles or hydration bladders to distribute the weight, making your trip a little easier. Using a filtration straw can reduce or eliminate water weight entirely - other than your backup. Just make sure your path has water readily available.

When choosing a water bottle, I suggest one made of stainless steel. These are pricier but won't break or crack if dropped. As an added bonus, stainless steel will retain the temperature of the water, so you won't need to worry about the water heating up in the sun. I prefer having two smaller 750ml or 1-liter bottles and packing them on either side of my backpack to distribute the weight.

Hydration bladders are helpful as you can drink while you walk. They can be bought in any size up to 5 liters. However, that is a little too heavy, so I propose sizing down. These fit into your backpack near the square of your back, so the weight is distributed evenly. If you opt for a hydration bladder, purchase the more durable ones, as they can puncture or leak, especially during lengthy treks.

Some people use filter straws, some bottles, some bladders, and some prefer to use a combination. Your choice will ultimately depend on your situation and your personal preference. You will need 1-2 liters of drinkable water for food rehydration throughout the day. Always rehydrate your food with clean water. Most meals need ½-1 cup of water per serving so make sure you have enough purified water!

There also needs to be about 2-4 liters for cooking and cleaning. Ensure you set up camp close to a viable water source. Consider carrying a lightweight, collapsible water container, which allows you to collect and carry water short distances for cooking and cleaning without tampering with your drinking water.

Filtering and Purifying Water

At no point should you drink directly from a water source. It may contain harmful bacteria, viruses, and even parasites. You must purify or filter the water to ensure it's clean enough to drink. Thankfully, there are several lightweight ways to do this.

Boiling

The most tried and true method of purification. The general rule of thumb is to keep the water at a steady boil for at least one minute. For altitudes above 2000 meters, let it boil for three minutes. Let's be honest, two extra minutes is not the end of the world, and it's best to be safe rather than sorry later. This method kills most pathogens and parasites, and I recommend it for cleaner water sources.

Filtering

Filters are a convenient way to clean water, requiring little work. Filtration on the move can be achieved by using a bottle filter. A pump and gravity filter will require you to stop at water sources. The upside is that they don't require electricity or heat. The downside is that they can be a little bulky. While they remove bacteria, sediment, and parasites, they are ineffective against viruses. Use these with caution or as an added filtration method.

Chemical Treatments

Iodine or chlorine tablets are lightweight and easy-to-use forms of purification. These tiny tablets are easy to store in your pack, and you can pack a reasonable amount before feeling the weight. They kill off bacteria, viruses, and parasites but won't remove sediment. The downside to chemical treatments is that you will need to wait the recommended time after use to drink your water. Depending on the type or brand you use, this can be anywhere from 30 minutes to 4 hours. This is an excellent overnight purification method if you don't mind the taste.

UV Light

Portable UV lights are an effective purification method as they destroy all pathogens. They are lightweight and easy to use, but they do need batteries. UV Light does not remove sediment, so a separate pre-filter will be required. If you're planning a long trip and need help carting around extra batteries, there are better methods for you.

Supply Points

If you are planning an extended trip, you simply cannot carry the necessary amount of food. Additionally, long trips can cause severe wear and tear on your gear, and you may need to replace it and stock up on vital items such as batteries, first aid supplies, and clothing.

As you plan your route, you may pass near various towns, hostels, hiking lodges, and, depending on location, dedicated backpacking outposts. These places will be your lifeline during long trips. There are two ways that you can make use of these stops. You can purchase food items and gear from the towns you pass through, create supply boxes, and pre-ship them to designated locations. Buying food and gear can be costly, and some towns may not have what you need. It's best to rely on something other than your rest stops if you have allergies or specific dietary limitations.

Consider the types of locations you will be passing. Going through a town, you can use the local post office as a supply point. If you are venturing into a more remote location, you must find the nearest hostel or outpost and arrange for your parcels to be shipped to them. Keep in mind that you will need to work around the stop's opening hours. Make a note of hostels or campsites that you can use in these areas to have a backup plan if you arrive at your supply point late in the day.

Mark off these areas and then calculate how many days you will take to reach each point. If you estimate ten days, make sure you have packed enough food for twelve in case of emergencies. Calculate how many days you will take to reach the next supply point. You must stock your boxes with enough food for the next part of your trek. Pack up your supply boxes and ship them to the designated locations.

Food is your number one priority. Typically, food is a heavy component, but not so when freeze-dried. Remember, you can also stock your boxes with gear, clothing, and other essentials. This can be more difficult to plan, as you would rather not carry extra gear you don't need. Bounce boxes are a great way to combat this. You can stock one box with as much gear and food as you require for your trip and ship it to your first supply point. When you hit your supply point, remove what you need and reship to the next one.

Another way to do this is by delivering your extra gear and food packages to a friend or family member. If you can contact them during the trip, you can ask them to mail what you need to the nearest location. Fortunately, freeze-dried foods are extremely lightweight, so you can pack plenty of homemade Just-Add-Water meals in their individual or family-sized Mylar bags.

Leave No Trace Principles

"Leave No Trace" is precisely how it sounds. This principle is based on promoting sustainable and minimal-impact practices in the wilderness. As a responsible, nature-loving backpacker, you'll want to ensure that the space you walk through is untouched. This includes leaving natural and cultural features undisturbed and respecting the wildlife around you by ensuring that their habitats and food sources are not damaged. Every bit of waste you make must be carried with you until it can be disposed of in a dedicated refuse bin. This includes items classified as "biodegradable," such as toilet paper, paper wrappers, and food scraps.

Campsites can be equally destructive. Wildfires are common, and you must take the proper precautions when building your campfire. When you set up your tent, do not disturb the surrounding land to make yourself more comfortable. Once you pack up your camp, scan the area to ensure it is waste-free, and if you come across litter on your trail, be the better person and pick it up. By adhering to these principles, you preserve the environment, allowing many generations of backpackers to enjoy.

The seven principles of Leave No Trace are:

- Plan Ahead And Prepare
- Travel & Camp On Durable Surfaces
- Leave What You Find

- Respect Wildlife
- Minimize Campfire Impacts
- Dispose of Waste Properly
- Be Considerate Of Other Visitors

MAP YOUR ROUTE!

Mapping Out Your Route

As discussed already, mapping out your route is non-negotiable. It would be best to have your route, water sources, and supply points marked already. With these guidelines, you can mark out separate emergency routes that will allow you to cut your trip short safely and seek help.

If the area is regularly used for backpacking, source a reliable and up-to-date trail map. Stick to the recommended routes and make note of any zones that have been classed as dangerous. If there are no pre-made trail maps, you must mark out your routes on a topographical map, which requires a basic understanding of the map features.

These maps will display key landmarks such as roads, rivers, lakes, and towns. The most beneficial part of these maps is that they show the different vegetation types and terrain. For easier use, each landmark type has its own color. In most cases, green is for vegetation, blue is for water, black is for manufactured structures, and red is for roads. White is used for sparse locations, including anything from desert, snow, rocks, and grass. Boundaries are drawn with broken or dotted lines. These indicate the boundary between national parks, different states, or counties.

The contour lines will be the most important to you, determining the difficulty of your trip. Ideally, you would only pass through mountains, cliffs, or deep valleys with the appropriate equipment.

The first contour line marks the beginning of an elevation change. Each contour line within this marks an additional shift in elevation. The closer the lines are to each other, the steeper the slope. If they are spread out, the incline or decline will happen gradually. Contour lines that form a V facing uphill indicate the presence of a valley. In contrast, lines that form a V facing downhill indicate a ridge. A valley is an excellent marker to note, as these are usually accompanied by a river or stream.

A measurement key at the bottom of each map will allow you to judge the distance and height of each contour line. Getting to know your map well and getting used to calculating distance and elevation is essential.

staying on your toes

Staying On Your Toes

Taking care of yourself physically and mentally is vital to ensuring your health, safety, and enjoyment during your trip. To maintain a healthy body and a healthy mind, you will need to focus on four main aspects: sleep, hydration, fitness, and balanced meals.

Get Enough Sleep

This is crucial. Your body will be under immense strain, and without adequate rest, it will start to give out on you. Sleep not only allows your muscles and vital organs to rest, but it also gives your brain a chance to shut down. As much as you enjoy the scenery, your brain constantly takes in new sights, sounds, and smells and tries to navigate the unknown. It's exhausting.

Without enough sleep, your body will tire, you will become clumsy and disoriented, and you are bound to make mistakes in this state. It would help if you were sleeping for eight hours a night. Make sure you're set up and settled into your camp just before sunset, and plan to wake up at sunrise to have enough time to eat breakfast, pack up, and start your next hike.

Comfort will ultimately determine the quality of your sleep. You will likely wake up stiff and tired if you're continuously tossing and turning. There are a few tips and tricks that you can use to ensure a comfortable night of sleep. Buy a tent with an inner netting and a waterproof cover. When it's hot, you can open the windows and doors while protecting yourself from pesky bugs. Additionally, the waterproof cover helps to hold warmth and will protect you from the cold.

Choose the right sleeping bag! Purchase a good quality bag that is catered for cold climates. This will keep you toasty and provide a comfortable sleep, and if it gets too warm, you can open it up. Too warm is always better than too cold.

Select a good spot to place your tent. Avoid setting up on rocks, roots, or twigs, as they can be incredibly uncomfortable. Additionally, you should take along a sleeping mat, which provides an additional layer of insulation and cushion from the cold ground. Consider taking a pair of earplugs if you struggle with the sounds at night. I prefer ones that block out lighter, annoying sounds but still allow me to hear what is happening outside my tent.

HYDRATE !

Stay Hydrated

Backpacking is a strenuous activity that increases your body's water needs. You now understand how to source, carry, and purify the water you find on your trail. However, you need to know how much of an effect dehydration has on you.

Hydration plays a crucial role in the functioning of your vital organs, particularly digestion. High-water-content foods are easily digestible, but freeze-dried foods have all the moisture removed from them. If not rehydrated correctly or if too much is eaten dry, your body will pull moisture from itself to successfully digest the food. This can cause severe stomach upsets if you do not drink enough water. Hydrate before, during, and after every meal to maintain a properly functioning digestive system.

Dry mouth, dark yellow-colored urine, and dizziness are the most obvious signs of dehydration. These symptoms will get worse as your hydration levels drop. Another way to test your hydration is by pinching the skin on your hand and pulling it upwards. If your skin bounces back, your levels are good. If your skin stands in a tented position for a few seconds, hydrate as soon as possible. Regularly monitoring your hydration status is critical to ensure you drink enough water to meet your body's demands.

Fitness

A long backpacking trip is not for the weak, and if your fitness levels aren't where they should be, you're simply not going to make it. When out on the trail, you should stretch before you head out in the morning and before bed at night. This will keep your joints fluid and your muscles warm.

 To be fully prepared, start a training program at least eight weeks before your trip. You must incorporate several activities to build your core strength, develop lower body strength, and improve your overall endurance.

When participating in a workout routine, it's best not to overdo it. Set aside rest periods. Work on your lower body and core strength at the beginning of your eight weeks. Great workouts to strengthen your muscles and improve your balance include jump squats, hip rolls, squat curls, planking, step-ups, and heel downs. Incorporate short and long walks or runs every other day to increase your overall endurance.

Two weeks before your trip, slow down your exercises and plan at least four long hiking days. These should be around 2 hours long, and you must carry the same pack weight that you would have on your trip. Do this, and you will be ready for your adventure.

Balanced Foods

A balanced, nutritional diet is crucial for maintaining energy levels and fueling your body. It's easy to slip into the routine of eating quick packaged meals that require no preparation, but these meals will start to take their toll, especially when you're out on the trail. You will need to incorporate various wholesome ingredients to create delicious meals that meet your body's needs.

HEALTHY FOOD

Vegetables and fruits taste great and are sources of valuable nutrients, including dietary fiber, vitamins, and minerals. Whole-grain dishes, including pasta and bread, are good sources of complex carbohydrates. Lean proteins such as chicken, turkey, eggs, nuts, and lentils work to repair and build muscle and tissue.

Using these ingredients, you can prepare and freeze-dry the perfect, energizing backpacking meals. Later, adding healthy fats, including nuts, oils, and seeds, will give your body continuous energy. Your backpacking meals need to meet several other requirements and be extra nutritious.

Lightweight

The less you carry, the better. There is only so much weight you can shave off regarding vital gear. The remaining weight loss comes down to choosing suitable types of food. Water is the most significant contributor to the weight of food. The moisture is completely removed through freeze-drying, drastically reducing the weight of the food.

Selecting the correct packaging will also contribute to the weight of your pack. Every bit of packaging you use must be carried until you can reach a dedicated refuse area. If you pack non-freeze-dried foods, consider removing them from any bulky plastic or cardboard packages and repackaging them into smaller reusable bags. This will drastically reduce your waste, and you can reuse these bags throughout the trip.

Ready-to-Eat

Simplicity is key. After a long, hard day, you will not want to set up a camp kitchen and prepare a five-course meal, but you could boil some water. Freeze-dried meals can be packaged in Mylar bags; when you are ready to eat, you just have to add water. There is nothing more straightforward than that. This easy rehydration method will save you energy, time, and clean-up, making it a convenient way to refuel during lunch breaks and stops.

Packable

Your backpack has limited space. To pack efficiently, you want to avoid bulky or 'poofy' items that may be lightweight but take up an immense amount of space. These may include items like bread, bags of chips, and popcorn. Freeze-dried meals take up minimal space compared to bulky canned goods. With its nutrient-dense content, you will get a lot of goodness from a small package.

Non-freeze-dried items such as nuts, seeds, trail mixes, jerky, fruit leather, crackers, and flatbread are great lightweight sources of nutrition and can easily be stored in your backpack's pockets. Again, ditch any excessive packaging to maximize your pack space. If you plan to cook your meals take a small amount of oil. We like avocado oil, which is a healthy, high-heat, delicious oil with many uses.

Shelf-stable

Shelf life doesn't just refer to how long the food stays edible. It also indicates how long the food remains nutritious and flavorful. Freeze-dried food is a fantastic shelf-stable option, as it will retain its nutritional content and flavor for 5-30 years if stored correctly. When backpacking, your freeze-dried foods will easily weather different temperatures, altitudes, and conditions as long as they are packaged correctly. This also makes them ideal options for putting in your bounce boxes.

Non-freeze-dried items such as dried jerky and dehydrated fruit will last around a year if stored in the right conditions. These are also valuable items to have in your pack as on-the-go snacks. Ensuring these are packaged correctly is crucial, as moisture or oxygen can quickly deteriorate the product.

Survival

Surviving in the Wild

Ideally, you want to do as little "surviving" as possible during your trip. However, regardless of extensive planning and packing, there is always a chance that something could go wrong. In these unlikely cases, it's best to be prepared to tackle any challenges you may face.

Handling Emergency Situations

There is a big difference between preparing for an emergency and actually being in one. We all react differently; the most important thing is to keep a clear head. If you're in a situation where you can stop, take a minute to sit down, close your eyes, take a breath, and then plan your exit strategy.

Firstly, you will need to remove yourself from the dangerous situation. How you do this will greatly depend on the scenario, but the most important thing is to grab your pack and get to safety. If you have planned correctly, you will have mapped out an emergency exit route, which allows you to cut your trip short. Pull out your map and compass and calculate the distance to your exit route and safe zone. Depending on the type of emergency, your exit route may be blocked. It's okay; take your time, assess the environment, and develop a new plan. Remember: smart backpackers do not walk at night!

If it's late, set up a temporary camp, but be ready to move as soon as the sun comes up. If you need to move quickly, consider dropping some unnecessary equipment. This goes against the Leave No Trace principles, but occasionally, there is no other option. Pack up your gear and secure it to a nearby tree so that it has a limited impact on the environment. Mark the location on the map so that you can return to it at a later point.

Keep all communication and signaling tools near the top of your pack for easy access. If you hear or see other hikers, use your whistle to signal to them. If you're using a satellite phone, keep it handy and regularly check if you can contact anyone.

Finding Food

Depending on your situation, you may have to deal with a food crisis. You may lose or run out of food or need to ration it. For these events, you will need to understand how to source nourishing and safe food from the wilderness.

Foraging edible plants, berries, and fruits is usually the easiest method. However, this can be extremely dangerous as they can be challenging to identify, and some may be poisonous. Only eat wild berries if you're 100% able to identify them correctly. You can safely source your food by carrying a local guidebook to the region's edible plants. Avoid mushrooms at all costs, as these are extremely difficult to identify.

Another option for food is catching fish or hunting small game. Fishing is likely your best bet, especially if you have a net or tarp to create a trap. You can also use a sharpened stick as a spear. Small game are challenging to hunt as they move fast and will avoid you at all costs. You will need to construct a trap, which can be difficult if you do not have the right gear. Most survival pocketbooks will have diagrams and instructions on how to build such traps. You may also want to learn more about snares and knots.

Making Shelter

Shelter is vital for survival. It offers protection against the elements. Even in the warmer seasons, you need to ensure you have rain protection. Location is critical. You want to camp in a covered area to reduce the impact of wind and rain as much as possible. Setting up a shelter near water is ideal. Consider the type of shelter you are building, and ensure you are safe throughout the night. Avoid water sources in an area with alligators, bears, or mountain lions.

You can create a shelter in several ways, depending on what you have available. A tarp shelter is the easiest if you have the materials. Camping tarps will come with six tie-off points: one on each corner and two in the center of the width. Strap the two-center tie-off points to nearby trees and peg the two back corners into the ground. Find sturdy dead branches to use as makeshift poles for the front ties.

If you don't have the available materials, consider creating a lean-to or debris shelter. You will need to find three long, strong branches. Tie them together to make an arch. Lean this structure against two large trees at a 45-degree angle so that the opening of your shelter is between the trees. Tie this into place to secure it. You can now work on roofing; if you have a tarp, you can throw this over. If not, gather smaller branches and create a grid-like structure. Further, cover this with leaves to finish it off.

Keeping Warm

Maintaining body heat is crucial for survival. Hypothermia sets in much quicker than you think and can quickly become deadly. Having the correct type of clothing and shelter is vital. If you cannot keep warm through shelter alone, start layering your clothing. You want lightweight, quick-drying clothing near your body for the inner layer, a warmer thermal layer in the middle, and heat trappers like raincoats and jackets for your outer layer.

While maintaining your core temperature is vital, do not forget about your hands and feet. Layer your socks; if they get wet at any point, you must remove them immediately. If your shoes are wet, you must change your socks and wrap your feet in something waterproof before putting your shoes back on.

A campfire is an excellent source of warmth. Find a safe spot away from dense grass or foliage and dried leaves to avoid starting a forest fire. Dig out a shallow circle and place rocks around the edges of the circle. Please note where you took these rocks from so that you can put them back. Gather some kindling. This should include dried leaves, birch, and small twigs. You will now need to build a platform fire to cook food. To achieve this, lay two or three thicker branches horizontally. This will be your base. Add smaller branches on top in a teepee formation, and fill the teepee with more kindling.

You can now light your fire. Stay close to your fire to ensure no embers bounce out and ignite the surrounding area. Once you are done and your branches have burnt through, put the fire out using water and then fill the hole with soil.

Staying Safe

Safety should be your top priority during any outdoor adventure. When an emergency occurs, retreat to safety and wait it out. Do not panic and run. The moment it is safe to do so, plan your escape route. If you find yourself having to traverse new terrain, stop and take note of your current position. Check your map and plot out the safest way forward.

If you find yourself in danger at night, you have two options. One, climb a tree! If you find a thick, stable branch, you can secure yourself to the tree using a rope. If you are unable to do so, keep your campfire going. A fire will keep away most wildlife and provide you with a valuable source of warmth and light.

These are some ***basic safety rules*** you should stick to:
1. Do not hike routes that are out of your league
2. Do not go off trail unless necessary
3. Do not approach wild animals
4. Do not walk on rotten or broken logs
5. Do not eat food items that you can't identify
6. Do not cross fast-running rivers
7. Always watch your step!

Protecting Your Food From Wildlife

You can use two methods to protect your food from bears and other wildlife. Bear canisters and Ursacks are sealed containers that animals cannot get into. Bear canisters are the most popular and, in some states, mandatory. These are quite heavy and, unfortunately, have limited storage space.

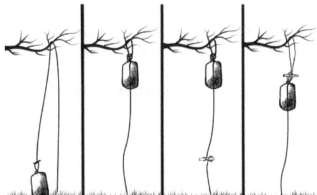

Ursacks are strong bags made from Kevlar. These can be tied to trees at night, and the animals won't be able to get into them. They are much lighter and easy to pack. A bear hang is another popular, lightweight method. You will need a light chord, a small carabiner, a small stuff sack, and a weatherproof sack.

Find a solid tree with a thick trunk and a tall branch that sticks out at least four feet from the base of the tree. Place a rock in your small stuff sack and tie it to the end of your chord. Tie the other end of the chord to an anchor tree. Toss the stuff sack with the rock up and over the tree branch. Aim for the edge of the branch furthest away from the trunk.

Remove the stuff sack and tie your carabiner to the end of the chord. Clip your weatherproof sack (filled with all your food) to the carabiner and thread the other end of your rope through the carabiner. Pull the rope until your food reaches the top of the branch.

You can now tie a stick to the rope. When you let the bag down, the stick will stop the rope from passing the carabiner, and your food bag will be suspended in the air.

Now that you've learned about the basics of backpacking, including ways to lessen dangers, you can feel good knowing you're ready to get started. The following section will prepare you with the gear and equipment to embark on your backpacking adventures. From selecting the right backpack and clothing to essential tools for navigation, hygiene, and safety preparations, we'll equip you with the knowledge and insights to ensure a safe, fun, and comfortable outdoor experience. So, stay with us as we jump into the world of backpacking gear and essentials, making your wilderness journeys even more rewarding.

2

GEARING UP AND PACKING UP

Before you head out on your adventure, you'll stock up on the necessary gear that will become vital to your survival. Your gear will include much more than just clothing and backpacks. You will need a variety of nifty tools, emergency kits, and shelter items to ensure your safety and comfort for the next few weeks.

Essential Backpacking Wear

Comfort and flexibility are key. Without the proper clothing, shoes, and backpack, the cold will seep in, discomfort will settle in, and blisters will develop. Your muscles will start aching, and your trip will become a nightmare. There are tons of products on the market, so you will need to research to find which items best suit your needs.

Backpacks

Choosing the right backpack will decide, in part, the success of your backpacking adventure. Consider a variety of factors before you select the perfect one for you. However, always remember to try on your pack before purchasing it, and don't let the cost be your deciding factor. This pack will become part of your body during your backpacking trip.

Capacity and Size: When selecting the appropriate pack, you need to consider your body shape and the length of your trip. Capacity is generally measured in liters; a standard day trip pack ranges from 20 to 30. For longer trips, look at packs ranging from 40 to 70 liters. Some take a day pack inside their backpack for shorter excursions during the backpacking trip.

The pack's size and shape depend on your body type, so "try before you buy." Find a pack that suits your torso length, hip size, and shoulder width. Each bag is adjustable to a point, so take your time and adjust the pack until it fits perfectly.

Weight Distribution: If the weight of your pack is not evenly distributed, you will continuously suffer from sore muscles and back pain. A good backpack has a padded back, straps, and a hip belt. These are vital as they keep the pack close to your body, removing the strain from your shoulders.

Durability: Don't be cheap when selecting your pack. You want one made from a sturdy material, either nylon or polyester. Check the pockets, zippers, and lining and make sure they are durable and well-stitched. Most backpacks will come with a built-in rain cover; if yours doesn't, purchase one. The padding on the back side of the pack should be well-ventilated to avoid sweat build-up.

Accessibility and Organization: A pack with a variety of compartments, attachment points, and straps will make your packing experience much easier and more convenient. You can separate your gear into appropriate sections, and the attachment points can be used to hold trekking poles, sleeping mats, and water bottles.

Clothing

The clothing you take will depend on the current season and altitude. If you're heading into cold weather, prioritize warm, layered clothes. If it's a hot, rainy season, prioritize waterproof clothing.

When choosing clothing items, opt for lightweight clothes that can be compressed for packing. Several warm but light options exist, such as thermal tights and long-sleeve shirts. Another great option is to select versatile clothing that can serve multiple purposes. Convertible pants are a great idea as you can easily unzip and remove the lower legs and have a pair of shorts instead.

Walking in wet clothing is a no-no, so you must have enough items to change if you do get wet. However, you also don't want to overdo the packing. Your goal will be to wash your clothing on the move, not have a new outfit each day.

Accessories are a necessity. A beanie hat and gloves will keep you warm during cold nights. Pack these regardless of the current season, as you never know when the cold may hit. A sun hat and sunglasses will save you from sunburn on hot days. The layering system is the key to staying comfortable and flexible in various conditions. It usually consists of three layers: a base, mid-layer, and outer shell.

Base Layer: Choose quick-drying, light fabrics such as synthetic blends or merino wool. These items keep your body dry from sweat and will help regulate your body temperature. Make sure to take a mixture of short-sleeve and long-sleeve shirts.

Mid-Layer: This is your insulating layer. Choose light items such as fleece, down, or synthetic jackets. Synthetic fabrics are generally more water-resistant, while down provides an excellent layer of warmth. Down can be bulkier to carry, so check that you will have sufficient space in your backpack.

Outer Shell: This should include jackets or coats that protect you from wind and rain. Waterproof materials are essential here. Select something a bit heavier in winter that will hold your body heat.

Footwear

Thick socks are non-negotiable, no matter the weather. These will provide much-needed padding for your feet, preventing blisters, adding traction, and preventing injuries. The route you take and the terrain you will cover will help you decide which hiking shoes you buy. Wear boots for rougher terrain, as these provide extra support for your ankles, lessening the chance of injury. These are a bit heavy but are often waterproof. If your route is relatively easy and flat, you can opt for a pair of lighter hiking shoes, which offer less support but make walking easier.

Regardless of which you choose, waterproof or water-resistant fabric is a must. You will also need to ensure that the soles of the shoes have enough traction to keep you from slipping. The price comes in at this point. The cheaper the shoes or boots, the more likely the soles will wear down and break.

Before purchasing your shoes, make sure they fit correctly! Take your hiking socks to your fitting, as these are thick and can change the fit of the shoes. Once you have purchased your shoes, wear them daily to break them in. If you don't do this, expect severe blisters on the first few days of your trek.

Necessary Equipment

Now that you're fitted with the appropriate wearable items, start filling that pack. I am about to go through the required, non-negotiable items. These are vital survival tools that will ensure your safety.

Shelter and Sleeping Systems

The quality and weather rating of your tent and sleeping bag will determine your sleep quality, warmth, and protection from the elements. Standard camping tents are heavy, so look for something lightweight with enough protection. Cheaper pop-up tents consist of a single piece. While very convenient and lightweight, moisture can settle on the tent, soaking into your sleeping bag and gear.

Good quality tents come in two pieces. The interior is mesh with an appropriate waterproof base and a rain cover that stays taut, even in heavy rain and wind. The rain cover should never touch the mesh, thus ensuring that you and your gear stay dry. When choosing size, opt for convenience over comfort. If you will be trekking solo, select a solo tent. The weight of the tent will ultimately be the deciding factor. A 3 lb tent is the standard weight for backpacking.

Sleeping bags are generally rated by expected temperatures. You will notice that each is labeled in degrees, and the weight of your bag will increase as the temperatures drop. If you struggle with the cold, opt for a bag that suits a colder temperature than what you expect. For a truly comfortable experience, invest in a sleeping pad. These will increase your comfort and keep the cold from seeping in from the ground. The thicker the foam padding, the more comfortable it will be; however, this will also increase the weight. Test out a few before you make your final decision.

I recommend investing in a camping tarp and emergency blanket as an added emergency measure. Emergency blankets are incredibly lightweight and can be an extra warmth layer for cold nights. Camping tarps are heavier but can be used to build an emergency shelter if your tent breaks. If you are preparing for a long journey in the rainy season, take a tarp!

Tools for Light and Heat

Many of the newer flashlights and headlamps are rechargeable through USB. While these are more environmentally friendly and economical, you may need help finding usable plug points to recharge them. Depending on the length of your trip, you may opt for battery-operated devices and carry extra batteries. Pack extra batteries in your bounce boxes.

Choose a flashlight with additional security settings, such as strobe lights and SOS signaling. Solar or wind-up flashlights are another practical solution, but remember that their light is not nearly as strong as battery-operated options. Fire-starting tools such as waterproof matches and lighters are extremely lightweight. They will allow you to start your campfire more efficiently and provide additional emergency light. A flint and stone tool is another reliable way you can learn to start up fires. Still, I recommend carrying matches or a lighter as a backup. Char cloth can be used as a quick fire-starting tinder. Made of vegetable matter, you only need a small piece to spark a flame. This cloth must be stored in a sealed, small tin to prevent unwanted sparks during your trip.

Reusable heat pads are surprisingly handy, especially on unexpected cold nights. They come in a variety of sizes; I prefer the pocket ones, which are roughly the size of your hand. The strong PVC pouch contains a supersaturated sodium acetate solution and a silver disc. When you bend the disc, the solution becomes solid and produces heat, lasting a few hours. To reset the pouch, you will need to boil it in water for a few minutes.

Navigation Tools

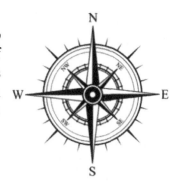

As discussed previously, you must carry a map of the area and a compass to navigate your trail successfully. Both of these should be kept in a waterproof case to prevent damage. Additionally, you can take along digital GPS devices or a smartphone equipped with offline maps. I recommend relying on something other than this, as it will become challenging to keep the devices charged. Excessive use makes you more likely to damage or break the device.

Electronics and Communication

Always keep your cell phone on you. Even if you cannot use it during your trek, you can use it when you get to your rest stops and supply points. However, it's best to pack a durable phone that boosts a long battery life and, if possible, carry a spare battery or charger. Keep the cell phone off when not in use.

If you take electronics, such as GPS devices or rechargeable flashlights, make sure you have a reliable charging source. A power bank is a great accessory, but even these can only hold a limited amount of battery, and they will add a noticeable amount of weight. Solar-powered power banks are your best option, but you must ensure they are adequately charged daily. Clip your power bank onto the top of your bag to charge as much as possible during your trek.

Always carry a whistle, whether you're backpacking, camping, or hiking, preferably attached for easy access. Whistles signal to other hikers, rangers, or members of your party that you need help. A signal mirror is another lightweight but efficient emergency communication tool. It reflects light and signals others in the area when you cannot make noise.

Protection and Self-Defense

Be sure to fully understand the most recent laws and regulations regarding pepper spray, tasers, firearms, and other personal protection tools in the state you've chosen to backpack. Keep in mind that certain nature parks will have additional regulations to follow. A few tools with dual use for safety include the strobe light function on your flashlight, pepper spray, multi-tool, and wildlife deterrents such as bear sprays. In some parks, bear sprays are a requirement. These work the same way as pepper spray and are filled with an irritant and spray at a range of 30 feet, which will immediately deter any charging or attacking bears.

Documents and Identification

I cannot stress this enough. Always ensure that you have all of your essential documents on you. To avoid damage, these should be folded and placed into a waterproof sealed bag or travel wallet. It's best to keep them in a section of your backpack that is easily accessible but won't be used regularly to avoid dropping them accidentally.

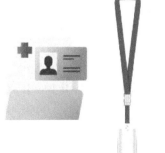

Your travel wallet should include your identification documents, such as your ID card, passport, and driver's license. Keep a copy of your medical documents, including your insurance plan, allergy information, and reliable emergency contacts. Carry your bank card and some cash for rest stops that don't take cards.

A copy of the local map and trail guides is essential. If walking through multiple locations, consider leaving maps in your bounce box to avoid carrying too many. Finally, always keep a notepad and pen. You can write down important information such as markers for direction and water sources and any relevant information that may be useful in emergencies.

Storage and Bags

You never quite know when rain will hit, and you must have a secure, dry place to store any of your electronic items or documents. Ziplock bags work well; I never hike anywhere without Ziplock bags. They are surprisingly handy in a pinch. Depending on the size, you can use them to collect berries or tinder. You can carry water in a pinch, store uneaten food, and seal any small loose objects. I like to use them for wet trash, especially sanitary items, as they prevent leaks.

However, I prefer sturdy, reusable, resealable, waterproof plastic bags and cases for expensive electronic items. These are readily available in the camping section. When compressed, stuff sacks contain no air and are best for storing foods, clothes, and other equipment. Another good option is dry sacks, which are a little bulkier and don't compress quite as well. These essential storage tools will separate your items and make them easier to find. It is best to carry at least one to store wet clothes or equipment.

Survival Tools

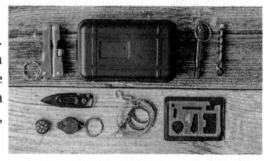

A multi-tool or Swiss Army knife is an all-in-one survival tool. These nifty gadgets come with several features depending on the model you buy. However, even the low-range models are fitted with two knives, a tweezer, pliers, a corkscrew, a can opener, and a bottle opener. Regardless of your chosen model, purchase a durable brand that will last you a lifetime.

Lightweight, strong rope or cordage, such as paracord, is a necessity that can be used in many situations. You can use it to hang your food, your laundry, or a tarp for shelter. It's a vital piece of safety equipment when attempting climbs or crossing rivers. You can also use it to tether yourself to other members of your party when an emergency forces you to walk at night. Duct tape is a surprisingly useful tool. It can be used for anything from patching up tears and cracks in your equipment to taping up poles or tarps to create a shelter. You can even use it to patch up your shoes.

You don't need to carry a textbook, but keep a Survival Guide pocketbook to guide you through the wilderness. These guidebooks will teach you with diagrams how to build shelter, start fires, find food, and perform first aid if necessary. These are great in an emergency; they remind you to do things right even if you have already learned the skills. I recommend purchasing a book that details how to forage for and identify edible plants in the area. If you can't accurately identify your food, don't eat it!

Hygiene and First Aid

Staying clean is vital to comfort and health. Bacteria and parasites breed in dirt; if you don't keep yourself clean, you may become ill and disorientated. Cuts should be treated and kept as clean as possible to avoid bacteria. However, staying clean isn't just important for you and the surrounding environment. Only use environmentally friendly cleaning products and toiletries to keep our rivers and streams clean.

Toiletries

Choose your toiletries carefully. You can either purchase travel-sized products or decant your products into travel-sized bottles. When it comes to dental care, buy a travel kit. These small kits come with a small toothpaste, a collapsible toothbrush, a reusable toothpick, and a reusable floss.

For body and hair care, buy an all-in-one shower and hair gel. I don't recommend carting around soap bars, as these are difficult to store and go mushy quickly if not completely dried. A compact, microfiber towel is best, as these are lightweight and dry rapidly. Body wipes are another nice addition.

Make sure that you pack a travel nail clipper. If you don't trim your toenails regularly, you will quickly find yourself in extreme pain and struggling to walk! Additionally, long fingernails can gather dirt and become a breeding ground for bacteria. A broken nail should be filed down as soon as possible, as it can snag on clothing and gear.

Your toiletry bag should include a small lip balm, insect repellent, and strong sunscreen. When backpacking, it's crucial to consider the environmental impact of your toiletry choices. Opt for eco-friendly options whenever possible to minimize your carbon footprint. Proper disposal of toiletry containers is essential to protect the environment and wildlife.

Sanitation

Leave no trace! Each time you pack up your tent, scan the surrounding area to ensure it is left pristine. Use a stuff sack for dry waste and a waterproof, sealable bag for wet waste. You must carry this waste until you reach a rest stop or supply point.

Human waste is a little more challenging to deal with. Urine does not necessarily pose a risk as long as you don't urinate in water sources.

Any toilet paper used must be packed in a sealed bag afterward. Different areas will have additional regulations regarding human solid waste. In highly sensitive ecosystems, you may also be required to pack your waste. You can use a portable toilet or "wag bag." These specialized waste disposal kits securely hold waste, making it safe and hygienic to carry it until you reach a designated refuse area.

For less sensitive environments, you can use the cat hole method, which involves digging a hole into the ground, doing your business, and then covering the hole with soil and natural vegetation. You must ensure you're at least 200 feet from trails, water sources, and campsites. Make sure to pack any toilet paper used into a sealed bag.

To avoid excessive packing, wash your clothes on the go. Ideally, you want to be able to do this at your rest stops, but in some cases, it's unavoidable. Gather water from a nearby water source and use an environmentally friendly laundry detergent to wash your clothes. Dispose of this water in a space void of vegetation. Do not rinse your clothes in a water source to avoid contaminating the water.

First Aid

You never know what may happen on your trip. It could be a splinter, a cut, a bruise, a burn, or a broken limb, so it is vital to have a well-equipped first aid. When packing your items, consider how many people you will be hiking with and calculate how many of each item you need.

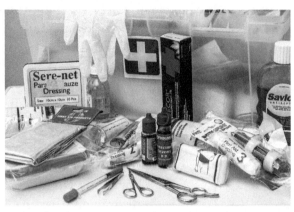

Store-bought first aid kits will stock a few of the most essential items, but you may need to add some extras. When buying supplies, there is no need to worry about going for bulk deals. Choose individually packaged items to ensure sterility. Your first aid bag will depend on your preference. You can purchase hard shells or fabric ones. Hard shells will keep your supplies safe but can take up a lot of space. Fabric is easy to compress into your bag, but make sure that you select a durable, waterproof material to keep your supplies safe.

Having a first aid guidebook on hand is excellent, but I strongly suggest you take a first aid course before starting your trip. You will need to thoroughly understand how to dress wounds, treat bites, and splint broken bones should the need arise. There is a checklist in Appendix 3.

First Aid Kit

1. Disposable gloves: Pack at least two pairs of disposable gloves. These should be put on before touching any open wounds to stop dirt, debris, and bacteria on your hands from entering the wound.
2. Scissors: Compact, strong scissors will help you cut bandages and clothing. The multi-tool you purchased will likely have a pair of scissors, but these are often not strong enough to cut through thick clothing.
3. Tweezers: Again, your multi-tool will be tweezer-equipped, but the one in your first aid kit will be more sterile. Use these to remove splinters, stingers, ticks, or debris from wounds. Sterilize your tweezers after each use, especially if used on open wounds.
4. Thermometer: A compact, battery-operated thermometer will allow you to monitor fevers, which is especially important if you have had an open wound that may be getting infected. Quickly identifying a fever will give you time to take the appropriate medication. Make sure that the battery is full before setting out.
5. Safety Pins: These can be used for so many things. They can secure bandages and are handy to use with temporary patches for any clothing or equipment tears.
6. Waterproof adhesive bandages: These are nice to have on hand for minor injuries such as cuts, blisters, and stings. Be sure to pack a variety of sizes.
7. Triangular bandages: These are generally used as slings, but due to their size, they can be used to secure splints or bandage larger wounds.
8. Elastic bandages: I suggest you take various widths and lengths. These will be used to cover wounds and secure sprains or breaks.
9. Adhesive tape: Tape secures bandages, gauze, and splints. In a pinch, medical tape can be used as a temporary stitch to hold cuts together. Still, any deep wounds will need medical attention immediately.

10. Moleskin: Pack a few of these to help alleviate blisters or hotspots on your feet. If you ever feel one coming on, stop immediately and treat it. Untreated blisters can become extremely painful and infected, especially on the feet.

11. Sterile gauze pads: Gauze pads can be used to stop bleeding and to clean wounds. They are also essential for dressing larger wounds and provide extra protection under a bandage. Gauze pads and tape can be used without a bandage to make a wound pad in a pinch.

12. Antiseptic wipes or solution: This will be used to clean wounds and equipment. Any wound must be thoroughly washed before being dressed and cleaned every time the injury is redressed. Keeping wounds clean will prevent bacteria from getting in and causing an infection.

13. Alcohol-based hand sanitizer: Opt for a fragrance-free hand sanitizer to disinfect your hands and equipment before and after use. While not recommended, it can also be used to clean a wound if you have run out of antiseptic solution.

14. CPR mask: These small devices are used to safely administer CPR to other people.

15. Instant cold packs: Cold packs can ease swelling from bites and sprains. Holding them on your forehead can relieve headaches and help reduce fevers.

16. Burn shield and burn cream: It's essential to take the appropriate precautions when lighting a fire and cooking, but still, accidents do happen, and burns are not as uncommon as they should be. A burn shield will provide immediate relief to the burned area and stop the burn from going deeper. You can carry an additional burn cream if you're accident-prone or plan to use campfires for cooking.

17. Antiseptic ointment: Apply thoroughly to cleaned wounds before they have been dressed. It will create an antibacterial barrier over the wound and promote general healing.

18. Pain relievers: Opt for common pain relievers that won't cause drowsiness or adverse reactions. These can include ibuprofen, acetaminophen, or paracetamol. These relieve pain but can also combat fevers.

19. Antihistamines: Pack tablets and ointments. These are used for allergic reactions, and the ointments will combat itchiness and rashes from skin contact allergens such as nettle or insect stings. If you're prone to severe allergies, ensure you have packed an EpiPen.

20. Antidiarrheal medication: Diarrhea is not something you want to deal with when you're in the wilderness. You can become severely dehydrated, and the consequences of no treatment can be fatal.

21. Charcoal Tablets: Depending on the brand, these can be taken directly or mixed with water. They soothe stomach upsets and combat food poisoning and other types of minor toxicity.

22. Personal medications and prescriptions: Pack enough stock of your prescription medications. Pack extras in your bounce boxes to ensure a continuous stock.

23. Snakebite kite: This is not always necessary, but you should have one if you are trekking through an area notorious for venomous snakes.

24. First aid manual: This guide will contain detailed diagrams of how to perform basic aid procedures.

Packing It All Up!

Once you have all your gear, it's time to perfect your packing strategy. Packing your supplies efficiently and effectively is crucial for a successful backpacking trip. You want to create a balanced, compressed backpack that fits all your gear while keeping your items accessible and secure.

Gather all your gear and place it into its appropriate category: clothing, shelter, cookware, food, hygiene, first aid, navigation, and miscellaneous tools. Use stuff sacks to pack similar bulky items together; you can further organize your gear from here. For example, pack your meals in order, from last to first. Your clothing can be loaded into separate sacks for cold or warm weather. The choice is up to you.

You will need to pack your backpack in layers. The bottom layer should contain your heavy and dense gear to distribute the weight and help you maintain balance. These items include those you won't need to grab in a hurry, such as your sleeping bag, rope, and extra shoes. I usually place any extra dry sacks and sealable bags here.

The middle layer should contain medium-weight items like cooking equipment, food, and clothes. Try to spread these items out evenly to maintain balance. The top layer should include items that you will use regularly. Pack your water purification supplies, snacks, and rain gear.

Depending on the pack you purchase, you should have several storage areas, including smaller compartments on the side, top, and hip belt. Use smaller compartments for small items, such as your compass, maps, multi-tools, and electronics. Keep your frequently used items in the most accessible areas.

Your pack should also have attachment points, loops, and straps. Use these to secure items such as a rain jacket or water bottles. At the bottom of your pack, you should have two loops to strap in your sleep mat and tent.

Final Weight Considerations

With all your gear packed, it's time for a trial hike. Take a walk on terrain similar to what you will be trekking for at least 60 minutes. You will be able to tell quickly whether your pack is too heavy or not. If it feels comfortable, then you packed successfully. Don't be cheeky and toss in extra items. Your backpack will feel heavier each day you walk, even if there is less in it.

If the pack is too heavy to bear, re-evaluate what you have packed. You may need to remove items or purchase more lightweight options.

A trial hike will also allow you to feel how well the weight is distributed. If you find that one side is heavier than the other, you may have to adjust your packing. Uneven weight distribution will lead to muscle strain and cramps.

As we conclude this chapter on essential backpacking gear and preparations, you've gained valuable insights to embark on unforgettable outdoor adventures. From selecting the right backpack to mastering vital skills, you're well on your way to becoming a seasoned backpacker. Now, let's focus on the benefits of freeze-dried food for backpacking. Discover how freeze-drying can revolutionize your outdoor culinary experience, providing lightweight, nutritious, and delicious meals fueling your wilderness adventures.

3

UNDERSTANDING YOUR FOOD

There's a big difference between buying pre-packaged foods and preparing your own. While the convenience is undeniable, and the foods may be tasty, the preservation methods often destroy the product's nutritional value. By preparing your food at home, you can avoid the extra sugars, salts, and preservatives that taint pre-packaged food.

You'll need to understand what ingredients your meals contain and how these ingredients and their nutritional value affect your body. In this chapter, I will walk you through food basics, meal preparation, and how to portion your food to create healthy, energy-filled meals.

Benefits of Freeze-Dried Food for Backpacking

There aren't really any downsides to using freeze-dried food. The meals are easy to prepare, store well, and are easy to rehydrate, making them incredibly convenient. These are all essential factors, beneficial for camping, hiking, and backpacking trips, where you must pack as many nutritious, lightweight meals as you can carry.

Lightweight and Space-Saving

When hiking with a backpack, every ounce matters. That bulky food may not feel too heavy initially, but once you have a few miles behind you, your back and joints will start to feel the stress from the weight. During freeze-drying, all the moisture is removed from the food, significantly reducing the weight. This lightweight alternative is a no-brainer regarding weight restrictions, allowing you to travel faster and enjoy even the most difficult paths. As a bonus, you can freeze-dry full meals, reducing or eliminating the need to carry any extra ingredients and cooking equipment. Due to this space-saving perk, you could fit a few extra meals into your pack and extend your journey.

Nutritional Value and Caloric Density

Backpacking is a physically demanding activity that can be difficult and even damaging to the body and mind if unprepared. You must be fit enough to carry your body weight and the added weight of your backpack and gear. Keeping up with the high-energy demands can be challenging. The best way to do this is to eat nutritional and calorie-dense foods.

Nutritional foods will provide your body with the essential vitamins, minerals, and macronutrients needed to thrive. However, more is required for backpacking. You will have to prepare meals with a high caloric density, which means a lot more energy from less food. High-calorie food with a low sugar content releases steady energy, allowing you to travel for an extended period without energy crashes or fatigue. Unlike other preservation methods, freeze-dried food retains its nutritional value.

Long Shelf Life and Convenience

One of the most notable benefits of freeze-dried food is its impressive shelf-life. If packaged and stored appropriately, these meals can retain nutritional value for anywhere between 5 and 15 years, dependent on ingredients. This advantage lets you pre-plan your meals and build a dependable food supply.

When planning a new adventure, all you'll have to do is go to the pantry and pack your bag with your favorite meals. Additionally, freeze-dried meals require minimal preparation, making them an ideal choice for quick, effortless meals on the trail. If you intend to use rest stops and bounce boxes, you can store your food in the boxes without worry of contamination or degradation.

Easy Preparation and Cleanup

Simplicity is vital whether camping, hiking or on a 3-week backpacking trip. You want to avoid the hassle of setting up a kitchen area and preparing meals from individual ingredients. Freeze-dried food is the key to simple cooking. It's easy to prepare and even easier to clean up, making it the perfect option for outdoor enthusiasts. Most meals require nothing more than adding water to the bag or container. Within a few minutes, your meal will be fully rehydrated and ready to enjoy. No cooking process or hard work is needed. For a hot meal, all that is required is boiling water!

This convenience extends to cleanup as well. When rehydrating and eating your meals directly from the Mylar bag, you only need hot or cold water and an appropriate utensil. Once your meal is finished, fold up the package and pack it away. There is no need to carry extensive cookware or wash a pile of dishes after every meal. Plus, you don't have to worry about carrying tons of trash! This easy preparation and cleanup allows you to focus on what truly matters during your backpacking trip—immersing yourself in nature, enjoying the scenery, and embracing the endless adventure.

Freeze-dried food and the many positives in our adventures

Freeze-dried food is a true lifesaver in keeping our backpacks light. Removing moisture during processing makes these meals remarkably lightweight—a game-changer for our family's treks. Even better, we can carry complete freeze-dried meals without the weight of extra ingredients or bulky cookware. It's like having a pantry in our backpacks, extending our journey without the excess weight. Our family appreciates being well-prepared for the physical demands of backpacking, and freeze-dried meals play a crucial role in this process. They're packed with essential nutrients and offer the high caloric density we need to keep us going. These meals provide steady energy, preventing fatigue and energy crashes. And the best part? Freeze-drying preserves all the good stuff, ensuring we stay in top form on the trail. Freeze-dried food's impressive shelf life is a blessing for our family's adventures. Whether it's a spur-of-the-moment trip or a well-planned expedition, we can count on these meals to be nutritious and delicious.

We've had our fair share of moments on the trail, but one thing's for sure—freeze-dried food has made life easier. Our trusty freeze-dried chicken salad pouch and crackers have become staples in our backpacks. The pouch transforms into a flavorful and nourishing meal with just a bit of water. There is no need for complex cooking equipment; there is just simplicity in the wild, letting us enjoy the great outdoors without the fuss.

Preparation is a breeze, a process we've cherished over the years. And cleanup? A cinch! Most meals can be enjoyed directly in the packaging, reducing the hassle and letting us focus on what matters—quality time together amidst nature's beauty. Freeze-dried food is a convenient and enjoyable addition to our family's outdoor experiences. It keeps our packs light, our bellies satisfied, and our adventures unforgettable.

Nutritional Considerations for Backpacking

Not all food is the same; everyone knows that. We have a range of food types that provide us with different benefits and energy sources. Each type contains various vitamins and minerals that keep our immune systems up and our bodies functioning correctly. At the same time, fats, proteins, and carbohydrates are our primary energy sources. Understanding your ingredients and creating meals that will provide you with what you need for a long, taxing backpacking adventure is essential.

Balanced Macronutrients: Carbohydrates, Protein, and Fat

Macronutrients are your primary energy source and should be the bulk of your meals. Creating meals with a balanced ratio will ensure that you have a steady flow of energy and that your body can recover after extended physical exertion. Your macronutrients are split into three main groups: Carbohydrates, Fats, and Proteins. As the primary fuel source for your muscles, carbohydrates are essential for quick and sustained energy during taxing physical activities. For this reason, they should form a significant portion of your meals, at around 50-65% in each meal. Aim to include healthy carbohydrates that provide steady energy without spiking your blood sugar levels. These include whole grains (brown rice, quinoa, oats, whole wheat pasta, bread, and couscous), vegetables (sweet potato, butternut, and corn), and legumes (lentils, chickpeas, and beans).

Fats provide long-lasting energy, which is vital for endurance activities. They also support various bodily functions and assist in the absorption of several vitamins. Including around 20-35% fat in your meals is ideal. When choosing fatty foods, ensure that you opt for the healthiest options. Avocado, coconut chips, and chia seeds are rich in healthy fats and will freeze-dry well. Other vital fat-filled foods include dark chocolate, nuts, and seeds (flaxseed, almonds, walnuts, and pumpkin seeds) and various kinds of nut butter. While these fats can't be freeze-dried, you can carry single-serving packages.

Proteins are a valuable energy source, but most importantly, they offer vital muscle repair and recovery, which is crucial when partaking in strenuous activities. Each meal should contain around 10-25% protein. Some of the healthiest options include lean meats, cheese, beans, lentils, and tofu. These ratios and ingredients are guidelines, and you need to consider that everyone's body works a little differently. You may function better on a higher carb vs. fat ratio, which is also acceptable. The most important part of meal planning and preparation is choosing healthy macronutrient sources.

Micronutrients: Vitamins and Minerals

Micronutrients are just as essential as macronutrients, as they provide your body with a variety of vitamins and minerals that promote overall health and well-being. Most of the macronutrients I suggested already contain valuable micronutrients, with the most important being nuts, seeds, quinoa, and chia seeds, which contain vitamin B, magnesium, and zinc.

You can also add ingredients to beef up the nutritional value of your meals. Dark leafy greens, like kale, tatsoi, and spinach, are excellent sources of iron, calcium, and vitamins A, C, and K. A variety of fruits, such as apricots, mangoes, and figs, contain potassium and vitamins A and C. I recommend taking powdered greens and seaweed snacks for an added boost. These are easy to carry and can be mixed into drinks or meals.

Hydration and Electrolyte Balance

The obvious solution to maintaining proper hydration is drinking water. However, there are other ways to maintain hydration and essential electrolyte balance. Sodium, magnesium, and potassium play vital roles in balancing fluid levels and muscle function. Incorporating foods rich in these minerals into your meals can boost your body's hydration when out on the trail. The best food items that can be successfully freeze-dried include bananas, spinach, oranges, and coconut.

Meal Planning and Portioning for Backpacking

Pre-planning your meals is absolutely vital. Without the right kind or amount of food, your trip could take a dark turn. When planning your meals, you will need to consider a few factors, the most important being the ability to pack enough food to last the trip while still being physically able to carry the weight.

Creating Balanced Meal Plans

Having a balanced meal plan is crucial for a backpacking trip. You will be expending energy and will need to keep your body nourished and hydrated. Aim to get your calories spread out during the day with 25% at breakfast 15% at lunch 25% at dinner, and 35% in snacks scattered throughout the day.

While you don't want to carry an excessive amount of food, you also can't risk running out. Document the number of days you plan to hike. If this is an estimation, document two extra days to be on the safe side. Next, calculate how many meals per day you intend to eat.

Minimum requirements include one breakfast, one dinner, and appropriate snacks to provide energy throughout the day. But you may want to have three meals plus snacks every day when going on a 3- or 5-day hike. You should carry at least twenty meals plus snacks for a ten-day hike. If you're in a position where you can use rest stops or bounce boxes, I recommend that you use them! But also be sure you carry two to four extra meals between each stop in case of emergencies. When deciding which meals to pack, consider several factors, such as your personal taste, caloric needs, and the physical demands of your route.

Determining Caloric Needs

Backpacking is a strenuous activity that requires a significant amount of energy. The meals you pack and eat may be quite different from the ones you eat every day. Calculate your caloric needs based on your body weight, metabolism, and, most importantly, the duration and difficulty of the trip. You will also have to consider the weather patterns. On colder days, you may need to eat more, as your body will expend more energy to keep warm. While on hotter days, hydration is your main priority. Note in advance which days may impact your appetite, and pack your meals to suit them.

Backpacking typically requires a higher energy expenditure, with recommended daily caloric intake ranging between 2500 to 4500 calories. To meet these needs, we suggest consuming approximately 2-4 servings for each meal. For those creating your own meal plans for backpacking or outdoor activities, it's important to consider your caloric intake. Adequate nutrition is key to maintaining energy and health during your backpacking adventures.

If you are an amateur backpacker embarking on a demanding trip, I recommend consulting with a nutritionist to be safe. Online calorie calculators can also be used, but it's important to remember that these can be inaccurate as they don't consider things like the weather, your walking speed, and your metabolic rate.

Another way to calculate your caloric needs is to use your body weight. Simply multiply your weight (in pounds) by an indicator of activity from 15 (resting) to 30 (all day hike). See Appendix 3 for more information about this. Once you calculate your daily caloric needs, add the total to your meal plan. You will need to pack meals that, when added together, total this need per day.

Portion Control and Food Weight Management

To ensure that you have enough food while maintaining a balanced pack weight, you will need to seriously consider the weight of each meal and portion your food correctly. Stocking up on calorie-dense foods will reduce your need for larger portions.

You can portion your meals into single-person packages or two-person meals if you plan to feed more than yourself. Most importantly, don't try to save on packaging by packing too large a portion, which will take up extra space and likely go to waste. Even worse, by forcing yourself to finish larger portions, you can end up feeling bloated and uncomfortable, which is a serious no-no when out in the wild.

The best time to portion is before you put your meal into the freeze-dryer. Once your food is prepared, you can use a digital scale to create meal portions of equal portions. Using tray dividers to separate the portions during freeze-drying makes it a cinch. Once the process is finished, reweigh your portions and mark down how much water will be required to rehydrate each one.

Organizing for Variety

When deciding which meals to pack, I recommend making a diverse selection. Nothing is worse than having to eat the same food for days. Choose nutritious meals with a variety of flavors, textures, and ingredients to truly enjoy your food experience. If you decide to take a few of the same meals, at least spread it out so that you aren't eating the same thing two days in a row. Mark these meals down on your Meal Plan (See Appendix 3) and ensure their calorie content matches your daily requirements.

Then, pack them into your backpack backward. If you will be on the trail for ten days, pack your tenth-day meal first and work your way to day one. Packing this way will make it much easier to remove the desired food without unpacking everything. I also like to label my food with the day, which helps me monitor my stock and ensure that I am only eating what I should.

Helpful Kitchen Tools

Numerous kitchen tools can simplify your preparation process. You may already have some of these around the house, but I like to keep a drawer of freeze-dry-only tools so that when I start my food prep, I have everything I need in one place.

Measuring Cups and Spoons

There is a big difference between a pinch of salt and a teaspoon of salt. Measuring cups and spoons are vital to avoid these mistakes when preparing food. Measuring seasonings becomes even more important when planning to freeze-dry your meals for backpacking. You likely won't be taking any extra ingredients or spices to "fix" flavor disasters.

Digital Scale

An accurate digital scale is crucial for preparing freeze-dried food. The scale can weigh your trays of food and the portion amounts for the trip. Weighing and separating your meal portions beforehand will make your life much easier when you start rehydrating your food.

Your scale will also be used to calculate the moisture loss of your food, which aids you in testing the dryness of your dishes once freeze-dried. Place an empty tray on the scale and press "tare" to clear the weight of the tray. Load your food and write down the weight. Once your food has been freeze-dried, you will do the weight check until dry. Then, you can take the final weight and mark down the lost moisture. Use this difference to measure the water needed to rehydrate your meals. See the rehydration worksheet in Appendix 3 to figure this out quickly. This difference can be written on your freeze-dried package, making the rehydration process easier, especially on the trail.

Food Processor

A food processor is helpful for so many things. This versatile tool can finely chop, slice, and grate ingredients and blend them to create purées and sauces. It can prepare a larger portion of ingredients in a very short amount of time, saving your hands and fingers a lot of trouble. You can purchase different types of food processors which have different capabilities. Since you will be preparing your food in bulk, I suggest purchasing a high-end product capable of performing multiple functions without hassle.

Utensils

You will be preparing a lot of food in one go. A durable, sharp knife, a variety of serving spoons and spatulas, and a large ladle can make preparation easier. Figure out what kinds of food you will be freeze-drying and find or purchase the appropriate tools to cook them.

Blender

Blenders work slightly differently from food processors. They generally have a blade for wetter recipes such as soups and smoothies. Others are made specifically for dry ingredients. They will blend ingredients seamlessly while your processor works better at chopping your ingredients. The blender is your best option to make nutritional powders to rehydrate into smoothies. We recommend using a Vitamix blender, which has the power and capabilities to do many tasks, including crushing ice.

Instant-Pot

An instant pot can save a considerable amount of time as it can cook many meals in a much shorter time span. Most instant pots have seven basic functions. These are rice cooker, slow cooker, pressure cooker, steamer, sauté pan, yogurt maker, and food warmer. There is SO MUCH you can do with an instant pot! These are ideal for preparing meals that traditionally take a long time to cook, such as stews, soups, and roasts, but they are not limited to that. You can cook anything from rotisserie chickens to hard-boiled eggs and delicious desserts. Leaving your meals to cook in an instant pot will give you the time to prepare the rest of your food.

Mandoline Slicer

I did not realize how much I needed a mandoline slicer until I got one. Now, I can't live without it. These devices are made up of a flat surface with a sharp blade, similar to a grater but much more precise. The blades can be changed depending on which brand you purchase. The blade types will accommodate your need for different cutting and chopping techniques and your preferred food size. I love this device as it reduces my cutting time and produces much more uniform slices of food, all while keeping my fingers intact.

Meat Thermometer

Food safety is critical when preparing freeze-dried meals. Meat can become a dangerous vector for bacteria if not cooked correctly. When you think your food is cooked, you can push the thermometer into its thick center and get an accurate reading of the current internal temperature. Different meats have different ideal temperatures, which are needed to kill off any bacteria and pathogens. Ground meats, including beef, lamb, and pork, must be between 155°F and 160°F. Whole meats, such as chops, steak, and roasts, need to be between 145°F and 150°F, and chicken should always be between 165°F and 170°F for safe consumption.

Other Useful Kitchen Tools

Having an array of kitchen tools at your disposal will make your preparation time more effective. Some helpful tools you likely already have include peelers and corers, enabling you to remove centers and stems from fruits and vegetables and peel off any hard, unwanted skins.

Colanders and strainers are just as handy and will help you rinse and drain your food without losing any pieces. You can never go wrong with sharp knives, quality cutting boards, and a knife sharpener. These will help with efficiency and give you more space when slicing and dicing the foods.

As we conclude our exploration of the many benefits that freeze-dried food brings to the world of backpacking, you've gained valuable insights into how it can revolutionize your outdoor culinary experience. From its lightweight and space-saving advantages to its long shelf life and easy preparation, freeze-dried food offers a game-changing solution for adventurers like yourself. Now, let's venture into the fascinating world of freeze-drying equipment. In the next chapter, we'll delve into the essential tools and techniques required to harness the power of freeze-drying and transform your favorite ingredients into backpacking-friendly meals.

4

LEARNING FREEZE-DRYING BASICS

Freeze-drying can initially seem daunting, but as long as you understand the process and stick to the basic rules, it's super simple and so rewarding. In this chapter, I will cover the basics of freeze-drying that you need to know, including some tips and tricks learned along my journey. For comprehensive information on how to get started with a freeze-dryer, check out "The Only Beginner Freeze Drying Book You'll Ever Need," which can be found on Amazon.

Freeze-Drying Equipment

I purchased my freeze-dryer from Harvest Right when it was the Home model. Harvest Right is the largest manufacturer and has the longest track record. Other manufacturers, such as Stay Fresh and Blue Alpine, also have good machines. This book will sometimes reference Harvest Right, as that is the one I have experience with.

Freeze-dryers from Harvest Right come in four sizes and three colors: black, white, or stainless steel. In 2023, Harvest Right announced its PRO line. Stay Fresh offers tray and pump options for its medium-sized machine, Blue Alpine offers three sizes, and Prep4Life has different varieties of one. Deciding which one is right for you can be challenging, especially if you are new to the world of food preservation. Check out the different capacities in Appendix 3.

If you don't own a freeze-dryer yet, ask yourself a couple of questions and be truly honest with your answers. How often do you intend to use your freeze-dryer? What will you use it for? How often will you go backpacking? How big is your family? Do you have a garden? How large are the batches you want to make? Do you want to create food storage for an emergency? Do you want to reduce your daily waste and grocery costs? Once you have answered these, you can determine which size will best suit your needs.

Freeze-Dryers

Your freeze-dryer needs a clean and dry environment that maintains a temperature between 45°F and 75°F. Ensure there is adequate space and ventilation on both sides and use fans when warm. Essential components of your freeze-dryer include the following.

1. The main chamber is where the magic happens. Ice rings adhere to the sides of the chamber. Be sure to defrost your machine each time you use it. Keep the rubber gasket clean and latch the acrylic door.
2. The shelving unit sits inside the chamber and is equipped with orange mats, the primary heat source for your freeze-dryer. The mats are located on the underside of each shelf so they can heat the trays. The shelving unit plugs into the chamber.
3. The vacuum pump is a component that supplies the freeze dryer with the pressure it requires. It connects to your freeze-dryer in two places: the power cord goes into the plug in the back, and the hose connects to the right side. The freeze-dryer controls when the pump is turned on and off. Make sure you do NOT plug the pump into a wall outlet.
4. The drain line is located on the left side of the machine, but can be switched to the right side if needed. After a freeze-drying cycle, the water from the machine will drain out of this tubing. The freeze-dryer shows a prompt to close the valve before starting the cycle. You will open the valve up slowly afterwards. When defrosting, the ice melts, and the water drains from the hose into your waste bucket.
5. The interface control panel is located on the front of the machine. This screen displays the current temperatures, pressure, and processing time. You can customize and adjust your freeze-drying settings. Set your Extra Dry Time to 12-24 hours.

When purchasing a Harvest Right freeze-dryer, you will also receive Mylar bags, Oxygen absorbers, a set of trays, an impulse sealer, an oil filter, and oil to prepare you for your first batches.

Accessories

Several accessories can make your freeze-drying experience more efficient and enjoyable while producing top-quality batches. Most of these products can be purchased with your freeze-dryer. Some items, such as pump oil and Mylar bags, need to be replaced as they are used to keep your operation running effectively.

Extra Trays

You can never really have enough. Pre-freezing your food in your household freezer is a great way to reduce your batch cycle time. To reduce the amount of time between batches, I lay out my food on a second set of trays and pop them in the freezer while my already pre-frozen food is going into the freeze-dryer. I am lucky enough to have a third set of trays to prepare while waiting.

Tray Lids

The tray lids from <u>Harvest Right</u> protect your food and save a ton of space by stacking your trays on top of each other. Remove your lids before placing your trays into the freeze-dryer, as this can hinder the process. An added benefit is that you can use these lids as extra trays. You can pre-freeze food in the lids, which have dividers, and are perfectly safe to use in the freeze-dryer.

Vacuum Pump Oil

Pump oil is non-negotiable. Without it, your machine doesn't run! It is best to change to fresh oil after a set number of uses (Standard pump: every 5 uses; Premium pump: after 30 uses). You can reuse old oil by properly filtering it, but I like to be prepared and have a spare bottle or two of new pump oil on hand in case something goes wrong during the filtering process.

Mylar Bags and Oxygen Absorbers

Another non-negotiable product. These are the best Harvest Right-approved packaging materials that you can use. 7mil Mylar bags are thick, silver bags that seal airtight with an Impulse sealer. They are top-rated as they completely protect your freeze-dried food against moisture, light, and oxygen, three of the enemies of food. Oxygen absorbers protect foods inside the bag. They are placed within the bag to keep your food fresh by removing the oxygen left behind after sealing.

Silicone Mats and Parchment Paper

These are used to line the bottom of your freeze-dryer trays. Silicone mats work fantastically for juicy fruits, making it easy to get them off the trays and into the bags. I use parchment paper primarily to freeze-dry candies, but it also works well for other sticky items. The paper stops the food from sticking to the tray, making it easy to remove and separate your batch once it's done.

Parchment paper can be bought in rolls or pre-cut, depending on your preference. Silicone mats are pricier but reusable, making them worth it in the long run. Never use silicone mats or parchment paper when processing liquids, as it will seep below the mat, making cleanup a nightmare. If you know you'll be freeze-drying an item that will puff up significantly (such as caramels or taffy), it can be helpful to place parchment paper on top of the foods so if they swell, they won't get stuck to the shelf above.

Oil Filter Replacement Cartridges

When purchasing your freeze-dryer, you will receive an oil filter and cartridges, which can be used to clean your old oil for reuse. These are simple to use and help your vacuum pump run smoothly. See the maintenance section to learn more about oil changes. It's best to replace the filter cartridge after every 20-30 uses to ensure proper filtration. These cartridges can be purchased from Harvest Right.

Tray Scoop

Another inexpensive and completely worth-it tool, these scoops are designed to work well with stainless steel trays. Some are wide scoops, and some have a funnel on the other. Scoop up your freeze-dried food and easily place it into your Mylar bags.

Tray Dividers

Tray dividers are essential for portioning food for individual servings. They can also separate different food groups on the same tray. I like to use them to portion out my food so that I don't have to try to cut and separate it after the cycle.

Roller Berry

The roller berry from Frozen Right may look a bit terrifying, but it is pretty handy when dealing with fruits and berries. Roll this tool over your food to easily pierce the skins of the fruits and accelerate your freeze-drying process. Berries and other foods with an outer skin, like tomatoes, need to have the skin pierced or sliced so the moisture can easily sublimate out.

Ice Guards

When freeze-drying high-moisture foods, the ice forming around the circular chamber may become too thick. If the ice starts to form on the trays, your machine will work harder as it attempts to dry the food thoroughly. This has two unfortunate results: a batch that's not fully dry and needs to be rerun or a prolonged cycle that takes additional time and hikes up your electricity bill. Always stay within the recommended weight limits for your machine size. Lower the amount of high-moisture foods on your trays, or get some ice guards. Ice guards are specially designed to fit around the top and bottom of your shelving unit and catch any excess ice that may form.

Chopper

A chopper is a kitchen tool designed for efficient and consistent chopping, dicing, and mincing of vegetables and other foods. I love my PL8 Professional Chopper. It includes a ½-inch chopper, ¼-inch dicer, and ⅛-inch mincer, along with a removable bin for easy ingredient transfer. You can also chop right over your freeze-drying tray. Made from stainless steel and silicone, it is durable and rust-resistant. This chopper is a lifesaver, reducing meal prep time and providing convenience.

Necessary Extras

To make your life easy, find or purchase an oil funnel, a fan, a bucket, and permanent markers. While you may already have these in your home, you may want to buy a few new ones and mark them for freeze-dry-use-only. I have two funnels. One is used to avoid spills while refilling my oil, and the second is a special large funnel for putting food into canning jars. Make sure you know which one is which. The bucket is non-negotiable, as it stays under the drain hose to catch water during defrosting. Without this, you can expect a flooded floor.

My fan is used to keep the ambient temperature in the room down and keep the machine from getting too hot. The permanent markers I use for package labeling. While they seem insignificant now, nothing is worse than packing up your food only to realize you can't remember which package is which.

Setting up your Machine

Properly setting up your freeze-dryer is crucial for optimal performance and safe operation. Read your owner's manual and follow the steps. Assuming you already have your freeze-dryer set up, below is a brief reminder list so you can check the steps and avoid causing machine damage or ruined batches.

1. Find a suitable location. As fantastic as these machines are, they aren't exactly the quietest. If you intend to run continuous cycles, find a space where the noise won't bother you. A spare room or basement works well as long as it's clean and well-ventilated. The freeze-dryer must be placed on a level surface (or slight slope to the back for drainage), such as a countertop or a strong table. Ensure that the surface you choose is strong enough to support its weight.

2. Ensure proper ventilation. To maintain optimal airflow during operation, ensure that the freeze-dryer's side vents remain unobstructed and have sufficient open space. Dust or debris in the room can cause the vents to become dirty and clog the cooling fins. The machine functions best in a relatively cool (45°F-75°F) environment. Anything too hot can overheat your machine or lengthen the cycles by as much as double. If everything looks good, leave the machine to rest for 24 hours before running a test. But complete the other tasks.

3. Check inside the chamber and ensure the shelving unit is right-side up. The stainless steel trays should slide on the stainless steel shelves, with the orange heating mats on the underside. Inspect and clean the inside of the door and the rubber gasket around it. You should have inspected the rest of the machine and accessories upon arrival. (Do not accept a damaged machine; contact the manufacturer for a replacement.) Securely close the door using the two-stage locking system.

4. Do not turn it on, but plug your freeze-dryer into a wall outlet prepared for your size machine. For large and X-large machines, a dedicated 20 amp circuit for a 110-volt NEMA 5-20 outlet is required. For small and medium machines, a 110-volt outlet will work, though upgrading the electrical for all freeze-dryers is recommended. Be sure to double-check the manufacturer's instructions.

5. Securely attach the drain tubing to the fitting on the left side of the machine. To avoid water suction, insert two ⅜" Y fittings (purchased separately). Find the drain valve and make sure it's turned perpendicular to the vinyl tubing. The valve must be securely closed while running and opened slowly once the cycle is complete. The vinyl tubing should hang loosely in a bucket to catch the sublimated water when it melts.

6. The vacuum pump should be positioned to the right or below your freeze-dryer. Set it up by adding pump oil to the midpoint and connecting the pump hose to the right side of the machine. Your vacuum pump supplies your freeze-dryer with the pressure it needs to function, so ensure that everything is secure, but don't overtighten. Plug the vacuum pump into the receptacle on the back of your machine and flip the switch to ON. The freeze-dryer will operate the pump as needed.

Once 24 hours have passed, you can turn on your freeze-dryer, check out the control panel, run some functional tests, and start the bread run.

1. The control panel is straightforward to use and should start up 3-5 seconds after the freeze-dryer is flipped on (the switch is on the back.) When you turn your machine on, you will see two options. "Customize" and "Start."
2. If you have a Harvest Right, you will see the logo at the top left of the screen. Click this logo to move into the functional testing menu. Follow your manufacturer's instructions to complete the functional tests of 'Freeze' and 'Vacuum.'
3. Now that your machine is fully functional, it's time for the "bread run." All you need to do is lay a few slices of bread on your trays and select "Start" on the control panel, beginning a complete freeze-drying cycle. The bread run is used to rid your machine of that "new car smell" so it doesn't taint your future batches.

Maintenance

Regular and consistent maintenance is essential to ensure your freeze-dryer performs optimally and continuously produces top-quality products. It is important to check your manufacturer's guidelines and change your oil as often as necessary. There are a couple of home maintenance tasks that you can perform to ensure the longevity of your machine. You can keep track of maintenance tasks on the worksheet in Appendix 3.

Exterior Cleaning

Use a soft cloth, dish soap, and warm water to wipe down the outside of your freeze-dryer, including the handle and screen. Remove any debris or food residue on the outside of the machine and keep the surrounding area clean.

Interior Cleaning

Cleaning the inside of your machine is a bit more complicated, as several parts must be considered. You can use warm water with dish soap, isopropyl alcohol, or Everclear. It's imperative to avoid using abrasive household cleaners, vinegar, and scourers, as they can damage the interior. Before you start an interior clean, turn the freeze-dryer off and unplug it from the wall. Be careful not to get any water on the plug or socket.

When you're ready to clean, and your machine is safely unplugged, you can open the door and remove the black rubber gasket and the shelving unit. The shelving unit is heavy, so be prepared. It is connected to the machine by a cable, which can be unlocked by pressing the tab. Wipe down the shelving unit and gasket and allow them time to dry.

Clean the chamber, making sure that no food debris remains. You may also need to clean out the drain hose, which can be done by pouring soapy water or alcohol down the line to flush out any debris. If necessary, you can use a tube scrubber. Dry the chamber, shelving unit, and gasket with a soft towel. Placing a fan to blow in the chamber will speed up the drying process.

You can now reconnect the cables and put the shelving unit back into place. Fit the rubber gasket back on and close the door to test if it is tight. If the door doesn't seal, move the gasket out a bit and reseat it. Plug your freeze-dryer back in, turn it on, and you are all set!

Inspections

You can inspect your machine for abnormalities during your routine cleaning. Focus on the seals, gaskets, and trays, as these suffer from wear and tear. Check for any cracks, tears, rust, and general deterioration. If you find something you're unsure of, especially loose or damaged components, contact your manufacturer or a qualified technician to conduct a proper inspection. The quicker you identify the problems, the easier they are to fix.

Regular Use

As with any machine, regular use is required for optimal functionality. If this isn't done, some components can deteriorate and seize. If you are not using your freeze-dryer regularly, run maintenance cycles occasionally to keep it in check. To plan for an extended period of downtime, empty and refill your pump with fresh oil and store it with the door and valve open to avoid mold in the chamber. Check your manufacturer's guidelines for how to store your machine properly when not in use.

Oil Changes

To maintain the vacuum pump and remove any potential contaminants, change the oil after a set number of batches. Your freeze-dryer should notify you when it is time, but the general rule of thumb is every 4–5 batches for a standard pump and every 20-30 batches for a premier pump. If the oil inside the pump appears cloudy, contaminated, or has an unusual coloration, then it's time to change the oil, no matter what.

The process of changing the oil is straightforward with five simple steps:

1. Begin by opening the oil drain valve on your oil pump, allowing all the oil to flow into a suitable container, such as an old yogurt container.
2. If necessary, gently tilt the pump to remove as much oil as possible without causing it to enter the demister.
3. Close the drain valve securely.
4. Slowly replenish it with clean, high-quality new or well-filtered vacuum pump oil. Pour the oil gradually until it reaches the midpoint at the front of the pump (sight glass). Avoid overfilling.
5. Seal the fill port securely after refilling it.

Always adhere to the pump's guidelines for oil changes, as outlined in the accompanying manual. Filtered and clear oil can be reused, but cleanliness is essential.
The oil filtration procedure is equally straightforward:

1. Place the used oil in the freezer for a minimum of several hours, with overnight being more effective. This step is crucial as it separates water from the used oil during freezing.
2. Pour the chilled oil into the filter that came with your freeze-dryer. Discard any ice or sediment settled at the container's bottom instead of letting it go into the filter. Ensure the container is thoroughly cleaned for future use.
3. Allow the oil to pass slowly through the filter over time.
4. Transfer the filtered oil into the original quart container used previously. For most pumps, around 600ml of oil is required to be filled adequately.

You can purchase new vacuum pump oil directly from Harvest Right or reuse old oil. The Oil-free pumps are louder and hotter than the premium pumps and quieter than the (old) standard pumps. They are more expensive, may require regular maintenance, and need an adapter (which you can get from Harvest Right for free). I like the Premium pumps, as they are easy to use, and the oil changes aren't too often - maybe once every month or two.

Safety Precautions

Your freeze-dryer is an expensive piece of machinery and should be treated with care. Following the set-up instructions and performing maintenance tasks regularly will ensure that your machine continues to perform without issue. However, several other safety precautions must be considered to ensure your safety.

Using a well-ventilated room and following the proper electrical procedures will prevent overheating and potential electrical fires. Use outlets with the recommended voltage, ensure your power cables are intact, and keep the electrical sockets dry.

Your machine is capable of running long cycles without supervision. The freeze-drying process involves heat, cooling, and high pressure to freeze-dry food effectively. Do not open the door or interrupt these cycles or components during the drying part of the process. If, for whatever reason, you need to interrupt the cycle for safety purposes, make sure you release the pressure slowly by opening the drain valve before opening the door.

As always, it is best to read through the manufacturer's user manual before starting your first cycle and get a refresher before trying anything new with your machine. Next, we will discuss prepping and processing foods, including your favorite home-cooked meals, so you can enjoy them while trekking through the wilderness.

5

PROCESSING FOOD IN YOUR FREEZE-DRYER

Nothing is more satisfying than eating the comforts of home while on the backpacking trail. Another reason why creating your very own healthy freeze-dried meals is so awesome! We have complete control and get to select the recipes and ingredients that we use.

Prepping Foods for the Freeze-Dryer

Proper food preparation will make all the difference in the success of your batches and the overall quality of your food. Not all ingredients or meals will freeze-dry at the same rate, and you will want to consider the differences between moisture-rich and drier foods. Considering all these factors, you can set your freeze-drying experience up for success and have meals that suit your needs.

Preparing Complete Meals

Pre-cooking and portioning complete meals will be the most convenient and space-saving option for your backpacking trip. Packing full meals will significantly reduce your packaging and, therefore, your waste, helping you better stick to the "leave no trace" principle. The downside to packaging entire meals is that they may store for less time than individual ingredients.

Meals containing fatty ingredients will last 1–5 years and should be rotated regularly. Fattiness won't be a factor if you are prepping meals for use within that time frame. Try to stick to simple meals that pack a nutritional, tasty punch. Since pre-made meals are the easiest to prepare and use while backpacking, it is what we recommend. There are recipes in Appendix 2, from meals to treats.

Family Backpacking Meals

For backpacking, we've discovered that pre-cooking and portioning one-pot meals is convenient and sustainable. Our family takes pride in minimizing waste and protecting the environment. One strategy we've found particularly effective is preparing double or triple recipes for dinner and then freeze-drying the excess. This way, we have hearty, homemade meals ready for our outdoor adventures (and emergency meals). While it's true that meals containing meats or fatty ingredients won't store as long as individual ingredients, we've found that they

remain perfectly edible for 1–5 years, often much longer, giving us plenty of time to enjoy them. Regular rotation ensures that we always have fresh, delicious options on hand. We understand that complex meals with multiple ingredients can pose challenges during the freeze-drying and rehydration processes. Different food items may dry and rehydrate at different rates, potentially making meal preparation more complex.

The recipes in Appendix 2 have been tested during our backpacking adventures, ensuring they satisfy our taste buds and streamline the cooking process in the great outdoors. Preparing whole meals for backpacking has become a family tradition that adds a personal touch to our trips. It's a way to savor the flavors of home while reveling in the beauty of nature.

Freeze-drying Individual Ingredients

Typically, freeze-drying individual ingredients is done with long-term storage in mind. But, if you enjoy sitting by a campfire as you prepare, assemble, and cook meals, you may want to consider freeze-drying individual ingredients. This will take a bit more preparation and planning, but it can be worth it if done right. You will still need a rough idea of what you want to eat on your backpacking journey, and then prepare your ingredients separately.

Start with a base for your meals; good options include grains, oats, pasta, or rice. Then, decide which proteins best suit your taste and dietary restrictions. Make sure that these will go well with your bases. Lastly, add some tasty, nutritional extras, including vegetables, cheeses, pastes, or fruits. Appendix 1 has instructions for freeze-drying over a hundred of the most common foods available.

The most difficult part of preparing these meals is ensuring you don't overpack. Calculate how much of each ingredient you will use per meal and portion your packages accordingly. Not everyone enjoys the same food, and when packing for a family, you can prepare a meal base and add additional ingredients according to each person's taste and dietary restrictions. When preparing your ingredients, you can either pre-cook them or keep them raw. Meat can be freeze-dried raw, but for convenience and safety, I recommend cooking it for backpacking meals.

The 3 preparation rules to follow:

Blanching

Blanching is a pre-treatment for food. It involves immersing the food in boiling water and then rapidly cooling it by placing it into ice water immediately after. Generally used for tubers and roots, like carrots and potatoes, as well as foods with a tough skin, like grapes. The process is essential to ensure the longevity of your food, as it deactivates the enzymes and microbes responsible for general decay. This deactivation helps preserve more sensitive food's color, flavor, and nutritional content, even during lengthy storage periods.

Slicing & Dicing

If you have ever had to defrost food, you know how frustrating it can be when the outer layer is ready to be cooked, but the inside is still as solid as a rock! Now, imagine how much harder your machine must work to sublimate the moisture from thick, chunky pieces. Slicing your ingredients into smaller, uniform pieces will enable your machine to dry the food quicker and more consistently, which means less dry time and fewer worries about some pieces retaining moisture. Cut your ingredients into pieces no larger than ½"-¾." For whole meals or portions, stick to the ¾" thickness rule.

Spicing

Spicing your food will make no difference to the actual freeze-drying process; however, it makes all the difference when you rehydrate it. Play with different spices and seasonings to create unique and delicious flavors that preserve well during freeze-drying and storage. You will eventually appreciate it when you enjoy a delightful, flavor-filled meal. Just remember that freeze-drying can make the flavors really pop, so avoid overseasoning your food and sprinkle in a bit more during rehydration if needed.

Using Canned Goods

There are plenty of ways to incorporate canned goods into your camping meals; even better, you can freeze-dry the contents. Freeze-drying can be especially useful if you have canned items reaching the expiration date. Most canned foods are preserved through heat after being placed in liquid, such as salt water, brine, oil, tomato sauce, or onion stock.

If you're using canned fruits or vegetables, drain and save the liquid before freeze-drying. Place vegetables directly on the trays. Canned fruits should be rinsed with water in a colander to remove any sugary syrup before freeze-drying. The result is a delicious snack with fruits as tasty as candy. The liquid can also be freeze-dried, and the powder can be used as flavoring. Canned meals such as chili and soups can be freeze-dried directly from the can. This option is very convenient for those who only cook a little or want to avoid the hassle of figuring out nutritional guidelines for home-cooked meals. Heavy oils can damage your freeze-dryer, so watch out for foods loaded with fats. Always check the ingredients before attempting a batch.

For general household use, freeze-drying canned items can significantly decrease waste. Tomato paste is my favorite example, as I can never seem to use it all before it expires. By freeze-drying the tomato paste, I can add the powder directly to my food or rehydrate it whenever needed.

Side Note on Trail Snacks

Trail snacks are essential for sustaining energy during your hike. They're a great way to give your body a boost when you're starting to tire out without having to stop and rest. The most common trail snacks include energy bars, nuts, raisins, and dried fruit. You wouldn't freeze-dry these items; just include them in your rations, if desired.

However, several snacks can be prepared and freeze-dried to add variety and keep your food experience interesting. Freeze-drying these snacks will help retain their original nutritional content, increasing the amount of energy you get from each one.

Choosing the right kinds of snacks will make all the difference. You want food items to be tasty even when not rehydrated while still maintaining a good balance of carbohydrates, proteins, and fats. I like to make my own trail mixes with various freeze-dried fruits and vegetables with a dash of seeds and nuts and the occasional sweet treat like chocolate or marshmallows. I then portion these into single-serving snack packs. Another option is to portion several days' worth of snacks into resealable bags to avoid excess waste while still protecting them from moisture and oxygen. Check out the snack recipes in Appendix 2 for some delicious snack ideas.

Including Non-Freeze-Dried Extras

Your freeze-dried meals will be the central part of your backpacking food. However, incorporating non-freeze-dried extras can make a pleasant difference to the taste and texture of your meals. The right ingredients can even increase the nutritional value of your meal. Textures like jerky and fruit leather are nice to have to mix it up. The taste and texture of seeds and nuts can be a game changer and a bonus of fats, which your freeze-dried foods could be lacking. Pack avocado oil if you plan to cook your meals over the fire. Depending on what kinds of meals you are taking, consider taking along single-serving packets of condiments or seasoning if you're packing pasta, meat, or stew meals.

If you want to avoid the cost of purchasing small, single-serving packages, you can use a FoodSaver or Impulse sealer to package the items yourself. Don't fret about buying tiny bags; you can use a bigger plastic bag and seal three sides. Add your spices or condiments and seal the fourth side. Ziplock bags also work well for temporary storage and come in many sizes to suit your needs.

When carrying liquids, I double-bag them to protect them from my equipment's punctures or pops. I store my condiment packages in a Ziplock bag, and seasonings and powders separately. Before adding your seasoning or extras to meals, make sure your food is fully rehydrated to avoid overpowering your meal with spices. Avoid taking anything fresh that can spoil in the heat. Dairy items are especially prone to go rancid and will usually last a day. Freeze-dry your dairy products beforehand for shelf-stable options that only need a bit of water. Also, consider taking individual packets of nut butter instead of regular butter (both of which cannot be freeze-dried.)

The Freeze-Drying Process

The freeze-drying process may seem complicated, but it will feel push-button easy once you learn it. When you start your freeze-dryer for its first cycle, you will notice that it goes through several phases until the entire process is complete. Understanding these phases and learning to use the customization menu when freeze-drying tricky foods is important for success.

The Phases

Pre-cooling

The pre-cooling phase happens first. This prepares your machine for freeze-drying by cooling the chamber to 32°F. The pre-cooling phase will take around fifteen minutes and works well for most meals and ingredients. However, you can adjust the temperature and time through the customization menu, which is especially useful when planning to freeze-dry more difficult foods such as ice cream. In this case, you'll want to pre-freeze for 60 minutes so the chamber can cool down much further.

Freezing

Once the pre-cooling phase is complete, you will place your trays full of food onto the shelving rack. Remember to close your drain valve and ensure the door is fully sealed. The freezing phase will begin, dropping the temperature within the chamber to an extreme low and completely freezing the food within it solid. The length of this cycle differs depending on the type of food you are freeze-drying. Foods with high moisture will extend the cycle. To cut down on time, you can pre-freeze your food in your home freezer overnight. I recommend always pre-freezing your batches.

Vacuum Freezing

At this point, your vacuum pump will turn on and create a vacuum, drastically decreasing the pressure in the chamber. This will further drop the temperature. Once the pressure hits around 500mT, the heaters on the shelving unit will kick in. These heaters will turn on and off, and the mTor pressure will change up or down depending on the pressure within the chamber. At this point, the water in the food will turn to vapor, and once it touches the chamber walls, it will turn into ice. This process will continue until all the moisture in the food has collected in ice form on the chamber walls.

Drying

The drying phase is the longest and technically the final phase, depending on the type of food you're freeze-drying. At this point, your machine is trying to remove the last little drops of moisture. The pressure should be consistently under 500mT, and the heaters will stay on for the rest of the process. This phase will take a long time to complete, so be patient.

⇒ Extra... Dry Time! ⇐

Extra Dry Time

After drying, your machine will switch into Extra Dry Time and run as long as you set your default. (We recommend 12-24 hours.) Foods cannot be over-dried, so don't worry about going too long. At any time after it's switched into Extra Dry Time, you will need to press Cancel so you can remove your food and test it for any moisture. Before you remove the food, remember that you need to release the pressure in the machine. You can do this by slowly opening the drain valve and allowing it to vent for five minutes. Double-check that your drain hose is not sitting in water from the previous defrost.

Now that it's safe to remove the food, it's time to perform the "Two Hour Weight Check" to ensure your food is completely dry before packaging. We will discuss how to do this shortly. I have also learned from experience to monitor the pressure gauge during the drying cycles. The lower the pressure, the dryer the food. Naturally, this will vary depending on your environment, especially your elevation. Once the pressure is consistently low, your food should be ready. After completing the two-hour weight check to determine your food is dry, you can package it up.

Always Defrost

Defrost

Once your food is out, you can start the defrosting process. Don't skip this super important step, as your chamber needs to be completely free of ice to ensure the success of your next batch. Make sure your drain valve is open, and the hose is in a bucket to catch the water. You can defrost your machine in two ways.

The first is a manual defrost. Leave the machine open and allow the ice to melt naturally. This method can take some time, but facing a fan into the chamber can speed this up to 30 min or so.

The second method is to use the machine's defrost cycle. The heaters will kick in and stay on for around 2 hours until all the ice has melted. We prefer the manual method as it's simple, uses no electricity, and is faster!

Freeze-Drying Technique

Now that you understand the process let's discuss techniques to make your experience more enjoyable. While following these tips will ensure your success, don't get frustrated if you make mistakes, especially in the beginning. You are learning, and eventually, you'll get the hang of it.

Again, if you are brand new to freeze-drying, you may want to check out the in-depth information in "The Only Beginner Freeze Drying Book You'll Ever Need." It has entire chapters dedicated to setup, maintenance, and food preparation.

Loading the Freeze-Dryer

How you load your trays can make or break the success of your batch. Each tray, depending on your freeze-dryer size, can handle freeze-drying a certain amount of weight without issue. Weigh your food to ensure that you stay within the guidelines. ALWAYS STAY WITHIN WEIGHT LIMITS.

Lay your food out in single layers with adequate space between foods. If plenty of weight is available, a second layer can be added (with parchment or silicone racks between). Overcrowded trays and thick chunks are a significant problem. They will not only take an extra long time to freeze-dry but also put more stress on your freeze-dryer, potentially shortening its lifespan.

Prepare the foods you plan to process in slices ½" to ¾" thick, pieces ¾" or smaller, or liquids ½" deep. Dilute sugary liquids 50:50 to avoid bubbling over. ALWAYS PRE-FREEZE LIQUIDS. We recommend pre-freezing everything.

Tray Maximum Amounts

Harvest Right HOME	Max Weight	Max Liquid	Machine Maximums	
Small, 3 tray	2.3 lbs	3.3 cups	7 lbs	10 cups
Medium, 4 tray	2.5 lbs	4.2 cups	10 lbs	16.8 cups
Large, 5 tray	3.2 lbs	5.9 cups	16 lbs	29.5 cups
X-Large, 6 tray	5.8 lbs	10.5 cups	35 lbs	62.4 cups

Harvest Right PRO	Max Weight	Max Liquid	Machine Maximums	
SmallPRO, 4 tray	2.5 lbs	3.7 cups	10 lbs	15 cups
MediumPRO, 5 tray	3 lbs	4.7 cups	15 lbs	23.4 cups
LargePRO, 6 tray	4.5 lbs	6.4 cups	27 lbs	38.3 cups
X-LargePRO, 7 tray	7.1 lbs	11.1 cups	50 lbs	78 cups

StayFresh	Max Weight	Max Liquid	Machine Maximums	
Medium, 4 tray	4.5 lbs	5.5 cups	18 lbs	22 cups
Medium, 7 tray	2.5 lbs	5.5 cups	18 lbs	38.5 cups
Mega, 6 tray	8.3 lbs	10 cups	50 lbs	60 cups

Blue Alpine	Max Weight	Max Liquid	Machine Maximums	
Medium, 5 tray	3 lbs	4 cups	15 lbs	20 cups
Large, 5 tray	5 lbs	8.1 cups	25 lbs	40.5 cups

Prep4Life	Max Weight	Max Liquid	Machine Maximums	
The Cube, 4 tray	3.5 lbs	5.7 cups	14 lbs	23 cups

Temperature and Time Customization

You can run most things using the default settings when your freeze-dryer is fully set up and ready. However, you can also use the customization menu when freeze-drying more advanced foods. Adjusting the temperatures can help reduce cycle time and ensure top-quality produce. When you go to the customization menu on the control panel, you will see that the machine is set to the following defaults:

- Initial Freeze: -10°F
- Extra Freeze Time: 0:00
- Dry Mode: Normal
- Dry Temp.: 125°F
- Extra Dry Time: 2:00 hours

From here, you can adjust these settings or restore your changes to default if necessary. You can lower the initial freeze temperature to -20°F, ensuring the food stays completely frozen before the process starts. I recommend using this setting when freeze-drying items like ice cream, eggs, soups, and other liquid items (All of which should be pre-frozen.)

You can also adjust your dry temperature from between 35°F to 150°F. How you adjust this will be highly food-dependent. As a general rule, most foods work well at the defaults. However, your herbs and probiotic dairy (such as yogurt) should be processed at 90°F. Most candy has extremely low moisture and should be processed at around 145°F. If you need more specifics on processing candy, check out Micro-Homesteading Education's book 'Making Freeze-Dried Candy for Selling and Fun!'

I recommend setting your extra dry time to 12–24 hours to give yourself as much time as possible to get to it. If your batch finishes in the middle of the night, your extra dry time will automatically kick in, saving you from getting up and packing your food. Your customization menu and machine capabilities will depend on the brand and model. Always check your manufacturer's manual before adjusting the machine settings.

WEIGHT CHECK ✓

Two-Hour Weight Check

The best way to monitor the dryness of your food is to use the two-hour weight check method. Once the cycle has ended, cancel the process and weigh all your trays. Put your food back in, and weigh your trays again after two hours. If any weight has been lost, the food still has moisture. Put your trays back in and run Extra Dry Time until you achieve a stable before-and-after weight.

This method also allows for super easy rehydration. Subtract the weight of your completed batch from the weight it was when you initially put it in. You can then convert these grams to cups of water for rehydration. In general, water weighs around 237 grams per cup. So, if your food has lost 500 grams, it will take about two cups of water to rehydrate successfully. See the worksheet Rehydration Information in Appendix 3.

Empty Your Bucket!

During freeze-drying, the moisture extracted from the food is released through the drain into your bucket. This water can be dumped or used for watering plants. However, problems occur when the bucket isn't emptied. Not only can stagnant water breed bacteria, but if the vinyl tubing is in the bucket when the valve is opened, the tubing will siphon the dirty water back up into your freeze-dryer, spraying it all over and ruining your freshly dried batch. Always remember to empty your bucket before starting a new batch!

If you're forgetful or want the security (like me!), you can purchase two ⅜" Y fittings. These will easily fit into your vinyl tubing and stop it from sucking water back into the machine, even if it's sitting in a bucket full of water.

What Not to Freeze-Dry

Several foods cannot be freeze-dried. Some of these make a horrible explosive mess, some can ruin your freeze-dryer or pump, and others don't freeze-dry effectively. While small amounts within recipes work just fine, large quantities are not recommended.

High Sugar Syrupy Foods

These foods don't freeze-dry well, mainly due to the specific structure of the sugars. Honey, jam, preserves, syrup, and jelly are definite no-nos. If you attempt them, you're in for an extreme clean-up, as these products are known to explode all over the walls of the freeze-dryer chamber when the pump turns on. However, these foods can be preserved well in other ways.

Oils, Butter, and Mayonnaise

The freeze-dryer is built to remove all water-based moisture from food to preserve it effectively. Oily and fatty foods such as butter, mayonnaise, cooking oil, Crisco, and chocolates contain oil-based moisture, which the freeze-dryer cannot remove. This oily residue can coat the interior of the chamber and gunk up the inside of the pump. The oils in foods go rancid over time and can become a breeding ground for bacteria.

Many of these oily, fatty ingredients will process well as an ingredient in a meal or baked good. These freeze-dried meals will be delicious, lightweight, and perfect for backpacking trips. The only thing to remember is that when these ingredients are added, they will drastically reduce the overall shelf-life of the food and should be used within 6-12 months. This timeframe is perfectly fine for backpacking meals, as these will only be stored briefly before use.

Nuts, Nut Butter, and Peanut Butter

These do not freeze-dry well due to their oil and fat content. The oil is the moisture, and a freeze-dryer does not remove it. Unsaturated fat is particularly problematic in storage, as it can quickly turn rancid when exposed to air. While we use airtight packaging and oxygen absorbers to remove air during packaging, it does not solve the problem. High-fat nut products can be affected quickly and will go rancid.

Odds and Ends that don't work

Alcohol and Vinegar are two liquids that will not freeze-dry. Instead, they act like water and are sublimated out. Small amounts in recipes won't be a problem, but a whole tray will turn into a whole lot of nothing. You also want to avoid freezing-dry bones, such as for bone broth. Instead, make the bone broth and freeze-dry it.

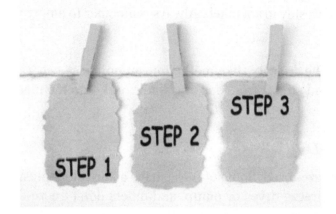

Step-by-Step Basics of Running the Freeze-Dryer

Before you start your first batch, make sure that you work through this comprehensive checklist. Following each step will ensure your freeze-dryer runs as efficiently as possible while achieving optimal, delicious results.

1. Wash and prepare your food, cutting it into slices or chunks no bigger than ¾" thick and ½" deep. Place the food on your trays, leaving adequate space between each slice to allow for ventilation.
2. Put your trays of prepared food into your regular freezer and leave them to pre-freeze for 24–48 hours. Pre-freezing will decrease your freeze cycle, avoid explosive messes, and potentially increase the life of your machine.
3. Check that your vacuum pump is ready. Make sure that the oil is clean and clear. If running low, top it up until it is between half full and max.
4. Plug your freeze-dryer in and flip the switch to the on position. Position the gasket and close the door. After latching it, make sure to check that it is fully sealed. If not, try again by reseating the gasket.
5. Press the "Customize" button on the start screen to modify the temperature or time if needed. (Probiotics or herbs: dry temp 90*. Ice Cream: freeze temp -20*.)
6. Press "Start" to begin the pre-cooling chamber. Depending on your settings, This step should take 15–90 minutes.
7. Plug your fan in and point it toward the left side of the freeze-dryer to keep your machine well-ventilated and cool.
8. Once the pre-cooling cycle is done, the screen will prompt you to close the drain valve. Make sure that the valve handle is perpendicular to the drain hose.
9. Before placing your food into the freeze-dryer, weigh it and write the weight per tray on your batch log. Then, put your trays in, close the door, ensure it is completely sealed, and latch the handle with two quarter-turns.

10. Press continue on the control panel to begin the full process. The freeze-dryer will cycle through the freezing, vacuum-freezing, and drying cycles. This should take between 24 and 60 hours, depending on the type of food. While you wait, prepare your next batch.

11. Extra Dry Time will begin and run for up to 24 hours when the phases are complete if you've configured it as recommended. If not, the default time is two hours. When the display indicates "Extra Dry Time," it's time to halt the machine by pressing the Cancel button. You can assess the food and perform weight checks to determine if it requires additional drying time. It's worth noting that certain types of food will consistently need extended drying periods.

12. Before opening the chamber, ensure your drain hose is in an empty bucket. Press Cancel and open the drain valve slowly to release the pressure. It may take up to five minutes to depressurize so you can open the door.

13. Make sure that your hands are clean and the surrounding area is dry. Open the door and remove your food. Weigh your trays and make a note on your batch log for moisture loss comparison.

14. Put your trays back into the chamber, close the valve, and latch the door. Press Extra Dry Time on the control panel to add more dry hours. Overshoot by setting it to four hours, but check on your food after two. When you remove your food to check, weigh the trays again and take note. If there was a weight change, your food still has moisture and needs to go back in the freeze-dryer for more dry time. Once the weight is the same as the previous weight, your food is completely dry, and you can proceed with packaging.

15. Work quickly to package freeze-dried food, as it can start absorbing moisture from the air. Make sure you have your packaging supplies on hand. Remove your food from the trays and place it into proper packaging with oxygen absorbers. For backpacking trip food, package your meals according to how you'll be using them, either as individual meals (MRE mylar bags) or group meals (large mylar bags). The next chapter will focus on the best packaging products and how to seal them correctly.

16. Once your food is packaged, start defrosting using the Defrost button or select No Defrost to defrost manually by opening the door to allow ambient air to melt the ice. After 15 minutes, you can remove the shelves and slide out the ice rings to speed up the defrosting process. Direct a fan into the chamber to speed things up further.

17. Clean the freeze-dryer with a soft cloth and warm water. Ensure thorough cleaning after accidental spills. You can use Isopropyl alcohol or Everclear, but avoid any abrasive products. Remove any debris particles and allow the chamber to fully dry. You are now ready to start your next batch.

Now You Can Freeze-Dry!

As we wrap up our exploration of the intricacies of freeze-drying equipment and techniques, you've gained a comprehensive understanding of the processes and tools that make freeze-drying a culinary marvel. Now, let's focus on the critical aspect of safe packaging and storage. In the upcoming chapter, we will unravel the secrets to preserving the quality and longevity of your freeze-dried creations. Discover the right materials, techniques, and storage conditions to keep your backpacking meals fresh and flavorful, ensuring you're well-prepared for outdoor adventures.

6

PACKAGING & STORING FREEZE-DRIED FOOD

Arguably, one of the most critical parts of freeze-drying food is storage. You can prepare your food and freeze-dry it to perfection, but you need to package it properly so it can be a good use of time and money. A dedicated storage location and a rotation plan are necessary to keep track of your food, whether for backpacking trips or storing it for 25 years.

Packaging Materials and Techniques

Before you freeze-dry your first batch, you must have all the necessary packaging items ready. I like to have a dedicated, clean working station for my items so I can work as quickly as possible when my food is ready to be packaged.

Materials

Your packaging materials will significantly affect how long you can store your food. Long-term food storage versus short-term backpacking food will be a little different. You need to consider the thickness of the bag, its size, and its durability. If you plan to eat your food in the bag while on the trail, you need to make sure it can withstand holding water (hot water for some meals.)

Mylar Bags

Mylar bags are the most popular choice for packaging freeze-dried meals and the ones I recommend for backpacking. These durable, lightweight bags protect against moisture, oxygen, and light. They come in various thicknesses, and your choice will depend on how long you want to store your food. The best long-term option is the thicker 7-mil bags, which can store food for 25+ years (7 mil on both sides, not total.) Thinner 5-mil bags are great for short-term storage, keeping your food fresh for around ten years.

For backpacking trips, Mylar is durable and can withstand the heat of boiling water during rehydration. Package your meals according to how you'll be using them: as individual meals in MRE mylar bags (6.5" x 8.5") which hold 5 cups, as group meals in large, gallon-sized mylar bags (10" x 14") or as individual ingredients in proportionally sized bags. Add the appropriate amount of oxygen absorbers and seal your packaging.

Vacuum Sealed Bags

While created for storing food in the freezer, vacuum-sealed bags can also be used to package fresh and freeze-dried meals. It is easy to remove the air from the package and create an airtight seal with a FoodSaver, which retains your food's quality while keeping it fresh. Be careful not to vacuum-seal too tightly, as some dry food can puncture these bags. They do not protect against light as they are clear plastic. These are recommended for short-term storage and should not be expected to store food longer than 6–12 months.

Vacuum-sealed bags are also a good backpacking option, as you only need the food to store for a short time. These bags can also withstand the heat of boiling water. Be cautious not to allow the bags to get punctured. Vacuum seal bags come in a few different sizes and rolls that can be cut to make custom sizes.

Canning Jars

Canning jars are great for 5-10-year storage and also for immediate use. I recommend using them for any individual ingredients you plan to use daily or weekly. Using the same FoodSaver (with a jar attachment), they are easy to seal and, with the addition of an oxygen absorber, can retain your food's freshness for years. A bonus part of using jars is seeing and monitoring your food.

Oxygen Absorbers and Moisture Control

When storing food long-term, it is best practice to include oxygen absorbers with your packaged food. These small packages contain an iron powder and are made so the powder can't get out, but oxygen can seep in. The absorbers remove the oxygen from the package, leaving behind nitrogen, which protects food. Placing a few of these into your packaged meals will reduce the risk of microbial growth, oxidation, and general decay of your food. Just remember to remove them before rehydrating with water!

They come in a variety of sizes to best suit the size of the package. A 300cc oxygen absorber is perfect for a 1-gal Mylar bag, while a 100cc one works well in a 1-quart canning jar or Mylar MHE bag. If packaging larger bags, you can double up or purchase 500cc absorbers. Adding too many oxygen absorbers won't hurt the food one bit. Oxygen absorbers are finite; once the powder has fully oxidized, it will stop absorbing oxygen. For this reason, it's essential to work as quickly as possible with them. Only remove them from their sealed packaging when you are ready to place them with your food and seal the bag immediately after. If they are stiff and crunchy then they are spent.

Sealing Techniques

The proper sealing technique is critical to successful storage. Without it, your oxygen absorbers won't work, and your food is in danger from oxygen, pests, and moisture. Heat is the best sealing method, and your heat sealer must be compatible with your chosen packaging.

Sealing Mylar Bags

Mylar bags are relatively easy to seal. I prefer the Impulse Sealer that came with my freeze-dryer, but you can also use a clothes iron and even a hair straightener if you're in a pinch. Place your food in the Mylar bag, followed by an oxygen absorber. Push air out of the package without crushing the food, and then hold down your sealer on the top edge. Test it to check for any leaks or holes. Create another seal below the first and above the tear tabs of the bag.

On the side of your Impulse Sealer, you will see a dial that changes the temperature. The thicker the bag, the higher your settings should be to seal effectively. 7-mil needs about 7 seconds, 5-mil needs about 6 seconds, and plastic bags need about 5 seconds. You may have to adjust your settings up or down to get the proper seal.

Sealing Vacuum Bags and Canning Jars

The FoodSaver Vacuum Sealer should be used to seal vacuum-sealed plastic bags. These sealers are great because they vacuum out the air within the bag before sealing it tightly. (Use with caution as this can crush freeze-dried food.) If the bag inflates after sealing, the package has a hole or tear. Remove the food and repackage it in a new bag.

The best part of the FoodSaver Sealer is that you can purchase an attachment to vacuum seal mason jars. Before sealing, an oxygen absorber should be put in each jar. When sealed, these can last 5–10 years, but they do need to be kept out of sunlight, or the food will lose its color.

For immediate use, you can reseal your canning jars between each use, reducing the oxidation that will occur. Keep in mind that opening and resealing your jars will drastically reduce the shelf life of your food. Any opened food should be used within 6–12 months.

Labeling and Date Marking

Proper labeling is the only way to keep track of your freeze-dried meals and ensure you rotate your stock correctly. Labeling should be done immediately after packaging. Please don't listen to those intrusive thoughts telling you you'll remember to label them later. You definitely won't, and I can tell you from experience that it is very difficult to figure out what food is in a bag just by feeling it and listening to a specific crunch.

Beef Chili
Packaged 11/14/23
Add 1c Hot Water to each 1c of FD chili.

Good information to include on each bag:

1. The contents of the package, including the type of meal and noteworthy ingredients.
2. The date that it was freeze-dried and packaged to monitor the shelf-life and freshness of the meal.
3. The weight of the food before it was freeze-dried (or the current freeze-dried weight) and the amount of water needed for rehydration.
4. Cooking instructions. These are not vital, but if you prepare many foods, you may not remember the instructions ten years from now.

I also include the specific batch number (from my batch log) for each of the foods freeze-dried during the same cycle. If I open a package and find that the food is compromised, I can quickly and easily go through my storage and take out all the packages with that batch number.

Storage Considerations

So now your meals are freeze-dried, packaged, labeled, and ready to be stored! You have worked through the most challenging parts. Now, it's time to organize your food and determine the best storage method for your situation.

Six Enemies of Food Storage

To ensure the quality and longevity of your freeze-dried food, you will need to create a healthy, clean storage environment. While a pantry or garage may seem like the best option, you will need to consider how much food you plan to store and consider the following factors: temperature, light, moisture, oxygen, pests, and time.

Temperature: It is essential to keep your freeze-dried meals in a cool, dry place. Ideally, the room temperature should be between 50°F-70°F (21°C). High temperatures cause the foods to lose flavor and nutrients and degrade their texture and appearance.

Light: Light, both artificial and natural sunlight, greatly diminishes food quality and nutritional content. Light breaks down foods' color and flavor. This is one of the reasons I prefer to use Mylar bags over vacuum-sealed plastic bags. However, it's still best to use a dark pantry or large, dark totes.

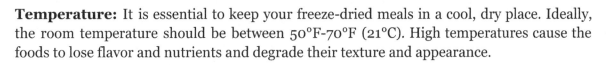

Moisture: A warm, moist environment is the perfect breeding ground for mold and bacteria, precisely what you don't want in your freeze-dried food. Choose an area that has low humidity. If this is not possible, set up a dehumidifier in the storage space.

Oxygen: We have already discussed how harmful oxygen can be to freeze-dried food, making fats rancid and encouraging microorganism growth. Oxygen provides the environment in which bacteria and microorganisms need to thrive. If oxygen enters your packages, your food will lose flavor and texture and ultimately spoil. The best way to combat this is to use sealed packaging with oxygen absorbers.

Pests: Another reason to use solid storage totes is pests. Rodents, insects, and other pests will quickly destroy your food if given the chance. Select a suitable storage area that rodents, pets, or children won't be able to access and place all your Mylar bags inside totes. Consider using food-grade Diatomaceous earth as a natural deterrent. Spreading a ring of this around your storage will help keep out insects and ants.

Time: Freeze-dried food can last many years, depending on how you package and store your meals. However, no food will last forever. Labeling your meals correctly and including the dates on each package is crucial. Developing a rotation system will ensure that you eat the oldest stock first.

Organizing, Inventorying, and Storing Freeze-Dried Meals

It's time to create a rotation plan. How you do this will depend on your storage space, the amount of food you have to store, and the available time. There is no one-size-fits-all organizational method, but I can give you some tips, and you can then modify them to suit your needs.

Firstly, determine how you want to store your food and clean your storage area. Plastic storage bins, totes, metal shelving, or racks can be used. Ultimately, it's your choice, but I do not recommend using wooden cabinets, closets, or shelves. Wood holds moisture, which breeds mold and attracts insects and pests.

Categorize your meals based on their purpose. I organize my meals into breakfasts, lunches, dinners, snacks, and individual ingredients. If you are creating a large storage area, you can place your meals in alphabetic order to make it even easier to access them. You can use an App for a QR code-type system to track what is in each tote or on each shelf on your phone. I use - and love - this simple system.

Follow FIFO!

Follow the first-in, first-out principle by organizing your meal types by date. Whenever you freeze-dry new food, place your packages at the back of the storage area so that you can easily access the older packages in the front, which are closer to expiration. If you have created a dedicated emergency tote or storage area, keep these packages swapped out first so they remain viable.

You can also keep an inventory logbook of all the food added to storage and all the food removed to be used. It doesn't matter how well you organize; you will likely miss a package here and there. Your logbook will help you to locate any older packages. The logbook is also a great way to monitor which types of food you have in storage and which ones you are running low on without digging through all your packages. Just be sure to note when you add to your storage or when you remove foods to use.

Rechecking Seals and Packaging Integrity

Occasionally, you will want to inspect your freeze-dried meals to ensure the seals and packaging remain intact. Doing this regularly, or any time you reorganize or move your stock, will catch problems quickly.

Check each bag for punctures, tears, or holes. As oxygen seeps into the package, the bag will expand and look bloated. Squeeze each bag, and if they deflate, your food has been compromised.

Do the same for any of your sealed jars. Lightly try to lift the lid; if this happens easily, then they have come unsealed. If you find any packages or jars like this, remove the food and inspect it carefully. You can transfer it to new packaging if it was recently processed and still looks and smells good, but it must be used as soon as possible. When in doubt, it's best to toss it out.

Troubleshooting When Food Goes Bad

Sometimes, despite our best efforts, freeze-dried food can go bad. If your food has an off smell, or you notice that the color and texture aren't quite right, don't eat it. There are several reasons why this can occur, and it's usually due to a mistake made along the way. Don't fret; it's all part of the learning process. You will need to figure out why it has happened so that it doesn't happen again.

The most common cause of spoilage is packaging food that is not completely dry. Even the slightest amount of moisture can lead to bacteria growth and mold, especially if your package has been stored in a warm room. Take extra care when weighing your foods for moisture content; always do a proper weight check and add extra dry time. Note which type of food was affected, as it can help you plan your dry time in the future.

If your packaging is not sealed, moisture and oxygen will get in. The moisture will create a breeding ground for bacteria and mold, and the oxygen will accelerate the rate at which your food degrades. This is a disaster, and the food cannot be eaten.

Fatty foods don't have a long shelf life, so it's best to remove the fat when freeze-drying meats. If your food smells greasy or rancid, it likely contains too much fat. Note which type of food was impacted and take the proper preparation precautions in the future, such as washing meats after cooking to remove as much oil as possible or entirely avoiding a fatty ingredient in a recipe.

If one meal from a batch is spoiled, the others could also be. If you have dated your food correctly or used a batch number, you will be able to find and remove other packages from the same batch. Check each package for tears and holes; discard the meal if found. If you suspect the food wasn't dried correctly, it's best to open the packages to check for spoilage.

As we conclude our journey through safe packaging and storage, you've equipped yourself with the knowledge and skills needed to protect your freeze-dried treasures. Now, let's dive into rehydration methods and techniques so we can feast on the foods we've prepared. In the upcoming chapter, you'll discover the secrets to bringing your freeze-dried creations back to life, ensuring that every meal on your backpacking adventure is a delicious and satisfying experience. From cold water rehydration to perfecting hydration times and ratios, we'll cover it all to make your outdoor culinary endeavors successful.

7

ENJOYING YOUR FREEZE-DRIED MEALS

There is nothing quite like relaxing by a campfire and eating a delicious meal after a hard day trekking through the wilderness. However, there are a few things you need to know and a few things to pack to make your food enjoyable. In this final chapter, I will walk you through how to savor the meals you worked so hard to prepare. I will also cover adding fresh ingredients and seasonings and perfecting your rehydration ratios. Packing the right cookware and tools will ease your pack weight and guarantee an easy mealtime, whether you're on the move or taking the time to relax.

Rehydration Methods and Techniques

Freeze-dried meals offer flexibility in rehydration, allowing you to choose the method that best suits your meal and conditions. Whether you're on the go or setting up a warm campfire meal, these methods will ensure delicious results. Our favorite method is cold water rehydration followed by cooking over the fire. But as long as you add in enough water and enjoy the final product, it's good.

Cold Water Rehydration

One of the simplest and quickest methods is using cold water to rehydrate food. This is especially useful when preparing quick, on-the-move meals during your trek. Following these steps will ensure proper cold water hydration and a delicious meal.

1. Open your food package. If you packaged your meal in a Mylar or Vacuum-sealed bag, simply cut off the top of the package. Remove oxygen absorber. If you have used another form of packaging, transfer the meal into a suitable container—preferably one with a lid.
2. Add cold water. Pour enough cold water into the bag or container to cover the freeze-dried ingredients entirely. If you followed the recommended packaging suggestion, you would have written how much water is needed to rehydrate your meal on the package. If not, follow the general guideline of around ½ - 1 cup of water per serving.
3. Gently stir the contents to ensure that the water has fully seeped in.

4. Sit back, relax, and wait. Give your meal the time it needs to rehydrate fully. Cold water rehydration typically takes a little longer than hot water. Depending on your meal and its ingredients, this could be anywhere from a few minutes to an hour or more (such as raw meats.) However, most ready-to-eat, single-serving meals take 10 minutes or less.
5. Check your food. After giving it time to rehydrate, check your meal until it has reached the desired texture and consistency. You may need to add a little extra water. Take your time with the process, and if you are unsure, just let the food sit for a few more minutes.

Hot Water Rehydration

Using hot water for rehydration is much quicker, especially for larger meal sizes. However, it is more time-consuming overall as you will need to set up your stove or campfire to boil water. Regardless, it is entirely worth it, as there is nothing like a nice hot meal at the end of a hard day. Follow these steps to rehydrate your food with hot water correctly.

1. Open up the package. Mylar bags and vacuum-seal bags are both heat-resistant, so you can simply cut off the top of the package. Remove oxygen absorber. Add water or tansfer your meal into a heat-resistant container, bowl, or pot.
2. Add boiling water directly to the bag or pot, completely covering the freeze-dried food. Follow the recommended water-to-meal rehydration ratio written on your bag, or use the ½ - 1 cup water per serving guideline. Make sure you're careful when rehydrating food in bags with boiling water, as the bag will be hot. You also don't want any water to spill or splash and burn you.
3. Stir the contents and close your container (or cover your pot) to trap the steam and heat inside. If you have used a vacuum-seal or Mylar bag, you can fold it over the top. Some mylar comes with a zip top that makes this super easy. I prefer to use zip-top gusseted mylar bags so they can sit independently. Other bags can be placed in a stable container to keep them upright, or the food can be transferred to another container.

4. Allow your meal the time it needs to rehydrate. Boiling water will seep in and soften your ingredients much quicker than cold water. Your food will be rehydrated within just a few minutes, often less than 5 minutes.
5. Open your container and check if your food is ready. If not, allow it a few extra minutes or add more water if necessary. Once it's done, wait for it to cool down before enjoying it.

Cooking with Freeze-Dried Foods

For freeze-dried foods meant to be served hot, heating after rehydration is highly recommended to improve texture, flavor, and overall quality. This method works especially well for hearty meals like chilis, stews, and casseroles.

1. Transfer the freeze-dried food straight from the Mylar bag into your camping pot. Pour enough water to fully cover the ingredients. Hot water will speed up rehydration, but use cold water if you're working with raw items like uncooked meats or eggs. Any temperature water will work.

2. Allow the ingredients to soak for a few minutes before heating to start the rehydration process. For tougher items like steak or other dense meats, soak in the Mylar bag beforehand until fully rehydrated.

3. Place the pot over your stove or campfire and start cooking. Stir occasionally to ensure even heating and monitor the texture. Add extra water as needed, especially if the mixture thickens during cooking.

4. Continue cooking until the meal is hot and the ingredients are at the desired texture. Check that meats and denser items are fully rehydrated, adjusting water and cook time as necessary.

Heating after rehydration brings out the best in freeze-dried ingredients, providing a satisfying, home-cooked taste and texture. This method ensures that your freeze-dried meals achieve flavors and textures similar to a freshly cooked dish.

Tip for Quick Meals on the Go:
Pre-pack freeze dried ingredients with seasonings in a Mylar bag. When you're ready to eat, transfer everything to your pot, add water, soak briefly, and heat until fully rehydrated. This approach is perfect for a hot, satisfying meal with minimal cleanup.

Some Foods are Better When Not Rehydrated

While some freeze-dried ingredients and meals are best rehydrated before eating, many delicious food items can be enjoyed in their freeze-dried state. Fruits such as strawberries, apples, and peaches are incredibly delicious to eat when freeze-dried. They become crunchy and delightfully sweet and can be eaten as a dry snack or used to add texture and a punch of flavor to granola or yogurt.

Freeze-dried vegetables can also be delicious in their freeze-dried state. The crunchy texture is an excellent addition to salads, and if you feel like a light snack, you can eat them as is. Crunchy veggie sticks I can dip in ranch are my personal favorite.

Even some freeze-dried meats can be eaten as is. However, they will need to be cooked before they are freeze-dried. You can also eat them as snacks, sprinkle shreds on salads, or toss in a soup for a protein kick. Crumbled lunch meat is so tasty over fresh salad.

While desserts and sweet breads can be rehydrated, some are more delicate than others. Getting the rehydrated texture right with some bread items can take some practice, and some don't work as well and just crumble. If you want to try rehydrating, you can quickly dip it in water and pan fry it nicely with the steam, which gives it a toasted feel. I prefer the crunchy, sweet, freeze-dried taste better.

One of the most significant benefits of freeze-drying food is the ability to lengthen the shelf-life of ingredients without the risk of them losing their flavor, nutrition, or vibrancy. Fresh herbs and spices can be hard to eat before they reach their expiration date. Once freeze-dried, they don't need to be rehydrated at all. Just add them to whichever dish you're cooking.

At the end of the day, it will all come down to your personal preference. While I thoroughly enjoy eating these items in a freeze-dried state, you may not. So, it's best to experiment with different foods and figure out what you enjoy most. Most importantly, remember to drink plenty of water whenever you eat freeze-dried food in its dry state.

Hydration Times and Ratios

Rehydration time and water ratio may vary depending on the ingredients in your freeze-dried meal, so it is crucial to note these instructions on your packaging. However, if you are unsure or can't test any of your meals before the trip, you can follow these general rules.

Breakfasts: These will typically rehydrate within 5–10 minutes. Scrambled eggs and oatmeal can be rehydrated using a 1:1 water ratio. If you have made a breakfast casserole or incorporated meats such as bacon, aim for ¾ cup of water per cup of food.

Snack items: These generally won't be rehydrated, but some fruits can be lightly soaked in cold water until the desired texture is achieved.

Soups, Gumbo, Chili, and Stews: These typically rehydrate within 5–20 minutes. You can rehydrate these at a 1:1 ratio and add extra water if desired.

Pasta and Rice-based Meals: These can take 1–5 minutes to fully rehydrate into the correct texture. Pasta and rice will quickly soak up moisture, so stick to the 1 cup per serving rule and only add more if necessary.

Breads: These can be tricky. Many bread items are best enjoyed crunchy. Dip briefly in a shallow dish of water and pat dry with a paper towel. Alternatively, it can be pan-fried after the quick dip in water.

Protein-heavy dishes: Any meal containing meat will likely need a longer rehydration time to achieve the best texture. This will typically take around 20–30 minutes. If you have chosen to freeze-dry raw meat, you must rehydrate and then cook your meal, which can be so worth it! Meat can't be over-hydrated, so it's best to cover it with water, allowing it to soak up what it needs, and remove it when you're happy with the texture. When rehydrating a meal, other ingredients can become mushy, and the flavor may be destroyed if too much water is added.

Hydration times and ratios can be adjusted based on your personal preference. If you want a softer texture, allow your food to rehydrate longer. If you prefer crispier foods, add less water. Add water to your meals slowly if you consistently have overhydrated or mushy food. Pour half the amount needed, give it a few minutes, and add more until you are happy.

Attaining Flavor Perfection

Tips for Achieving Optimal Texture and Flavor

How a freeze-dried meal is rehydrated can significantly impact the texture, flavor, and consistency of the meal. Here are some tips that will enhance your experience.

Soaking Time

Patience is key. Allow your meal sufficient time to soak in moisture. It usually takes 10–15 minutes to rehydrate a single-serving meal. However, this can be affected by the thickness of your food and certain ingredients. If you rush the process, your meal will have a tough or chewy texture. It's best to give it a couple more minutes and a few more stirs.

Water Temperature

Cold water hydration is convenient and so easy. Fruits, breakfasts, and sweet treats, such as freeze-dried oatmeal or smoothies, should only be rehydrated with cold water to recreate the same delicious flavor and texture. Hot water accelerates the process and generally improves the overall eating experience of some meals, particularly meats, soups, and stews. That being said, it must be noted that some ingredients and vegetables may turn mushy when left to soak in hot water for too long. So, make sure to get your timing right!

Stir Frequently

Stirring will help to distribute the water evenly. It will break up thicker pieces of food, giving all pieces an equal chance to absorb the water. This will improve the overall texture and flavor of your meal.

Water Amount

Not all freeze-dried meals will rehydrate at the same rate or with the same amount of water. The ½ - 1 cup water to 1 serving is just an estimation, and even your recommended rehydration ratio may not be precisely what your food needs. It's best to test different ratios to see which works best for your meal.

Food Flavors

Seasonings are easy to store and lightweight enough to pack. The freeze-drying process accentuates flavors and seasonings, so it's best to under-season your food when you prepare it. Pack a few small packets of your favorite condiments and add these to your meals after the rehydration process. This will help you achieve the perfect flavor without going all out and adding extra fresh ingredients.

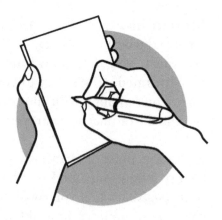

Remember, achieving the best-tasting meals may take some trial and error. Keep notes of what works and what doesn't, and adjust your meals for future trips.

What Could Go Wrong?

Thankfully, nothing terrible can go wrong with rehydration. If you overhydrate your food, it can become quite mushy and soupy. While this won't taste the best, it is still edible, and you can work at fixing it by adding some extra ingredients. Under-rehydrated food is also edible; you will need a couple of extra minutes and a bit more water to fix it.

If you find one of your packages punctured, open it and inspect your food. If the food looks okay, eat it as soon as possible! If the food smells rancid or off, place it into your designated waste bag. No matter how hungry you are, if you are unsure, do not eat it. Depending on the ingredients, this can cause severe stomach upsets.

Enhancing Rehydrated Meals with Fresh Ingredients

Freeze-dried meals are designed and prepared to be eaten as is once rehydrated. However, don't let that stop you from adding fresh ingredients, as this can enhance the flavor of the meal and add extra nutrition. While this is best done at home, where you will have regular access to fresh ingredients, it's also nice to add a bit of variety, even on a backpacking trip.

Several long-lasting fresh ingredients can be packed whole, such as onions, garlic, bell peppers, or fruits like apples and oranges. Decide if the added weight is worth the flavor they will add to your meals. If you do choose to take these items with you, make sure to buy only one or two of each, as you want to avoid dealing with waste and extra weight.

Another option is gathering food on your trail. Fresh fruits are ideal for sprucing up your morning oatmeal and giving you that added sweet sugar boost for your trek to come. If you have an edible plants book and are confident in your foraging skills, you can pick some edible berries as you hike and incorporate these into your breakfast. Do NOT eat anything you cannot confidently identify.

I like to stock up on a few fresh ingredients when I pass through supply points. I purchase a limited number of items from local stores and make sure that I stick to ingredients that will complete the meals I plan to eat within the next two or three days. If I have fish on the menu, I will grab a lemon and squeeze it onto my meal to enhance the flavor. You can then use the remaining lemon for other meals as an extra flavor for your water.

If you will be using heat keep in mind that camping stoves heat up rapidly. When cooking or rehydrating, keep the setting low so you don't burn your food.

Cooking Equipment

When it comes to cooking equipment, you will need to source the most lightweight, durable items. Keep your camping kitchen to a bare minimum for long trips to reduce your pack weight while ensuring you have everything you need to prepare your food.

Remember, when it comes to freeze-dried food, you will only need to cook if you want to use hot water hydration to make a cozy, warm meal.

Pots, Pans, and Cutlery

If you are backpacking solo, go simple and purchase only one of each item. Collapsible silicone bowls, mugs, and plates are ideal as they are lightweight and can be condensed in your pack. If you enjoy hot coffee in the morning, you can opt for an open mug or a sealable flask that will retain heat. Whichever one you choose, make sure it is lightweight and easily packable. Keep your utensils to a minimum as well. Opt for a foldable knife, spoon, and fork, or pack a handy spork.

Purchase a camping pot and pan set. These are small pots that fit into each other and a small pan that can be used as a lid for your pot. To save space, store dry items such as your fire-starting tools inside your pot to keep your cooking items together. These are a good size to fit well on fires and mini camping stoves. You may also want a heat-resistant container with a lid to rehydrate meals on the go. To save space, store your utensils in it when not in use.

Stoves and Fuel

A lightweight, gas-fueled camping stove is ideal for an outdoor adventure. It will reduce your need to start campfires each night and morning, positively impacting your environment. These stoves come in different sizes, so source the most space-efficient one possible.

If you take along a stove, you must also take an appropriate amount of fuel. Different stoves consume different types and amounts of fuel, so research to find a fuel-efficient one. Test your stove out at home and boil a few pots of water to measure how quickly you will burn fuel.

Canister fuels will come in different sizes. It is easier to carry two smaller canisters over one large canister, as the weight in the pack can be distributed more efficiently. You can choose from three fuel types: isobutane, propane, and butane. Butane has the highest boiling point, but these canisters do not perform well in winter, and I don't recommend them. Isobutane works well in three seasons but starts to lag on cold winter nights. Propane performs well all year round. In general, a fuel canister is often a mix of two fuels. Look for an all-season fuel blend with around 80% isobutane and 20% propane.

Most compact camping stoves come with a storage container that can hold the stove and two fuel canisters. If not, storing the canister in one of your pots or an outside pocket is best to avoid it being damaged or pierced by other equipment. Keeping extra fuel in your bounce box is also wise.

Measuring Device or Cup

Being able to measure water is essential when it comes to rehydrating your food. If you have labeled your food correctly, you will have written down the water needed to rehydrate it. Now, all you need is something to measure that amount of water. Depending on your preference, there are a few different choices.

For easy meals, like soup, you can use your mug to pour in some water, but this will be a rough estimate that may not work for sensitive meals. Some plastic water bottles have measurements engraved into them. These are nice as you don't have to pack extra items. Silicone collapsible measuring cups are another option. These fold completely flat and will fit well in your pack.

Helpful Tools

Lightweight, collapsible utensils are also recommended, including a spatula, which is especially useful for breakfasts, or tongs for cooking meats. A reliable, collapsible knife is also valuable, but this knife should be dedicated to food use only.

Pack a pair of heat-resistant gloves or pot grippers! Your stove reaches extreme temperatures, the handles are compact, and you can feel the heat. I love my camping pot and pan set but am careful when using them. Be safe and protect your hands.

Cleaning

Keeping your cookware clean is essential for maintaining hygiene and preventing the spread of bacteria. Pack a small, environmentally friendly dishwashing soap, a dishwashing sponge, and a drying cloth.

Scrape all food scraps from your pot, pan, or dish into a designated, sealed waste bag. Collect water using a collapsible bucket and add a touch of biodegradable dishwashing liquid. You can then wash your cookware, dry it, and pack it away. The used water can be poured into an open area away from water and food sources and then covered with dirt. Do not wash your cookware directly in a water source, as you can contaminate the source.

Safety

For safety, you must learn, understand, and abide by strict fire safety rules when cooking. Set up your stove in a clear area away from debris and dead vegetation. It must be placed on a flat surface to heat up effectively and ensure your pot or pan doesn't topple over.

If it is windy, your stove might not light effectively or continuously blow out. Do not try to create a wind barrier or set up the stove in your tent, as this is a serious fire hazard. Instead, opt for cold water rehydration or wait for the wind to die down.

Once your fire pit is set up, you can ignite it and start cooking. Don't fill your pot or pan more than ¾ deep. A full pot of water is difficult to lift without spilling. Additionally, any food rehydrated in the pot could bubble over if it is too full.

When you are done cooking, turn off the stove and allow it to cool down. Place your hot pot or pan away from the fuel canister and allow it to cool. You can now disconnect your fuel canister and pack it away, unless you need to wash your pot first. Once your stove has cooled, wipe it down to remove any dirt or food scraps. Most importantly, ensure the connection to the fuel canister is clear of debris.

Never leave your stove or campfire unattended. Camp stoves are designed for safe cooking, and unless they topple over, they are unlikely to start a fire. Campfires, however, continuously produce sparks and embers. Typically, these will burn out before even touching the ground, but a tiny spark is all it takes, and if you don't notice it quickly enough, you may be dealing with a much larger fire.

If you notice an ember that hasn't burned out, stomping on it should put it out immediately. Water and sand can also be used to extinguish a flame quickly. Water will create a large amount of smoke, so sand or soil is the best option. Double-check that your fire is fully extinguished before you go to bed or leave your campsite.

Armed with the knowledge of rehydration techniques, the importance of optimal texture and flavor, and the nuances of water ratios, you're well-prepared to savor delicious meals during your backpacking adventures. You've learned to select essential cooking equipment for your freeze-dried meals, adjust hydration for variations, and safely prepare meals while backpacking. You've also learned that some foods shine best without rehydration. You are equipped to enhance your rehydrated dishes with any desired fresh ingredients, and you can elevate your outdoor culinary experience.

CONCLUSION

Embarking on a backpacking adventure can be difficult. It's extremely taxing on the body and takes immense planning to ensure its success. However, there is nothing else in this world quite like it. This journey will be one of self-discovery and exploration and will be a sure way to build a strong connection to the world around you. Throughout this book, we have covered the essentials of backpacking, from planning and selecting the right gear to navigation, finding water sources, and staying safe.

As you set out to travel through challenging terrains and breathtaking landscapes, remember that backpacking is not about the destination. It's about the journey, the memories you will make, and the beautiful moments and experiences that will free you from yourself. What good is an outstanding journey if you don't have the delicious food to match it?

Freeze-drying is a revolutionary food preparation and preservation method that changes the lives of families, emergency preppers, and adventurers alike. This cost-effective method provides an exceptional shelf-life, reduces overall food waste, and, as a bonus, is incredibly easy to prepare and enjoy. Moisture-free, lightweight food is ideal for backpacking as it takes up a minimal amount of space while still retaining its nutritional value—freeing you of the extra weight and empowering you to journey further.

Throughout the last few chapters, we have uncovered the science behind the freeze-drying process, its benefits, and how to pre-plan and package your meals correctly. I have provided everything you need to know to successfully freeze-dry backpacking foods, from single ingredients to calorie-dense whole meals. You now have the knowledge and techniques to rehydrate and spice up these meals while on the trail, making your backpacking journey a food journey. The following three appendices contain recipes, meal plans, supplies lists, batch logs, and other worksheets to help you get on your way.

This comprehensive guide will give you the ability to begin your adventure. As you experiment with your ingredient choices, rehydrating and using freeze-dried ingredients to enhance your meals, you will realize that the possibilities are endless. With endless options also comes endless chances to fail. Never take these to heart; we have all been there, and those who take these failures as a challenge are the ones who succeed. Use these failures to further your knowledge and push yourself to create something better and tastier.

You are now equipped to embark on an unforgettable backpacking journey with delicious and nutritious meals to fuel your adventure. May your backpack be filled with well-prepared freeze-dried meals and your heart with the joy of exploring the great outdoors. Remember to respect and preserve the natural environment by practicing Leave No Trace principles. Be mindful of your impact on the trails and wilderness areas, ensuring that future generations can also enjoy the beauty and serenity of these spaces.

Safe travels and bon appétit!

KNOWLEDGE IS POWER... LET'S SHARE IT!

With your knowledge of freeze-drying and its numerous advantages, you're well-equipped to assist others in uncovering its potential.

Sharing your honest review of the book "Freeze Drying Food at Home for Backpacking Trips" on Amazon will provide valuable insights for those interested in exploring freeze-drying. Your feedback will serve as a guide for them on their own freeze-drying journey and contribute to the book's enhancement for future readers.

We sincerely value your support and your active participation and contribution to the growing freeze-drying community. Remember, as more individuals discover the advantages of freeze-drying, it benefits the entire industry.

We genuinely appreciate you reading this book. Your support means a great deal to us.

To leave a review scan the QR code or visit: BPR.2MHE.COM

APPENDIX ONE: INSTRUCTIONS FOR 154 FOODS

A wide variety of foods can be freeze-dried effectively, with guidelines here for common options. Freeze-drying times and rehydration methods are approximate and will vary based on ingredients, environment, and techniques. Exercise good judgment and adhere to hygiene and safety protocols. All shelf life recommendations are approximate and dependent upon process and ingredients.

FRUITS 70
Apples
Apricots
Avocados
Bananas
Blackberries
Blueberries
Cantaloupe
Cherries
Coconut Meat
Cranberries
Grapefruit
Grapes
Honeydew
Kiwi, Golden
Lemons
Limes
Mandarins
Mangos
Nectarines
Oranges
Peaches
Pears
Pineapple
Plums
Pomegranate
Raspberries
Rhubarb
Strawberries
Tangerines
Watermelon

DAIRY & EGGS 78
Cottage Cheese
Cream Cheese
Sour Cream
Sweet Cream
Ice Cream
Milk
Hard Cheeses
Soft Cheeses
Kefir
Yogurt
Eggs
Deli Meat

VEGETABLES 73
Asparagus
Beets
Bok Choy
Broccoli
Brussel Sprouts
Cabbage
Carrots
Cauliflower
Celery
Corn
Cucumber
Eggplant
Garlic
Green Beans
Kale
Leeks
Lettuce
Mushrooms
Okra
Onions
Parsnips
Peas, Green
Peas, Snap/Snow
Peppers, Hot
Peppers, Sweet
Potatoes
Pumpkin
Radish
Rutabaga
Scallions
Spinach
Squash, Butternut
Squash, Spaghetti
Squash, Yellow
Squash, Zucchini
Sweet Potatoes
Swiss Chard
Tomatoes
Turnips
Yams

BEEF 80
Ground
Filets
Kabobs/Strips
Meatballs
Patties
Pot Roast
Steak
Stew Meat

PORK 82
Bacon
Ham
Chops
Loin/Roast

POULTRY 82
Ground
Roasted
Slices or Strips
Turkey Bacon

FISH 83
Bass
Herring
Tilapia
Mackerel
Tuna
Salmon
Other White
Other Oily

SHELLFISH 84
Mixed Shellfish
Crab
Clams
Lobster
Mussels
Oysters
Scallops
Shrimp

LEGUMES 84
Beans, dry
Chickpeas
Lentils
Peas, dry
Edamame
Sprouts
Tempeh
Tofu

GRAINS 85
Barley
Buckwheat
Oats
Quinoa
Rice
Wheat Berries
Couscous
Seitan
Pasta
Cake
Breads
Sweet Breads

HERBS 87
Basil
Chives
Cilantro
Dill Weed
Fennel
Ginger
Horseradish
Lemon Balm
Marjoram
Nettle
Oregano
Parsley
Peppermint
Rosemary
Sage
Spearmint
Stevia
Tarragon
Thyme
Turmeric

Fruits   Approximate Shelf Life: 20-25 yrs

Apples
Serving: 200 grams (1 medium) 104 calories
Prep: Wash, cut in half, remove center, and peel if desired. Slice or dice to ½" max pieces and dip in lemon water to prevent browning. Drain, place on trays, and pre-freeze. For powder: blend with water, pour measured amount on trays, and pre-freeze.
Freeze-Dry Time: 25-35 hours - default settings
Use: Snacks, smoothies, pies, and desserts.
Rehydrate: Add ½ cup of water to 1 cup of apples. Sit for 5-10 min.
Tip: Use an apple corer and slicer for quick preparation.

Apricots
Serving: 105 grams (3 small) 51 calories
Prep: Wash, cut in half, remove pit, and peel if desired. Slice or dice to ½" max pieces, place on trays, and pre-freeze. For powder: blend with water, pour measured amount on trays, and pre-freeze.
Freeze-Dry Time: 35-45+ hours - default settings
Use: Snacks, smoothies, jams, and desserts.
Rehydrate: Add ½ cup of water to 1 cup of apricots. Sit for 5-10 min.
Tip: Freeze halved apricots and slice when ready to freeze-dry.

Avocados
Serving: 100 grams (½ large) 160 calories
Prep: Wash, cut, remove seed and skin. Slice or cube to ½" max thickness and dip in lemon water to prevent browning. Drain, place on trays, and pre-freeze. For powder: mash or blend with water, spread measured amount on trays, and pre-freeze.
Freeze-Dry Time: 25-35 hours - default settings
Use: Instant guacamole and smoothies.
Rehydrate: Add ⅓ cup of water to 1 cup of avocado pieces. Add ⅔ cup water to 1 cup avocado powder for a puree. Sit for 5-10 min.
Tip: An avocado slicer quickly halves, pits, and slices.
Note: Shelf Life is 5-10 years for Avocados.

Bananas
Serving: 100 grams (1 medium) 105 calories
Prep: Peel, slice to ½" max thickness and dip in lemon water to prevent browning. Drain, place on trays, and pre-freeze. For powder: blend with water, spread measured amount on trays, and pre-freeze.
Freeze-Dry Time: 30-40 hours - default settings
Use: Snacks, smoothies, pancakes, and desserts.
Rehydrate: Add ½ cup of water to 1 cup of banana pieces. Add ¾ cup water to 1 cup of banana powder. Sit for 5-10 min.
Tip: Freeze bananas before slicing to make handling easier.

Blackberries
Serving: 144 grams (1 cup) 62 calories
Prep: Gently rinse, pat dry, place on trays, and pre-freeze. For powder: blend with water, strain out seeds, pour measured amount on trays, and pre-freeze.
Freeze-Dry Time: 50-60 hours - default settings
Use: Smoothies, pancakes, and desserts.
Rehydrate: Add ½ cup of water to 1 cup of blackberries. Sit for 5-10 min.
Tip: Buy frozen berries to skip prep.

Blueberries
Serving: 148 grams (1 cup) 84 calories
Prep: Wash and pat dry. Slice or pierce individual berries, place on trays, and pre-freeze. For pre-frozen berries: thaw, drain, place on trays, and pre-freeze. For powder: blend with water, pour measured amount on trays, and pre-freeze.
Freeze-Dry Time: 35-45 hours - default settings
Use: Snacks, pies, jams, smoothies, salads, pancakes, muffins, & desserts.
Rehydrate: Add ½ cup of water to 1 cup of blueberries. Sit for 5-10 min.
Tip: Make berry powder from freeze-dried blueberries for baking or smoothies.

Cantaloupe
Serving: 177 grams (1 cup or ¼ medium) 60 calories
Prep: Rinse, cut, de-seed, and remove the rind. Use a melon baller, slice, or cube to ½" max thickness, place on trays, and pre-freeze.
Freeze-Dry Time: 40-50+ hours - default settings
Use: Dry snacks and desserts.
Rehydrate: Soak pieces in water or add ½ cup of water to 1 cup of cantaloupe. Sit for 5-10 min.
Tip: Use a melon baller for quick, bite-sized pieces.

Cherries
Serving: 138 grams (1 cup or 20 cherries) 87 calories
Prep: Wash, remove stems, cut in half and remove pits, place on trays cut side up, and pre-freeze.
Freeze-Dry Time: 50-60+ hours - default settings
Use: Snacks, smoothies, pie, and desserts.
Rehydrate: Soak or add ½ cup of water to 1 cup of cherries. Sit for 5-10 min.
Tip: Use a cherry pitter for quick preparation.

Coconut Meat
Serving: 45 grams (2" x 2" piece) 159 calories
Prep: Drain liquid via the soft eye, crack open, and pry the flesh from the shell. Slice, dice, or shred, place on trays, and pre-freeze.
Freeze-Dry Time: 30-40 hours - default settings
Use: Desserts, toppings, granola, baking, and flour.
Rehydrate: Soak or steam pieces of coconut over boiling water for 5-10 min.
Tip: Toast your coconut flakes for added flavor before freeze-drying.
Note: Shelf Life is 5-10 years for Coconut Meat.

Cranberries
Serving: 100 grams (1 cup) 32 calories
Prep: Detach stems and wash. Slice, shred, or coarsely chop, spread on trays, and pre-freeze.
Freeze-Dry Time: 50-60 hours - default settings
Use: Breads, pies, and sauces.
Rehydrate: Soak or add ½ cup of water to 1 cup of cranberries. Sit for 5-10 min.
Tip: Whole cranberries are challenging and not recommended.

Grapefruit
Serving: 123 grams (½ large) 52 calories
Prep: Cut into ½" slices or peel and separate segments. Remove pith, skin, and seeds, place on trays, and pre-freeze. For powder: blend (with or without peel) with water, pour measured amount on trays, and pre-freeze.
Freeze-Dry Time: 35-45+ hours - default settings
Use: Water flavoring, salads, or croutons.
Rehydrate: Soak segments in water 10+ minutes and drain off excess. For juice, combine ¼ cup of powder with 1 cup of water. Sit for 5-10 min and shake.
Tip: Make sure each segment is pierced for even drying.

Grapes
Serving: 92 grams (1 cup or 22 grapes) 62 calories
Prep: Wash and destem. Cut in half, place on trays cut side up, and pre-freeze. To maintain shape, blanch whole grapes 2 min followed by an ice bath, cool, place on trays, and pre-freeze.
Freeze-Dry Time: 45-60+ hours - default settings
Use: Snacks, salads, jams, and smoothies.
Rehydrate: Soak pieces in water 10+ minutes and drain off excess.
Tip: They are hard and crunchy when fully done and should not be sticky.

Honeydew
Serving: 177 grams (1 cup) 64 calories
Prep: Rinse, cut, de-seed, and remove the rind. Use a melon baller, slice, or cube to ½" max thickness, place on trays, and pre-freeze.
Freeze-Dry Time: 30-40 hours - default settings
Use: Dry snacks and desserts.
Rehydrate: Soak pieces in water or add ½ cup of water to 1 cup of honeydew. Sit for 5-10 min.
Tip: Use a cookie cutter to shape honeydew slices into fun shapes.

Kiwi, Golden
Serving: 75 grams (1 medium) 42 calories
Prep: Rinse and peel very ripe kiwis. Slice or dice to ½" max pieces, place on trays, and pre-freeze.
Freeze-Dry Time: 40-50+ hours - default settings
Use: Snacks, smoothies, and granola toppings.
Rehydrate: Soak or add ⅔ cup of water to 1 cup of kiwi. Sit for 5-10 min.
Tip: Invest in a good quality vegetable peeler for removing the outter peel.

Lemons
Serving: 58 grams (1 small) 17 calories
Prep: Cut into ½" slices or peel and separate segments. Remove pith and seeds, place on trays, and pre-freeze. For powder: blend (with or without peel) with water, pour measured amount on trays, and pre-freeze.
Freeze-Dry Time: 30-40+ hours - default settings
Use: Water flavoring, salads, pie, dressings, marinades, and desserts.
Rehydrate: Soak segments in water 10+ minutes and drain off excess. For juice, combine ¼ cup of powder with 1 cup of water. Sit for 5-10 min and shake.
Tip: Create lemon vinaigrette by blending with oil and herbs after freeze-drying.

Limes
Serving: 67 grams (1 small) 20 calories
Prep: Cut into ½" slices or peel and separate segments. Remove pith and seeds, place on trays, and pre-freeze. For powder: blend (with or without peel) with water, pour measured amount on trays, and pre-freeze.
Freeze-Dry Time: 30-40+ hours - default settings
Use: Water flavoring, dressings, guacamole, salads, pie, and salsa. Use freeze-dried lime powder to flavor grilled fish or chicken.
Rehydrate: Soak segments in water 10+ minutes and drain off excess. For juice, combine ¼ cup of powder with 1 cup of water. Sit for 5-10 min and shake.
Tip: Add a pop of flavor to your drinks by tossing in a freeze-dried lime.

Mandarins

Serving: 88 grams (1 medium) 47 calories
Prep: Cut into ½" slices or peel and separate segments. Remove pith and seeds, place on trays, and pre-freeze. For powder: blend (with or without peel) with water, pour measured amount on trays, and pre-freeze.
Freeze-Dry Time: 35-45+ hours - default settings
Use: Flavored waters, dressings, marinades, and salads.
Rehydrate: Soak segments in water 10+ minutes and drain off excess. For juice, combine ¼ cup of powder with 1 cup of water. Sit for 5-10 min and shake.
Tip: Blend mandarin juice with oil and vinegar for a quick salad dressing.

Mangos

Serving: 165 grams (1 cup) 99 calories
Prep: Wash, peel, cut in half, and cut out pit. Slice or cube to ½" max pieces, place on trays, and pre-freeze. For powder: blend with water, pour measured amount on trays, and pre-freeze.
Freeze-Dry Time: 35-45+ hours - default settings
Use: Snacks, toppings, marinade, and desserts.
Rehydrate: Soak or add ⅔ cup of water to 1 cup of mango pieces. Sit for 5-10 min.
Tip: Avoid touching the mango peel with sensitive skin. Always use sharp knifes for quick slicing.

Nectarines

Serving: 140 grams (1 medium) 62 calories
Prep: Wash, cut in half, remove pit, and peel if desired. Slice or dice to ½" max pieces, place on trays, and pre-freeze. For powder: blend with water, pour measured amount on trays, and pre-freeze.
Freeze-Dry Time: 35-45+ hours - default settings
Use: Snacks, pies, smoothies, and desserts.
Rehydrate: Soak or add ½ cup of water to 1 cup of nectarine pieces. Sit for 5-10 min.
Tip: Ensure every segment has been punctured.

Oranges

Serving: 140 grams (1 medium) 75 calories
Prep: Cut into ½" slices or peel and separate segments. Remove pith and seeds, place on trays, and pre-freeze. For powder: blend (with or without peel) with water, pour measured amount on trays, and pre-freeze.
Freeze-Dry Time: 35-45+ hours - default settings
Use: Flavored waters, salads, pies, and desserts.
Rehydrate: Soak segments in water 10+ minutes and drain off excess. For juice, combine ¼ cup of powder with 1 cup of water. Sit for 5-10 min and shake.
Tip: Select sweet varieties to avoid an unpleasant tartness.

Peaches

Serving: 130 grams (1 medium) 50 calories
Prep: Wash, cut in half, remove pit, and peel if desired. Slice or dice to ½" max pieces, place on trays, and pre-freeze. For powder: blend with water, pour measured amount on trays, and pre-freeze.
Freeze-Dry Time: 35-45+ hours - default settings
Use: Snacks, pies, cakes, jams, smoothies, muffins, pancakes, and desserts.
Rehydrate: Soak or add ½ cup of water to 1 cup of peache pieces. Sit for 5-10 min.
Tip: Make peach puree and freeze in ice cube trays for easy portioning.

Pears

Serving: 178 grams (1 medium) 101 calories
Prep: Wash, cut in half, remove center, and peel if desired. Slice or dice to ½" max pieces, place on trays, and pre-freeze. For powder: blend with water, pour measured amount on trays, and pre-freeze.
Freeze-Dry Time: 35-45+ hours - default settings
Use: Snacks, smoothies, and desserts.
Rehydrate: Add ½ cup of water to 1 cup of pears. Sit for 5-10 min.
Tip: Pears should be firm, but ripe. Overly ripe fruit can bubble up in the machine.

Pineapple

Serving: 165 grams (1 cup chunks) 82 calories
Prep: Rinse, remove crown, end, core, and rind. Slice into rings or cut into chunks ¼" - ½" thick. Place on trays and pre-freeze. Canned: drain well, place on trays, and pre-freeze.
Freeze-Dry Time: 40-60+ hours - default settings
Use: Snacks, desserts, tropical recipes, smoothies, flavoring, pizza, and stir-fries.
Rehydrate: Soak or add ½ cup of water to 1 cup of pineapple. Sit for 5-10 min.
Tip: Use a pineapple corer and slicer for quick preparation.

Plums

Serving: 66 grams (1 medium plum) 30 calories
Prep: Wash, cut in half, remove pit, and peel if desired. Slice or dice to ½" max pieces, place on trays, and pre-freeze. For powder: blend with water, pour measured amount on trays, and pre-freeze.
Freeze-Dry Time: 35-45 hours - default settings
Use: Snacks, smoothies, jams, and desserts.
Rehydrate: Soak or add ½ cup of water to 1 cup of plums. Sit for 5-10 min.
Tip: Removing the peel will enhance the sweetness of the fruit.

Pomegranate
Serving: 140 grams (½ medium) 117 calories
Prep: Wash, cut, and remove fruit from the pith. Place on trays and pre-freeze. For powder: blend with water, strain out seeds, pour measured amount on trays, and pre-freeze.
Freeze-Dry Time: 50-60+ hours - default settings
Use: Smoothies, toppings, and natural coloring.
Rehydrate: Soak or add ½ cup of water to 1 cup of pomegranate. Sit for 5-10 min.
Tip: Roll the pomegranate before cutting to loosen the arils for easier prep.

Raspberries
Serving: 123 grams (1 cup) 64 calories
Prep: Gently rinse, pat dry, place on trays, and pre-freeze. For powder: blend with water, strain out seeds, pour measured amount on trays, and pre-freeze.
Freeze-Dry Time: 45-55 hours - default settings
Use: Flavored water, pies, smoothies, and desserts.
Rehydrate: Add ½ cup of water to 1 cup of raspberries. Sit for 5-10 min.
Tip: Add freeze-dried raspberry powder to cocktails for a fruity twist.

Rhubarb
Serving: 122 grams (1 cup) 26 calories
Prep: Remove toxic leaves and rinse stalks. Dice to ½", place on trays, and pre-freeze. For powder: blend with water, pour measured amount on trays, and pre-freeze.
Freeze-Dry Time: 30-40 hours - default settings
Use: Jams, pies, and flavorings.
Rehydrate: Add ½ cup of water to 1 cup of rhubarb pieces. Sit for 5-10 min.
Tip: Use in savory sauces for pork or chicken.

Strawberries
Serving: 152 grams (1 cup sliced) 49 calories
Prep: Rinse, pat dry, and remove caps. Slice ¼ - ½" thick, place on trays, and pre-freeze. For powder: blend with water, strain out seeds, pour measured amount on trays, and pre-freeze.
Freeze-Dry Time: 35-45+ hours - default settings
Use: Snacks, pies, cakes, jams, smoothies, ice cream, muffins, toppings, and desserts.
Rehydrate: Add ½ cup of water to 1 cup of strawberries. Sit for 5 min.
Tip: Always needs extra drying time due to the seeds.

Tangerines
Serving: 76 grams (1 small) 40 calories
Prep: Cut into ½" slices or peel and separate segments. Remove pith and seeds, place on trays, and pre-freeze. For powder: blend (with or without peel) with water, pour measured amount on trays, and pre-freeze.
Freeze-Dry Time: 30-40+ hours - default settings
Use: Flavored waters, garnish, dressings, marinades, and salads.
Rehydrate: Soak segments in water 10+ minutes and drain off excess.
Tip: Select sweet fruits and puncture each segment.

Watermelon
Serving: 152 grams (1 cup diced) 46 calories
Prep: Rinse cut, and remove the rind. Use a melon baller, slice, or cube to ½" max pieces, place on trays, and pre-freeze.
Freeze-Dry Time: 50-60+ hours - default settings
Use: Dry snacks and desserts.
Rehydrate: Soak pieces in water or add ½ cup of water to 1 cup of watermelon pieces. Sit for 5-10 min.
Tip: Always needs lots of extra dry time because of the high water content.

Vegetables   Approximate Shelf Life: 20-25 yrs

Asparagus
Serving: 90 grams (½ cup) 20 calories
Prep: Rinse spears and remove tough ends. Leave intact, or chop into pieces, blanch for 2-4 min, cool, place on trays, and pre-freeze. Cooked: Sauté in water until tender, cool, place on trays, and pre-freeze.
Freeze-Dry Time: 25-35 hours - default settings
Use: Snacks, salads, soups, casseroles, chowders.
Rehydrate: Dip in water for 30 sec. Sauté with butter for 1-3 min.
Tip: Blend into pesto for a unique twist.

Beets
Serving: 68 grams (½ cup) 29 calories
Prep: Rinse and remove all but 1" of the stem. For raw, blanch 5-10 min, peel, shred or slice to ½", place on trays, and pre-freeze. Cooked: Boil for 20-40 min until tender, put in an ice bath, drain, remove the skin and stem, rinse, slice or chop into pieces no thicker than ½", place on trays, and pre-freeze.
Freeze-Dry Time: 30-40 hours - default settings
Use: Snacks, salads, smoothies, coloring, & stir-fries.
Rehydrate: Add ½ cup water to 1 cup beets. Let sit for 10+ min. Sauté with butter for 1-3 min.
Tip: Blend into hummus for a colorful dip.

Bok Choy

Serving: 70 grams (1 cup) 10 calories
Prep: Rinse, half, and cut out core. Slice, shred, or chop to bite size, place on trays, and pre-freeze. Blend with water (for green powder,) pour measured amount onto trays and pre-freeze. Cooked: Sauté in water for 3-5 min, cool, place on trays, and pre-freeze.
Freeze-Dry Time: 30-40 hours - default settings
Use: Stir-fries, soups, and stews.
Rehydrate: No. Best used as a recipe ingredient or as a nutrient powder.
Tip: Add to ramen for extra greens.

Broccoli

Serving: 91 grams (1 cup) 31 calories
Prep: Rinse, remove outer leaves, and cut into small florets. Blanch for 3-5 min, put in an ice bath, drain, place on trays, and pre-freeze. Cooked: Boil 15 min, drain, cool, place on trays, and pre-freeze.
Freeze-Dry Time: 30-40 hours - default settings
Use: Snacks, salads, casseroles, soups, and chowders.
Rehydrate: Add ⅓ cup water to 1 cup broccoli. Let sit for 5-10 min.
Tip: Incorporate into quiches for a protein-packed breakfast.

Brussel Sprouts

Serving: 78 grams (½ cup) 28 calories
Prep: Rinse, trim stem ends, and cut into halves. Blanch for 3-5 min, place in ice bath, drain, place on trays, and pre-freeze. Cooked: Sauté in water until tender, cool, place on trays, and pre-freeze.
Freeze-Dry Time: 30-40 hours - default settings
Use: Stir-fries, soups, and sautés.
Rehydrate: Add ⅓ cup water to 1 cup brussel sprouts and let sit for 5-10 min. Sauté with butter for 1-3 min.
Tip: Roast prior to freeze-drying to enhance flavor.

Cabbage

Serving: 89 grams (1 cup shredded) 22 calories
Prep: Wash and remove the core. Shred or chop the leaves or make ½" slices, and pre-freeze. Blend with water (for greens powder,) pour measured amount on tray, and pre-freeze. Cooked: Boil for 10-15 min, drain, cool, place on trays, and pre-freeze.
Freeze-Dry Time: 30-40 hours - default settings
Use: Soups, stews, roasts, sautés, and cole slaw.
Rehydrate: Add ⅓ cup water to 1 cup cabbage and let sit for 2-5 min.
Tip: Use a food processor to shred quickly.

Carrots

Serving: 61 grams (1 medium or ½ cup) 25 calories
Prep: Rinse, peel or scrub, shred, dice, or cut into ½" sticks, coins, or chunks. Blanch ALL Raw Carrots for 3-5 minutes, drain, place on trays, and pre-freeze. Cooked: Boil 20-40 mins till tender, drain, cool, place on trays, and pre-freeze.
Freeze-Dry Time: 25-35 hours - default settings
Use: Soups, stews, roasts, and stir-fries.
Rehydrate: Add ½ cup water to 1 cup carrots. Let sit for 10+ min.
Tip: Use a mandoline slicer for uniform slices.

Cauliflower

Serving: 107 grams (1 cup florets) 27 calories
Prep: Rinse, cut into small florets, place on trays, and pre-freeze. Riced: Pulse raw into granules, spread on trays, and pre-freeze. Cooked: Boil 10 min, drain, cool, place on trays, and pre-freeze.
Freeze-Dry Time: 25-35+ hours - default settings
Use: Snacks, soups, casseroles, side dishes, and flour.
Rehydrate: Add ⅓ cup water to 1 cup cauliflower. Let sit for 5-10 min.
Tip: Rehydrate and blend into soups to add a creamy consistency.

Celery

Serving: 40 grams (1 medium stalk) 6 calories
Prep: Separate and rinse stalks. Trim off leaves and ends. Slice or dice to a max of ½", place on trays, and pre-freeze.
Freeze-Dry Time: 35-45 hours - default settings
Use: Soups, stews, broths, and seasoning.
Rehydrate: Add ⅓+ cup water to 1 cup celery. Let sit for 10+ min.
Tip: Sauté with onions and butter for a savory side dish. No need to rehydrate prior to sautéing.

Corn, Sweet

Serving: 85 grams (¾ cup or 1 med cob) 88 calories
Prep: Remove husks and silk, blanch corn 3-5 min, put it in an ice bath, cut the corn from the cob, place on trays, and pre-freeze. Cooked or canned corn: drain, place on trays, and pre-freeze.
Freeze-Dry Time: 30-40 hours - default settings
Use: Snacks, soups, stews, and casseroles.
Rehydrate: Add ½ cup water to 1 cup corn. Let sit for 5-10 min.
Tip: Add to salads for a sweet, crunchy texture.

Cucumber
Serving: 52 grams (½ cup sliced) 8 calories
Prep: Rinse, peel if desired. Slice up to ½" thickness place on trays, and pre-freeze. To de-seed slice lengthwise, scoop out seeds, slice or chop into ½" pieces, place on trays, and pre-freeze.
Freeze-Dry Time: 40-50+ hours - default settings
Use: Snacks, salads, smoothies, flavored water, and sauces.
Rehydrate: Add ½ cup water to 1 cup cucumber. Let sit for 5-10 min.
Tip: Use in Tzatziki sauce for a tangy dip.

Eggplant
Serving: 41 grams (½ cup cubed) 11 calories
Prep: Rinse, remove stem, peel if desired, cut into slices or dice into pieces no thicker than ½", and pre-freeze. Cooked: After slicing sprinkle with salt and allow it to rest for 30-60 min. Rinse and pat dry. Sauté in water until tender, cool, place on trays, and pre-freeze.
Freeze-Dry Time: 25-35 hours - default settings
Use: Faux meatballs, fritters, dips, stews, casseroles.
Rehydrate: Dip in water for 30-60 sec per side, then sauté.
Tip: Microwave for faster tenderizing.

Garlic
Serving: 3 grams (1 clove) 5 calories
Prep: Separate cloves, remove end, and peel. Cut in halves or slices, mince or roughly chop, place on trays, and pre-freeze.
Freeze-Dry Time: 25-35 hours - default settings
Use: Soups, stews, stir-fries, and seasoning.
Rehydrate: Add 1 tsp water to 1 Tbs garlic for 3 cloves of garlic and let sit for 3-5 min.
Tip: Difficult to freeze-dry whole and must be punctured.

Green Beans
Serving: 100 grams (1 cup) 31 calories
Prep: Rinse, remove stems and strings, cut into pieces if desired, blanch for 3-5 minutes, place in ice bath, drain, place on trays, and pre-freeze. Cooked or canned beans: drain, place on trays, and pre-freeze.
Freeze-Dry Time: 25-35 hours - default settings
Use: Snacks, soups, stews, and casseroles.
Rehydrate: Add ⅓-½ cup of water to 1 cup of green beans. Let sit for 20+ min.
Tip: Buy frozen green beans to skip prep.

Kale
Serving: 21 grams (1 cup) 8 calories
Prep: Rinse whole or chopped leaves, use raw or blanch for 2-3 minutes, place in ice bath, drain, place on trays, and pre-freeze. Blend with water (for green powder,) pour measured amount onto trays and pre-freeze.
Freeze-Dry Time: 25-35 hours - default settings
Use: Snacks, smoothies, soups, stews, eggs, casseroles, and powdered greens.
Rehydrate: No. Best used as a recipe ingredient or as a nutrient powder.
Tip: Powdered kale can be added to most food for a nutrient boost.

Leeks
Serving: 45 grams (½ medium leek) 27 calories
Prep: Rinse, remove outer leaves, trim roots, slice or dice into pieces no thicker than ½", place on trays, and pre-freeze.
Freeze-Dry Time: 25-35 hours - default settings
Use: Soups, stews, sautés, and stir-fries.
Rehydrate: Add ⅓ cup water to 1 cup leeks and let sit for 2-5 min.
Tip: Cook leeks with onions and garlic, then blend and freeze-dry as a soup base.

Lettuce, Romaine
Serving: 72 grams (1 cup shredded) 10 calories
Prep: Wash and discard the root. Roughly chop the leaves, place on trays, and pre-freeze. Blend with water (for greens powder,) pour measured amount on tray, and pre-freeze.
Freeze-Dry Time: 25-35 hours - default settings
Use: Snacks, smoothies, and stir-fries.
Rehydrate: No. Best used as a recipe ingredient or as a nutrient powder.
Tip: Use a salad spinner to dry quickly after rinsing.

Mushrooms
Serving: 70 grams (1 cup sliced) 15 calories
Prep: Rinse gently, slice or chop into pieces no thicker than ½", place on trays, and pre-freeze. Cooked: Sauté 5-10 minutes in water. Cool, place on trays, and pre-freeze.
Freeze-Dry Time: 25-35 hours - default settings
Use: Snacks, soups, stews, salads, sauces, & stir-fries.
Rehydrate: Add ¼ cup water to 1 cup of mushrooms and let sit for 3-5 min.
Tip: Blend into sauces for extra flavor.

Okra

Serving: 80 grams (½ cup sliced) 18 calories
Prep: Rinse, remove cap and tip, slice into coins or pieces no more than ½" thick, place on trays, and pre-freeze. Cooked: Bake at 350°F for 20 minutes, cool, place on trays, and pre-freeze.
Freeze-Dry Time: 25-35 hours - default settings
Use: Soups, stews, curry, gumbo, and fried okra.
Rehydrate: Add ½-⅔ cup water to 1 cup okra and let sit for 5-10 min.
Tip: Eat freeze-dried for a crunchy non-slimy snack.

Onions

Serving: 110 grams (1 medium) 44 calories
Prep: Rinse, remove outer leaves, trim roots, slice or dice into pieces no thicker than ½", place on trays, and pre-freeze.
Freeze-Dry Time: 25-35 hours - default settings
Use: Soups, stews, casseroles, salads, stir-fries, sautés, sauces, marinades, and seasoning.
Rehydrate: Add ½-⅔ cup water to 1 cup onions and let sit for 3-5 min.
Tip: Blend for an incredible onion powder.

Parsnips

Serving: 100 grams (1 cup) 75 calories
Prep: Rinse, peel, shred, dice, or cut into ½" sticks, coins, or chunks. Blanch for 3-5 minutes, drain, place on trays, and pre-freeze. Cooked: Boil 20-40 mins till tender, drain, cool, place on trays, and pre-freeze.
Freeze-Dry Time: 25-35 hours - default settings
Use: Soups and stews.
Rehydrate: Add ⅓-½ cup water to 1 cup parsnips. Let sit for 10+ min.
Tip: Use a vegetable chopper for quick dicing.

Peas, Green

Serving: 80 grams (½ cup) 62 calories
Prep: Rinse, shell peas, blanch for 2-3 min, place in ice bath, place on trays, and pre-freeze. Cooked or canned peas: drain, place on trays, and pre-freeze.
Freeze-Dry Time: 25-35 hours - default settings
Use: Snacks, soups, stews, casseroles, and salads.
Rehydrate: Add ½ cup water to 1 cup peas and let sit for 3-5 min.
Tip: Freeze-dried peas can be used just like fresh.

Peas, Snap/Snow

Serving: 63 grams (1 cup) 27 calories
Prep: Rinse, remove stems and strings, cut into pieces if desired, place on trays, and pre-freeze.
Freeze-Dry Time: 25-35 hours - default settings
Use: Snacks, salads, and stir-fries
Rehydrate: Add ½ cup water to 1 cup snap peas and let sit for 5-10 min.
Tip: These make a nice, crunchy snack. Add seasonings for a different flavor.

Peppers, Hot

Serving: 14 grams (1 pepper) 4 calories
Prep: Wear gloves to avoid burns. Rinse, cut in half, remove seeds and stem, slice into strips or dice into pieces no thicker than ½", place on trays, and pre-freeze.
Freeze-Dry Time: 25-35 hours - default settings - default settings
Use: Chili, stews, soups, sauces, salsas, seasonings, and marinades.
Rehydrate: Add ⅓ cup water to 1 cup pepper and let sit for 3-5 min.
Tip: Mix powder 50:50 with salt for a spicy seasoning.

Peppers, Sweet

Serving: 149 grams (1 cup or medium) 39 calories
Prep: Rinse, cut in half, remove seeds and stem, slice into strips or dice into pieces no thicker than ½", place on trays, and pre-freeze.
Freeze-Dry Time: 25-35 hours - default settings
Use: Snacks, fajitas, creole, stews, soups, sauces, seasonings, and salsas.
Rehydrate: Add ⅓ cup water to 1 cup pepper and let sit for 3-5 min.
Tip: Make a powder with Red bell peppers to create your own paprika.

Potatoes

Serving: 173 grams (1 medium) 164 calories
Prep: Scrub well, peel, and cut into ¼-½" pieces. Soak and drain 3 times to remove starch. Blanch ALL Raw Potatoes for 1-3 minutes, place in ice-bath, drain, and pre-freeze. Cooked: Boil 20-30 mins till tender, drain, (mash if desired,) place on trays, and pre-freeze.
Freeze-Dry Time: 30-40+ hours - default settings
Use: Snacks, fries, mashed, casseroles, skillets, stir-fries, thickener, and flour.
Rehydrate: Add ½ cup water to 1 cup potato and let sit for 5-10 min. For mashed, add ¾ cup water to 1 cup potato powder and let sit for 5-10 min.
Tip: Very fragile. Potatoes can easily be turned into a powder.

Pumpkin
Serving: 245 grams (1 cup) 49 calories
Prep: Rinse, cut in half, remove seeds, slice or cube into pieces no thicker than ½", and pre-freeze. Cooked: Bake two halves at 350°F for 60-90 minutes or until tender, scrape out of skin, mash, cool, spread on trays and pre-freeze.
Freeze-Dry Time: 30-40 hours - default settings
Use: Snacks, pies, bread, soups, thickener, and flour.
Rehydrate: Add ½ cup water to 1 cup pumpkin chunks and let sit for 10+ min. For puree, add ¾ cup water to 1 cup pumpkin powder.
Tip: Add pumpkin powder and spices to pancake batter for a fall twist.

Radish
Serving: 116 grams (1 cup) 19 calories
Prep: Rinse, trim stem, slice, shred, or dice into pieces no thicker than ½", place on trays, and pre-freeze.
Freeze-Dry Time: 30-40 hours - default settings
Use: Snacks, stir-fries, and salads.
Rehydrate: No. Best used as a crunchy topping, snack, or ingredient.
Tip: Adds a nice spicy crunch to salads.

Rutabaga
Serving: 140 grams (1 cup) 52 calories
Prep: Rinse, peel, and cut into ¼-½" pieces, place on trays, and pre-freeze. Cooked: Boil 15-20 mins till tender, drain, cool, and pre-freeze.
Freeze-Dry Time: 25-35 hours - default settings
Use: Roasts, soups, and mashed.
Rehydrate: Add ½ cup water to 1 cup rutabaga and let sit for 10+ min.
Tip: Toss into a roasting pan with potatoes, carrots, onions, and beef roast.

Scallions
Serving: 15 grams (1 medium) 5 calories
Prep: Rinse, remove outer leaves, trim roots, slice or dice into pieces no thicker than ½", place on trays, and pre-freeze.
Freeze-Dry Time: 25-35 hours - default settings
Use: Garnish, stir-fries, soups, stews, salads, and seasoning.
Rehydrate: Add ⅓ cup water to 1 cup scallions and let sit for 2-5 min.
Tip: Excellent garnish, no need to rehydrate.

Spinach
Serving: 29 grams (1 cup) 7 calories
Prep: Rinse and lay out raw leaves or chop to bite size, place on trays, and pre-freeze. Blend with water (for green powder,) pour measured amount onto trays and pre-freeze. Cooked: Blanch for 3 minutes, drain, cool, and pre-freeze.
Freeze-Dry Time: 25-35 hours - default settings
Use: Smoothies, quiches, soups, sauces, stews, eggs, casseroles, and powdered greens.
Rehydrate: Add ⅛ cup water to 1 cup spinach and let sit for 3-5 min, then sauté. Powder is best used as a recipe ingredient or as a nutrient powder.
Tip: Perfect powder to use in smoothies or sauces to add in extra nutrition.

Squash, Butternut
Serving: 205 grams (1 cup) 82 calories
Prep: Rinse, peel, remove seeds, slice or cube into pieces no thicker than ½", and pre-freeze. Cooked: Bake at 350°F for 20-30 minutes, cool, place on trays, and pre-freeze. Blend with water (for soup powder), pour measured amount onto trays, and pre-freeze.
Freeze-Dry Time: 30-40 hours - default settings
Use: Soups, sautéed dishes, thickener, and flour.
Rehydrate: Add ¾ cup water to 1 cup squash pieces and let sit for 10+ min. For puree, add ¾-1 cup water to 1 cup squash powder.
Tip: Thin slices can be eaten as a snack, like chips.

Squash, Spaghetti
Serving: 155 grams (1 cup) 42 calories
Prep: Rinse, cut lengthwise, and remove seeds. Cooked: Bake at 400°F for 30-40 minutes and cool. Scrape strands out, place on trays, and pre-freeze.
Freeze-Dry Time: 40-50 hours - default settings
Use: Faux meatballs, fritters, sautées, thickener, and flour. Use as flour, 1:2 with regular flour.
Rehydrate: Add ⅓-½ cup water to 1 cup squash and let sit for 5-10 min.
Tip: Works well as a pasta substitute for low-carb meals.

Squash, Yellow
Serving: 113 grams (1 cup) 18 calories
Prep: Rinse, peel, remove seeds, slice or cube into pieces no thicker than ½", and pre-freeze. Cooked: Bake until tender, cool, and pre-freeze.
Freeze-Dry Time: 25-35 hours - default settings
Use: Snacks, casseroles, soups, thickener, and flour
Rehydrate: Add ½ cup water to 1 cup squash and let sit for 5-10 min.
Tip: Slice thin and sprinkle on different seasonings for tasty chips.

Squash, Zucchini
Serving: 124 grams (1 cup) 21 calories
Prep: Rinse, peel, remove seeds, slice, cube, or shred, into pieces no thicker than ½" and pre-freeze. Cooked: Bake until tender, cool, and pre-freeze.
Freeze-Dry Time: 25-35 hours - default settings
Use: Snacks, soups, baked goods, breads, flour, and powdered nutrition. Ratio: Use as flour, 1:2 with regular flour.
Rehydrate: Add ½ cup water to 1 cup zucchini and let sit for 5-10 min.
Tip: Great as chips! Easy and near tasteless powder can be used as a nutrient boost in many dishes.

Sweet Potatoes
Serving: 180 grams (1 large) 162 calories
Prep: Scrub well, peel, and slice, shred, or dice into pieces no thicker than ½". Soak and drain 3 times to remove starch & pre-freeze. Cooked: Boil 10-20 mins till tender, drain, cool, (mash if desired,) & pre-freeze.
Freeze-Dry Time: 30-40 hours - default settings
Use: Snacks, fries, mashed, soups, stews, casseroles, skillets, stir-fries, thickener, and flour.
Rehydrate: Add ⅓-½ cup water to 1 cup potato chunks and let sit for 5-10 min. For mashed, add ¾ cup water to 1 cup sweet potato powder.
Tip: Add cinnamon for a sweet flavor.

Swiss Chard
Serving: 36 grams (1 cup) 7 calories
Prep: Rinse and lay out raw leaves or chop to bite size, place on trays, and pre-freeze. Blend with water (for green powder,) pour measured amount onto trays and pre-freeze. Cooked: Blanch for 3 minutes, drain, cool, place on trays, and pre-freeze.
Freeze-Dry Time: 25-35 hours - default settings
Use: Soups, stews, casseroles, and powdered greens.
Rehydrate: Gently spray the swiss chard with water and let it sit for 3-5 min, then sauté. Powder is best used as a recipe ingredient or as a nutrient powder.
Tip: Cut out the spine to avoid any bitter flavor.

Tomatoes
Serving: 91 grams (1 small) 16 calories
Prep: Rinse and discard the stem. Slice to ½" max thickness and pre-freeze. Chunk or quarter, remove seeds for faster processing, place on trays, and pre-freeze. Blend with water (for powder,) pour measured amount on tray and pre-freeze. Cooked: Simmer into a sauce with seasonings, cool, blend, pour measured amount on tray and pre-freeze.
Freeze-Dry Time: 35-45+ hours - default settings
Use: Burger slices, salads, soups, stews, and sauces.
Rehydrate: Add ⅔-¾ cup water to 1 cup tomato chunks. For sauce add ¾ cup water to 1 cup powder. For juice, add 1 cup water to ¼ cup powder.
Tip: Always needs extra drying time due to the seeds.

Turnips
Serving: 156 grams (1 cup) 34 calories
Prep: Rinse, peel, and cut into ¼-½" pieces, place on trays, and pre-freeze. Cooked: Boil 20-40 mins till tender, drain, cool, place on trays, and pre-freeze.
Freeze-Dry Time: 25-35 hours - default settings
Use: Stews, roasts, and soups.
Rehydrate: Add ½ cup water to 1 cup turnips and let sit for 10+ min.
Tip: Add herbs before freeze-drying for a savory side.

Yams
Serving: 136 grams (1 cup) 158 calories
Prep: Scrub well, peel, and cut into ¼-½" pieces - slices or cubes, place on trays, and pre-freeze. Cooked: Boil 10-20 mins till tender, drain, cool, (mash if desired,) place on trays, and pre-freeze.
Freeze-Dry Time: 30-40 hours - default settings
Use: Soups, stews, casseroles, mashed, and flour.
Rehydrate: Add ⅓-½ cup water to 1 cup yam chunks and let sit for 5-10 min. For mashed, add ¾ cup water to 1 cup yam powder.
Tip: Can be used as a substitute for sweet potatoes.

Dairy   Approximate Shelf Life: 10-15 yrs

Cottage Cheese
Serving: 100 grams (3.5 oz) 84 calories
Prep: Spread measured cottage cheese evenly on the trays and pre-freeze.
Freeze-Dry Time: 20-30 hours - default settings
Use: Side dish, casseroles, or protein smoothies.
Rehydrate: Combine ¾ cup water with 1 cup crumbles. Add water gradually and stir. Best left to sit overnight in the refrigerator.
Tip: Process in a blender to make a protein powder.

Cream Cheese
Serving: 15 grams (1 Tbs) 51 calories
Prep: Cut into ½" thick slices or chunks. Place on trays and pre-freeze.
Freeze-Dry Time: 20-30 hours - default settings
Use: Spreads, dips, frosting, and cheesecakes.
Rehydrate: Add ½ cup water to 1 cup cream cheese chunks and let sit in fridge 3+ hours. If powdered, mix 1 Tbs of water with 2 Tbs powder.
Tip: Rehydration texture is best when allowed to sit overnight in the fridge.

Sour Cream

Serving: 29 grams (2 Tbs) 57 calories
Prep: Spread measured cream evenly on tray and pre-freeze.
Freeze-Dry Time: 20-30 hours - default settings
Use: Sauces, soups, dips, dressings, and toppings.
Rehydrate: Add ⅔ cup water to 1 cup powder and let sit in fridge 3+ hours. Best texture can be achieved with room temperature water and an immersion blender.
Tip: Add freeze-dried sour cream to mashed potatoes for extra creaminess.

Sweet Cream

Serving: Heavy: 30 grams (1 oz) 100 calories
Whipped Serving: 6 grams (2 Tbs) 15 calories
Prep: Pipe small dollops onto lined trays and pre-freeze. Place empty trays in freezer. Pour measured cream onto trays, cover, and pre-freeze.
Freeze-Dry Time: 20-35 hours - default settings
Use: Sauces, soups, stews, desserts, baked goods, and drinks like hot cocoa and coffee.
Rehydrate: Add ½-⅔ cup water to 1 cup powder and let sit in fridge 3+ hours. Best texture can be achieved with room temperature water and an immersion blender.
Tip: Keep it whipped to stop separation.
Note: Shelf Life is 1-3 yrs.

Ice Cream, any flavor

Serving: Vanilla: 134 grams (1 cup) 270 calories
Strawberry: 134 grams (1 cup) 250 calories
Chocolate: 134 grams (1 cup) 285 calories
Mint Chocolate Chip: 134 grams (1 cup) 300 calories
Cookies & Cream: 134 grams (1 cup) 330 calories
Cookie Dough: 134 grams (1 cup) 320 calories
Butter Pecan: 134 grams (1 cup) 270 calories
Pecan Praline: 134 grams (1 cup) 270 calories
Prep: Ensure ice cream has been frozen for at least 12 hours. Use a melon baller or a knife to create bite-sized pieces. Place on a cold tray. Pre-freeze for 12+ hours. Adjust initial freeze to -25°F. Allow the Chamber to cool 60-90 minutes after pressing Start.
Freeze-Dry Time: 20-30 hours - UPDATE settings
Use: Snacks, holiday gift, or treat.
Rehydrate: Not recommended.
Tip: The powder tastes great as a coffee creamer substitute.
Note: Shelf Life is 2-5 yrs.

Milk, any kind

Serving: Whole White: 244 grams (1 cup) 150 calorie
2% White: 244 grams (1 cup) 122 calories
1% White: 244 grams (1 cup) 100 calories
Skim White: 244 grams (1 cup) 80 calories
1% Chocolate: 244 grams (1 cup) 160 calories
Almond: 249 grams (1 cup) 60 calories
Rice: 240 grams (1 cup) 110 calories
Coconut: 226 grams (1 cup) 450 calories
Prep: Place empty trays in freezer. Pour measured milk onto trays, cover, and pre-freeze.
Freeze-Dry Time: 25-35 hours - default settings
Use: Rehydrated drink or powder for recipes.
Rehydrate: Add 1 cup of water to ¼ cup milk powder and blend well.
Tip: Tastes best when whisked and refridgerated.

Hard Cheeses

Serving: Cheddar: 28 grams (1 oz) 120 calories
Colby: 28 grams (1 oz) 110 calories
Parmesan: 28 grams (1 oz) 110 calories
Swiss: 28 grams (1 oz) 100 calories
Prep: Shredded: Shred cheese, lay paper towels on trays, spread shreds over towels, and pre-freeze. Sliced/Cubed/Curds: Cut to between ¼ - ¾ inches, lay paper towels on trays, place cheese, and pre-freeze.
Freeze-Dry Time: 20-30 hours - default settings
Use: Snacks, pastas, casseroles, and grilled cheese.
Rehydrate: For shreds, spritz with water. For slices and cubes, soak in water 5-10 min and drain off excess. Some cheeses need to soak overnight.
Tip: Freeze-dry in grated form for easy melting and for use in recipes.

Soft Cheeses

Serving: Brie: 28 grams (1 oz) 100 calories
Feta: 28 grams (1 oz) 80 calories
Mozzarella: 28 grams (1 oz) 90 calories
Ricotta: 28 grams (1 oz) 39 calories
Prep: Slice, crumble, or spread cheese onto trays. Maintain the original shape as much as possible and pre-freeze.
Freeze-Dry Time: 18-24 hours - default settings
Use: Salads, sandwiches, or pizzas after rehydration.
Rehydrate: Gently mist with water or let sit in a small amount of water until desired consistency is reached.
Tip: Freeze-drying soft cheeses can alter their texture, so experiment with small batches.

Kefir

Serving: 235 grams (1 cup) 139 calories
Prep: Place empty trays in freezer. Pour measured kefir onto trays and pre-freeze. Set Dry Temp to 90°F.
Freeze-Dry Time: 20-35 hours - UPDATE settings
Use: Smoothies, trail mixes, oatmeal, or desserts.
Rehydrate: Add ¾-1 cup water to 1 cup powder and let sit in fridge 3+ hours. Best texture can be achieved with room temperature water and an immersion blender.
Tip: Kefir grains freeze-dry as well and can be reactivated by soaking them in milk.

Yogurt

Serving: Plain: 235 grams (1 cup) 154 calories
Vanilla: 235 grams (1 cup) 208 calories
Blueberry: 235 grams (1 cup) 243 calories
Strawberry: 235 grams (1 cup) 243 calories
Prep: Place empty trays in freezer. Pour measured kefir onto trays and pre-freeze. Set Dry Temp to 90°F.
Freeze-Dry Time: 20-35 hours - UPDATE settings
Use: Snacks, smoothies, oatmeal, or desserts.
Rehydrate: Add ¾-1 cup water to 1 cup powder and let sit in fridge 3+ hours. Best texture can be achieved with room temperature water and an immersion blender.
Tip: Spread into molds and pre-freeze to create easy bites, saving your hands from squeezing manually.

Eggs

Serving: 50 grams (1 large) 78 calories
Prep: Raw: Blend cracked eggs. Place empty trays in freezer. Pour blended eggs onto trays and pre-freeze. Scrambled: Slightly undercook, let cool, then spread on trays and pre-freeze. Skillets & casseroles: Cook as desired, let cool, cut into slices or pieces with ¾" max thickness. place on trays, and pre-freeze.
Freeze-Dry Time: 25-35 hours - default settings
Use: Scrambled eggs, omelets, casseroles, and baking ingredient.
Rehydrate: For a single egg, add 2 Tbs water to 1 Tbs egg powder. For 8 eggs, add 1 cup water to ½ cup egg powder. Whip well and let sit for 5 min.
Tip: Avoid over-whipping the eggs as the air can cause it to bubble up and could make a mess.
Note: Shelf Life is 20-25 yrs for Eggs

Deli Meat, various

Serving: Ham: 51 grams (2 oz or 2-4 slices) 61 calorie
Chicken: 51 grams (2 oz or 2-4 slices) 58 calories
Turkey: 51 grams (2 oz or 2-4 slices) 67 calories
Roast Beef: 51 grams (2 oz or 2-4 slices) 70 calories
Prep: Roll up 2-3 slices depending on type and thickness. Place them on the tray and pre-freeze.
Freeze-Dry Time: 20-30 hours - default settings
Use: Snacks, salads, sandwiches, wraps, scrambles, toppings, or pizzas.
Rehydrate: Dip in shallow water 30-60 seconds to restore to original condition.
Tip: Becomes very delicate. Best packaged in glass jars to prevent crumbling.
Note: Shelf Life is 20 yrs for poultry deli meat and 10 yrs for red meats.

Beef   Approximate Shelf Life: 5-10 yrs

Ground Beef, 97% Lean

Serving: 85 grams (3 oz) 160 calories
Prep: Raw: Use 97% Lean, spread on trays, and pre-freeze. Bake Loaf: °F for min. Cool and slice to ¾" max thickness and pre-freeze. Pan Fry: 7-10 minutes and drain off fat. Cover beef with water and refrigerate overnight. Remove the fat cap the next morning. Drain off liquids, pat dry, place on trays, and pre-freeze.
Freeze-Dry Time: 25-35 hours - default settings
Use: Soups, stews, tacos, casseroles, or gravy.
Rehydrate: Soak raw meat in cold water in the fridge overnight. For cooked, use hot water and soak 10-15 min. Use excess water as broth.
Tip: Adding ¼ c breadcrumbs per 1 lb raw beef during cooking can assist with faster rehydration later.

Filets

Serving: 85 grams (3 oz) 227 calories
Prep: Raw: Trim off fat, cut to ¾" max thickness and pre-freeze. Pan Fry: 4-8 min each side. Grill: 4-5 min each side. Bake: 425°F for 15-20 min. Rinse, cool, place on trays, and pre-freeze.
Freeze-Dry Time: 25-35 hours - default settings
Use: Grill raw rehydrated filets for a fresh flavor.
Rehydrate: Soak raw meat in cold water in the fridge overnight. For cooked, use hot water and soak for 15-20 min, then cook on a grill or pan-fry.
Tip: Soaking filets in a marinade for at least 30 minutes before cooking gives incredible flavor.

Kabob Meat and Strips

Serving: 85 grams (3 oz) 220 calories
Prep: Raw: Trim off fat, cut to ¾" max thickness and pre-freeze. Pan Fry: 2-3 min each side. Grill: 2-4 min each side. Bake: 425°F for 10-15 min. Rinse, cool, place on trays, and pre-freeze.
Freeze-Dry Time: 25-35 hours - default settings
Use: Snacks, fajitas, sandwiches, or gravy.
Rehydrate: Soak raw meat in cold water in the fridge overnight. For cooked, use hot water and soak for 15-20 min.
Tip: On-the-stick kabobs with thinly sliced meats and veggies can also be freeze-dried together.

Meatballs

Serving: 113 grams (4 medium) 324 calories
Prep: Raw: cut to ¾" max thickness and pre-freeze. Pan Fry: 15 min. Grill: 6-8 min each side. Bake: 400°F for 20-25 min. Rinse, cool, place on trays, and pre-freeze.
Freeze-Dry Time: 25-35 hours - default settings
Use: Snacks, soups, sauces, platters, or sandwiches.
Rehydrate: Soak raw meat in cold water in the fridge overnight. For cooked, use hot water and soak for 30-60 mins or add dry to sauces.
Tip: Mix in grated vegetables (like carrots or zucchini) for added nutrition and faster rehydration.

Patties, hamburger (non-breaded)

Serving: 85 grams (3 oz patty) 200 calories
Prep: Raw: Use 97% Lean and keep to ¾" max thickness and pre-freeze. Pan Fry: 4-6 min each side. Grill: 3-5 min each side. Bake: 400°F for 15-20 min. Cool, place on trays, and pre-freeze.
Freeze-Dry Time: 25-35 hours - default settings
Use: Grill raw rehydrated patties for a fresh burger.
Rehydrate: Soak raw meat in cold water in the fridge 3+ hours or overnight. For cooked, use hot water and soak for 10-15 min, then cook on a grill or pan-fry.
Tip: Crumble patties into spaghetti sauce or chili for a quick meaty boost.

Pot Roast

Serving: 85 grams (3 oz) 255 calories
Prep: Raw: Trim off fat, cut to ¾" max thickness and pre-freeze. Bake: 325 °F for 2 hrs. Cool, slice or shred. Pressure Cooker: Slow cook with 1 cup of water until it shreds easily with a fork. Cover shreds with water and refrigerate overnight. Remove the fat cap the next morning. Drain off liquids, pat dry, place on trays, and pre-freeze.
Freeze-Dry Time: 25-35 hours - default settings
Use: Soups, enchiladas, tacos, or stews.
Rehydrate: Soak raw meat in cold water in the fridge overnight. For cooked, add ⅓ cup hot water to 1 cup of freeze-dried pork, stir & let sit covered for 10-15 min.
Tip: Roast decreases in weight by about 50% when cooked. Use the cooking liquid to make a gravy, freeze-dry separately, and rehydrate together for a complete meal.

Steak

Serving: 85 grams (3 oz) 180 calories
Prep: Raw: Trim off fat, cut to ¾" max thickness and pre-freeze. Pan Fry: 5-6 min each side. Grill: 4-6 min each side. Rinse, cool, place on trays, and pre-freeze.
Freeze-Dry Time: 25-35 hours - default settings
Use: Grill raw rehydrated steaks for a fresh flavor.
Rehydrate: Soak raw meat in cold water in the fridge overnight. For cooked, use hot water and soak for 15-20 min, then cook on a grill or pan-fry.
Tip: Cook the steak to medium-rare (135°F) before freeze-drying to ensure it isn't overcooked after rehydration.

Stew Meat

Serving: 85 grams (3 oz) 160 calories
Prep: Raw: Trim off fat, cut chunks to ¾" max thickness and pre-freeze. Pan Fry: 2-3 min each side. Boil: 1½ - 2 hrs. Rinse, cool, place on trays, and pre-freeze.
Freeze-Dry Time: 25-35 hours - default settings
Use: Chili, soups, stews, and gravy.
Rehydrate: Soak raw meat in cold water in the fridge overnight. For cooked, use hot water and soak for 15-20 min, then heat.
Tip: Add freeze-dried stew meat to instant pot recipes for a convenient and quick protein source.

Pork   Approximate Shelf Life: 5-10 yrs

Bacon
Serving: 35 grams (3 slices) 160 calories
Prep: Raw: Cut to size (¾" max thickness), place on trays, & pre-freeze. Pan Fry: 8-10 min each side. Grill: 4-6 min each side. Bake: 400°F for 15-20 min each side. Drain, rinse, cool, place on trays, and pre-freeze.
Freeze-Dry Time: 25-35 hours - default settings
Use: Snacks, soups, casseroles, salads, or sandwiches.
Rehydrate: Not recommended.
Tip: Lay paper towels on the freeze-drying trays to absorb excess grease.
Note: Shelf Life is 1-5 yrs for Bacon.

Ham
Serving: 134 grams (1 cup) 190 calories
Prep: Raw: Trim off fat, cut to ¾" max thickness and pre-freeze. Pan Fry Slices: 3-5 min each side. Bake: Whole ham at 350°F for 1½ -2 hrs. Cool, slice, place on trays, and pre-freeze.
Freeze-Dry Time: 25-35 hours - default settings
Use: Snacks, cold salads, eggs, casseroles, or soups.
Rehydrate: Soak raw meat in cold water in the fridge overnight. For cooked, use hot water and soak for 20+ min, then cook on a grill or pan-fry.
Tip: Slice ham thinly to reduce rehydration time.

Chops
Serving: 157 grams (1 chop) 328 calories
Prep: Raw: Trim off fat and bone, cut to ¾" max thickness, place on trays, and pre-freeze. Pan Fry: 4-5 min each side. Grill: 10-15 min each side. Bake: 425°F for 15-20 min. Cool, place on trays, and pre-freeze.
Freeze-Dry Time: 25-35 hours - default settings
Use: Soups, stews, stir-fries, or serve as a main dish after rehydration.
Rehydrate: Soak raw meat in cold water in the fridge overnight. For cooked, use hot water and soak for 15-20 min, then cook on a grill or pan-fry.
Tip: Trimming excess fat improves shelf life.

Loin Roast, Shredded
Serving: 85 grams (3 oz) 160 calories
Prep: Raw: Trim off fat, cut to ¾" max thickness, place on trays, & pre-freeze. Grill whole: 60-90 min. Bake whole: 400°F for 55-75 min. Cool, slice or shred, cover with water, and refrigerate. Remove fat cap, drain, place on trays, and pre-freeze.
Freeze-Dry Time: 25-35 hours - default settings
Use: Snacks, sandwiches, tacos, enchiladas, soups, casseroles, or stews.
Rehydrate: Soak raw meat in cold water in the fridge overnight. For cooked, add ⅓ cup hot water to 1 cup of freeze-dried pork, stir & let sit covered for 10-15 min.
Tip: Add seasonings after removing the fat.

Poultry   Approximate Shelf Life: 20-25 yrs

Ground
Serving: 85 grams (3oz) 220 calories
Prep: Raw: Spread out on trays and pre-freeze. Pan Fry: 15-20 min. Drain fat, rinse, cool, place on trays, and pre-freeze. Boil: boil meat, cover with water, and refrigerate. Remove fat cap, drain, place on trays, and pre-freeze.
Freeze-Dry Time: 25-35 hours - default settings
Use: Tacos, casseroles, gravy, creole, and soups.
Rehydrate: For raw, soak in cold water overnight. For cooked, add hot water or broth, cover and let sit.
Tip: Quick addition to pasta sauces and casseroles.

Roasted or Shredded
Serving: 85 grams (3 oz) 190 calories
Prep: Raw: Trim off fat, cut to ¾" max thickness, place on trays, and pre-freeze. Grilled strips: 6-8 min each side. Cool, place on trays, and pre-freeze. Bake: whole at 325°F for 2-3 hrs. Cool, cut, and place on trays, pre-freeze.
Freeze-Dry Time: 25-35 hours - default settings
Use: Snacks, soups, stews, tacos, and stir-fries.
Rehydrate: For raw, soak in cold water overnight. For cooked, add hot water or broth, cover and let sit.
Tip: 5 lb whole chicken gives about 2.5 lbs of meat.

Slices or Strips
Serving: 74 grams (2 strips) 220 calories
Prep: Raw: Trim off fat, cut to ¾" max thickness, place on trays, and pre-freeze. Pan Fry: 3-5 min each side. Grill: 5-7 min each side. Bake: 425°F for 20-30 min. Cool, place on trays, and pre-freeze.
Freeze-Dry Time: 25-35 hours - default settings
Use: Snacks, soups, stews, gravy, and sandwiches.
Rehydrate: For raw, soak in cold water overnight. For cooked, add hot water or broth, cover and let sit.
Tip: Crumble for recipes or add as a topping to salads.

Turkey Bacon
Serving: 33 grams (4 slices) 120 calories
Prep: Raw: Cut to size (¾" max thickness), place on trays, and pre-freeze. Pan Fry: 4-5 min each side. Grill: 5-7 min each side. Bake: 400°F for 8-10 min each side. Drain, cool, place on trays, and pre-freeze.
Freeze-Dry Time: 25-35 hours - default settings
Use: Snacks, soups, casseroles, salads, or sandwiches.
Rehydrate: Not recommended.
Tip: Handle with care to prevent it from crumbling. Use in place of croutons for a low-carb salad topping.

Fish   Approximate Shelf Life: White: 5-10 yrs   Oily: 1-5 yrs

Bass (white)
Serving: 85 grams (3 oz) 105 calories
Prep: Raw: cut to ¾" max thickness, place on trays, and pre-freeze. Sauté: 3-4 min each side. Grill: 4-6 min each side. Bake: 375°F for 12-15 min. Cool, place on trays, and pre-freeze.
Freeze-Dry Time: 25-35 hours - default settings
Use: Soups, stews, or served with vegetables.
Rehydrate: Soak in cold water, in refrigerator overnight until fully hydrated.
Tip: Ensure that your fish is thoroughly cleaned and deboned.

Herring (oily)
Serving: 85 grams (3 oz) 134 calories
Prep: Raw: cut to ¾" max thickness, place on trays, and pre-freeze. Sauté: 3-4 min each side. Grill: 2-3 min each side. Bake: 375°F for 20-25 min. Cool, place on trays, and pre-freeze.
Freeze-Dry Time: 25-35 hours - default settings
Use: Salads and pasta dishes.
Rehydrate: Soak in cold water, in refrigerator until fully hydrated.
Tip: Sauté with a light brushing of sesame oil for added flavor after rehydrating.

Tilapia (white)
Serving: 85 grams (3 oz) 110 calories
Prep: Raw: cut to ¾" max thickness, place on trays, and pre-freeze. Sauté: 4-6 min each side. Grill: 7-9 min each side. Bake: 375°F for 17-20 min. Cool, place on trays, and pre-freeze.
Freeze-Dry Time: 25-35 hours - default settings
Use: Tacos, salads, or served with rice.
Rehydrate: Soak in cold water, in refrigerator overnight until fully hydrated.
Tip: Season well before cooking to enhance flavor after rehydration.

Mackerel (oily)
Serving: Filet: 85 grams (3 oz) 223 calories
Prep: Raw: cut to ¾" max thickness, place on trays, and pre-freeze. Sauté: 3-5 min each side. Grill: 5 min each side. Bake: 375°F for 10-15 min. Cool, place on trays, and pre-freeze.
Freeze-Dry Time: 25-35 hours - default settings
Use: Salads and dip or served with potatoes.
Rehydrate: Soak in cold water, in refrigerator until fully hydrated.
Tip: A very strong-flavored fish so season well and use within a year.
Note: Shelf-Life is 6-12 mo.

Tuna (white)
Serving: Filet: 85 grams (3 oz) 110 calories
Canned: 172 grams (1 can) 220 calories
Prep: Raw: cut to ¾" max thickness, place on trays, and pre-freeze. Sauté: 2 min each side. Grill: 2 min each side. Bake: 450°F for 8-12 min. Cool, place on trays, and pre-freeze. Canned: drain water, spread evenly on trays, and pre-freeze.
Freeze-Dry Time: 25-35 hours - default settings
Use: Sandwiches, salads, and casseroles.
Rehydrate: Soak in cold water, in refrigerator overnight until fully hydrated.
Tip: Canned tuna (in water) works well too.

Salmon (oily)
Serving: Filet: 85 grams (3 oz) 175 calories
Smoked: 85 grams (3 oz) 100 calories
Prep: Raw: cut to ¾" max thickness, place on trays, and pre-freeze. Sauté: 4-5 min each side. Grill: 5-8 min each side. Bake: 450°F for 12-15 min. Cool, place on trays, and pre-freeze.
Freeze-Dry Time: 25-35 hours - default settings
Use: Salads and pasta dishes or served with greens.
Rehydrate: Soak in cold water, in refrigerator until fully hydrated.
Tip: Great protein source for long hikes or camping trips.

Other White Fish
Serving: Catfish: 85 grams (3 oz) 122 calories
Cod: 85 grams (3 oz) 89 calories
Haddock: 85 grams (3 oz) 77 calories
Snapper: 85 grams (3 oz) 109 calories
Prep: Raw: cut to ¾" max thickness, place on trays, and pre-freeze. Sauté: 3-5 min each side. Grill: 6-8 min each side. Bake: 375°F for 10-12 min. Cool, place on trays, and pre-freeze.
Freeze-Dry Time: 25-35 hours - default settings
Use: Casseroles, salads, tacos, and soups.
Rehydrate: Soak in cold water, in refrigerator overnight until fully hydrated.
Tip: You can make fish cakes by mixing with potatoes.

Other Oily Fish
Serving: Carp: 85 grams (3 oz) 140 calories
Trout: 85 grams (3 oz) 162 calories
Sardines: 85 grams (3 oz) 177 calories
Anchovies: 85 grams (3 oz) 111 calories
Prep: Raw: cut to ¾" max thickness, place on trays, and pre-freeze. Sauté: 3-5 min each side. Grill: 5-10 min each side. Bake: 400°F for 15-25 min. Cool, place on trays, and pre-freeze.
Freeze-Dry Time: 25-35 hours - default settings
Use: Casseroles, salads, and soups.
Rehydrate: Soak in cold water, in refrigerator until fully hydrated.
Tip: Try fish stew with tomatoes, vegetables, & spices.

Shellfish   Approximate Shelf Life: 5-10 yrs

Mixed Shellfish (Boiled) **Prep:** Boil your combination of pre-cooked seafood for 2-5 min, cool, remove shells, place on trays, and pre-freeze. **Freeze-Dry Time:** 25-35 hours - default settings **Use:** Soups, stir-fries, and salads. **Rehydrate:** Soak in cold water, refrigerate overnight. **Tip:** Season the boiling water with herbs or spices for added flavor.	**Crab** **Serving:** 118 grams (1 cup) 100 calories **Prep:** Cook, remove from shells, break into chunks, place on trays, and pre-freeze. **Freeze-Dry Time:** 25-35 hours - default settings **Use:** Seafood salads, sushi rolls, and soups. **Rehydrate:** Soak in cold water, refrigerate overnight. **Tip:** Consider adding a squeeze of lemon juice before freeze-drying to enhance flavor.
Clams **Serving:** 85 grams (3 oz) 130 calories **Prep:** Pat dry, spread on trays, and pre-freeze. **Freeze-Dry Time:** 25-35 hours - default settings **Use:** Seafood pastas, stews, chowders, soups, and spreads. **Rehydrate:** Briefly soak in cold water. Cook if raw. **Tip:** When rehydrating, add the clams to the dish towards the end of cooking to prevent overcooking.	**Lobster** **Serving:** 85 grams (3 oz) 120 calories **Prep:** Cook, remove from shell, break into chunks, place on trays, and pre-freeze. **Freeze-Dry Time:** 25-35 hours - default settings **Use:** Seafood salads, sushi rolls, and soups. **Rehydrate:** Soak in cold water, refrigerate overnight. **Tip:** Use lobster in stew with tomatoes and saffron.
Mussels **Serving:** 85 grams (3 oz) 150 calories **Prep:** Pat dry, spread on trays, and pre-freeze. **Freeze-Dry Time:** 25-35 hours - default settings **Use:** Seafood pastas, stews, and spreads. **Rehydrate:** Briefly soak in cold water. Cook if raw. **Tip:** Serve mussels with a spicy tomato sauce and crusty bread.	**Oysters** **Serving:** 96 grams (4 med) 160 calories **Prep:** Pat dry, spread on trays, and pre-freeze. **Freeze-Dry Time:** 25-35 hours - default settings **Use:** Seafood pastas, stews, soups, and spreads. **Rehydrate:** Briefly soak in cold water. Cook if raw. **Tip:** Garlic butter dipping sauce: 8 Tbs butter, 4 minced garlic, 1 ½ Tbs lemon juice, + seasonings.
Scallops **Serving:** 85 grams (3 oz) 60 calories **Prep:** Pat dry, spread on trays, and pre-freeze. **Freeze-Dry Time:** 25-35 hours - default settings **Use:** Seafood pasta, soups, stews, and stir-fries. **Rehydrate:** Briefly soak in cold water. Cook if raw. **Tip:** After rehydrating, sear scallops in a hot pan with butter for a crispy exterior.	**Shrimp** **Serving:** 85 grams (17 pieces) 85 calories **Prep:** Raw or cooked, remove shells and devein, lay flat on trays, and pre-freeze. **Freeze-Dry Time:** 25-35 hours - default settings **Use:** Stir-fries, soups, salads, and shrimp cocktails. **Rehydrate:** Soak in cold water for 20-30 min. **Tip:** Try making a shrimp ceviche with lime juice, avocado, jalapeno, and cilantro.

Legumes & Veg Protein   Approximate Shelf Life: 20-25 yrs

Beans, dry **Serving:** 175 grams (1 cup) 240 calories **Prep:** Sort and wash. Soak overnight. Drain. Boil in fresh water until tender, season, cool, place on trays, and pre-freeze. **Freeze-Dry Time:** 25-35 hours - default settings **Use:** Soups, stews, chili, veggie burgers, grain bowls, or flour. **Rehydrate:** Mix 1 cup beans with ¾ cup water. Let sit for 1-3 min. **Tip:** Excellent to use for 'meals in a jar' recipes.	**Chickpeas** **Serving:** 164 grams (1 cup) 270 calories **Prep:** Rinse, soak 8 hrs. Boil until tender. Season, cool, place on trays, and pre-freeze. **Freeze-Dry Time:** 25-35 hours - default settings **Use:** Snacks, salads, hummus, soups, casseroles, toppings, thickener, or flour. **Rehydrate:** Mix 1 cup chickpeas with ½ cup water. Let sit for 1-3 min. **Tip:** Rehydrate with lemon juice and garlic for a quick hummus.

Lentils
Serving: 198 grams (1 cup) 230 calories
Prep: Boil until soft, drain, cool, place on trays, and pre-freeze.
Freeze-Dry Time: 25-35 hours - default settings
Use: Soups, stews, chili, curries, veggie burgers, pasta dishes, spreads, or flour.
Rehydrate: Mix 1 cup lentils with ½ cup water. Let sit for 1-3 min.
Tip: Blend freeze-dried lentils into a powder for a protein-rich flour substitute.

Peas, dry and Split Peas
Serving: 196 grams (1 cup) 230 calories
Prep: Boil until soft, drain, cool, place on trays, and pre-freeze.
Freeze-Dry Time: 25-35 hours - default settings
Use: Soups, stews, casseroles, and spreads.
Rehydrate: Mix 1 cup peas with ½-⅔ cup water. Let sit for 1-3 min.
Tip: For a smoother texture in soups or spreads, blend rehydrated peas before adding to the dish.

Edamame Soybeans
Serving: 78 grams (½ cup) 90 calories
Prep: Raw: Rinse, shell beans, place on trays, and pre-freeze. Roasted: bake at 350°F for 15-20 mins. Cool, place on trays, and pre-freeze.
Freeze-Dry Time: 25-35 hours - default settings
Use: Snacks, salads, or flour.
Rehydrate: Mix 1 cup soybeans with ½ cup water. Let sit for 1-3 min.
Tip: Add freeze-dried edamame to soups for extra texture and nutrition.

Sprouts
Serving: 33 grams (1 cup) 10 calories
Prep: Rinse, place on trays, and pre-freeze. Lower Dry Temp to 90°F for nutrient preservation.
Freeze-Dry Time: 25-35 hours - UPDATE settings
Use: Soups, sandwiches, salads, or nutritional powder.
Rehydrate: Not recommended. Best as a topping or as a nutrient powder.
Tip: Freeze-dried sprouts add a delightful crunch when used as a salad topping.

Tempeh
Serving: 84 grams (3 oz) 150 calories
Prep: Slice thinly or crumble, spread on trays, and pre-freeze.
Freeze-Dry Time: 25-35 hours - default settings
Use: Sandwiches, stir-fries, or salads.
Rehydrate: Soak in water until soft, drain off and press out excess water.
Tip: Marinate before freeze-drying for more flavor.

Tofu
Serving: 91 grams (0.2 block) 80 calories
Prep: Cut into ½-inch cubes, season, place on trays, and pre-freeze.
Freeze-Dry Time: 25-35 hours - default settings
Use: Stir-fries, salads, or soups.
Rehydrate: Soak in water until soft, drain off and press out excess water.
Tip: For a crispy texture, after rehydrating, bake or air fry the tofu cubes.

Grains   Approximate Shelf Life: 20-25 yrs

Barley, pearled
Serving: 157 grams (1 cup) 193 calories
Prep: Boil barley, simmer for 30-40 minutes, cool, place on trays, and pre-freeze.
Freeze-Dry Time: 25-35 hours - default settings
Use: Soups, stews, salads, thickner, or flour.
Rehydrate: Add ½ cup hot water to 1 cup barley. Soak for 5-10 min.
Tip: Use freeze-dried barley in energy bars or granola for a nutrient boost.

Buckwheat
Serving: 168 grams (1 cup) 160 calories
Prep: Boil buckwheat, simmer for 15 minutes, cool, place on trays, and pre-freeze.
Freeze-Dry Time: 25-35 hours - default settings
Use: Cereals, soups, rice substitute, or flour.
Rehydrate: Add ½ cup hot water to 1 cup buckwheat. Soak for 5-10 min.
Tip: Toast before boiling for a nuttier flavor.

Oats
Serving: Rolled: 41 grams (½ cup) 140 calories
Steel Cut: 80 grams (½ cup) 305 calories
Prep: Cook oats (OF 5 min, SC 25 min.) Add toppings or sweeteners, cool, place on trays, and pre-freeze.
Freeze-Dry Time: 25-35 hours - default settings
Use: Snacks, porridge, soups, toppings, or flour.
Rehydrate: Add ¾ cup water to 1 cup oats and let sit for 2-5 min.
Tip: Add to baked goods for extra fiber and texture.

Quinoa
Serving: 93 grams (½ cup) 110 calories
Prep: Boil quinoa, simmer for 15 minutes, cool, place on trays, and pre-freeze.
Freeze-Dry Time: 25-35 hours - default settings
Use: Soups, smoothies, porridge, or flour.
Rehydrate: Add ½-⅔ cup water to 1 cup quinoa. Soak for 2-5 min.
Tip: Add freeze-dried quinoa to smoothies for a protein boost.

Rice, cooked
Serving: White: 158 grams (1 cup) 210 calories
Brown: 158 grams (1 cup) 218 calories
Wild: 158 grams (1 cup) 170 calories
Prep: Cook rice, cool, place on trays, and pre-freeze.
Freeze-Dry Time: 25-35 hours - default settings
Use: Instant rice, soups, stir-fries, thickener, or flour.
Rehydrate: Add ½ cup water to 1 cup rice. Wait 2-5 min and fluff.
Tip: Make a pudding by adding milk and sweeteners.

Wheat Berries
Serving: 48 grams (¼ cup) 170 calories
Prep: Boil wheat berries, simmer for 45-60 minutes, cool, place on trays, and pre-freeze.
Freeze-Dry Time: 25-35 hours - default settings
Use: Salads, soups, porridge, thickener, or flour.
Rehydrate: Add ½ cup hot water to 1 cup wheat berries. Soak for 15-20 min.
Tip: Rehydrate wheat berries with hot milk and honey for a quick breakfast porridge.

Processed Grains   Approximate Shelf Life: 5-10 yrs

Couscous
Serving: 157 grams (1 cup) 176 calories
Prep: Boil couscous, fluff, cool, place on trays, and pre-freeze.
Freeze-Dry Time: 25-35 hours - default settings
Use: Salads or as a side dish.
Rehydrate: Add ½ cup hot water to 1 cup couscous. Soak for 5-10 minutes and fluff.
Tip: Quick to rehydrate and great to add to soups.

Seitan
Serving: 85 grams (⅓ cup) 110 calories
Prep: Slice thinly or dice, spread on trays, and pre-freeze.
Freeze-Dry Time: 25-35 hours - default settings
Use: Vegan stews, tacos, stir-fries, burritos, and sandwiches.
Rehydrate: Soak in water until soft and drain.
Tips: Add spices and herbs before freeze-drying.

Pasta
Serving: 126 grams (1 cup) 210 calories
Prep: Boil until al dente, or slightly underdone. Cool, mix with sauce, if desired, place on trays, and pre-freeze.
Freeze-Dry Time: 25-45 hours - default settings
Use: Soups, baked dishes, casseroles, stir-fries, or pair with a sauce.
Rehydrate: Add ½ cup hot water to 1 cup pasta. Soak for 5-10 min and drain off any excess.
Tip: Handle with care. Some pasta has sharp edges and can puncture mylar.

Cake
Prep: Cut cake into thin, even pieces between ½" and ¾". Place on trays, and pre-freeze.
Freeze-Dry Time: 20-30 hours - default settings
Use: Biscotti-like snacks or crumbled toppings for ice cream or yogurt.
Rehydrate: Wrap in a damp paper towel & refrigerate in a plastic bag overnight. Or briefly dip in cool water & pan-fry until rehydrated.
Tip: Can be freeze-dried with the frosting.

Breads
Prep: Slice or cut bread into even pieces. Place on trays, and pre-freeze.
Freeze-Dry Time: 20-30 hours - default settings
Use: Salad croutons or breadcrumbs.
Rehydrate: Wrap in damp paper towel & refrigerate in a plastic bag. Or briefly dip in cool water & pan-fry.
Tip: Slice up to ¾" thick to ensure they don't break during rehydration.

Sweet Breads
Prep: Cut sweet breads into thin, even pieces. Place on trays, and pre-freeze.
Freeze-Dry Time: 20-30 hours - default settings
Use: Snacks or toppings.
Rehydrate: Wrap in damp paper towel & refrigerate in a plastic bag. Or briefly dip in cool water & pan-fry.
Tip: Crumble on ice cream, yogurt, or oatmeal for added texture and sweetness.

Herbs & Spices   Approximate Shelf Life: 20-25 yrs

Basil
Prep: Wash and place basil leaves on trays and pre-freeze if desired. For powder: Blend basil with water. Pour measured amount onto trays and pre-freeze. Set Dry Temp to 90°F.
Freeze-Dry Time: 25-35 hours - UPDATE settings
Use: Flake or powdered seasoning.
Rehydrate: No. Add to recipes dry.

Chives
Prep: Wash and chop into desired size. Place chives on trays and pre-freeze if desired. For powder: Blend chives with water. Pour measured amount onto trays and pre-freeze. Set Dry Temp to 90°F.
Freeze-Dry Time: 25-35 hours - UPDATE settings
Use: Chopped pieces or powdered seasoning.
Rehydrate: No. Add to recipes dry.

Cilantro
Prep: Wash and place cilantro leaves on trays and pre-freeze if desired. For powder: Blend cilantro with water. Pour measured amount onto trays and pre-freeze. Set Dry Temp to 90°F.
Freeze-Dry Time: 25-35 hours - UPDATE settings
Use: Flake or powdered seasoning.
Rehydrate: No. Add to recipes dry.

Dill Weed
Prep: Wash and cut into desired size. Place dill weed on trays and pre-freeze if desired. For powder: Blend dill weed with water. Pour measured amount onto trays and pre-freeze. Set Dry Temp to 90°F.
Freeze-Dry Time: 25-35 hours - UPDATE settings
Use: Chopped pieces or powdered seasoning.
Rehydrate: No. Add to recipes dry.

Fennel
Prep: Wash and cut into desired size. Place fennel weed on trays and pre-freeze if desired. Chop fennel bulb into pieces no thicker than ½", place on trays, and pre-freeze. For powder: Blend fennel weed and bulb with water. Pour measured amount onto trays and pre-freeze. Set Dry Temp to 90°F.
Freeze-Dry Time: 25-35 hours - UPDATE settings
Use: Chopped pieces or powdered seasoning.
Rehydrate: No. Add to recipes dry.

Ginger
Prep: Wash, chop or shred ginger into pieces no thicker than ½", place on trays, and pre-freeze. For powder: Blend ginger with water. Pour measured amount onto trays and pre-freeze. Set Dry Temp to 90°F.
Freeze-Dry Time: 30-40 hours - UPDATE settings
Use: Chopped pieces or powdered seasoning.
Rehydrate: No. Add to recipes dry.

Horseradish
Prep: Wash, chop or shred horseradish into pieces no thicker than ½", place on trays, and pre-freeze. For powder: Blend horseradish with water. Pour measured amount onto trays and pre-freeze. Set Dry Temp to 90°F.
Freeze-Dry Time: 30-40 hours - UPDATE settings
Use: Chopped pieces or powdered seasoning.
Rehydrate: No. Add to recipes dry.

Lemon Balm
Prep: Wash and place lemon balm leaves on trays and pre-freeze if desired. For powder: Blend lemon balm with water. Pour measured amount onto trays and pre-freeze. Set Dry Temp to 90°F.
Freeze-Dry Time: 25-35 hours - UPDATE settings
Use: Flake or powdered seasoning, or tea.
Rehydrate: No. Add to recipes dry.

Marjoram
Prep: Wash and place marjoram leaves on trays and pre-freeze if desired. For powder: Blend marjoram with water. Pour measured amount onto trays and pre-freeze. Set Dry Temp to 90°F.
Freeze-Dry Time: 25-35 hours - UPDATE settings
Use: Flake or powdered seasoning.
Rehydrate: No. Add to recipes dry.

Nettle
Prep: Wear gloves. Wash and place nettle leaves on trays and pre-freeze if desired. For powder: Blend nettle with water. Pour measured amount onto trays and pre-freeze. Set Dry Temp to 90°F.
Freeze-Dry Time: 25-35 hours - UPDATE settings
Use: Chopped pieces for tea.
Rehydrate: No. Add to recipes dry.

Oregano
Prep: Wash and place oregano leaves on trays and pre-freeze if desired. For powder: Blend oregano with water. Pour measured amount onto trays and pre-freeze. Set Dry Temp to 90°F.
Freeze-Dry Time: 25-35 hours - UPDATE settings
Use: Flake or powdered seasoning.
Rehydrate: No. Add to recipes dry.

Parsley
Prep: Wash and place parsley leaves on trays and pre-freeze if desired. For powder: Blend parsley with water. Pour measured amount onto trays and pre-freeze. Set Dry Temp to 90°F.
Freeze-Dry Time: 25-35 hours - UPDATE settings
Use: Flake or powdered seasoning.
Rehydrate: No. Add to recipes dry.

Peppermint
Prep: Wash and place peppermint leaves on trays and pre-freeze if desired. For powder: Blend peppermint with water. Pour measured amount onto trays and pre-freeze. Set Dry Temp to 90°F.
Freeze-Dry Time: 25-35 hours - UPDATE settings
Use: Flake or powdered seasoning, or tea.
Rehydrate: No. Add to recipes dry.

Rosemary
Prep: Wash and place rosemary sprigs or needles on trays and pre-freeze if desired. For powder: Blend rosemary with water. Pour measured amount onto trays and pre-freeze. Set Dry Temp to 90°F.
Freeze-Dry Time: 25-35 hours - UPDATE settings
Use: Needle or powdered seasoning.
Rehydrate: No. Add to recipes dry.

Sage
Prep: Wash and place sage leaves on trays and pre-freeze if desired. For powder: Blend sage with water. Pour measured amount onto trays and pre-freeze. Set Dry Temp to 90°F.
Freeze-Dry Time: 25-35 hours - UPDATE settings
Use: Flake or powdered seasoning.
Rehydrate: No. Add to recipes dry.

Spearmint
Prep: Wash and place spearmint leaves on trays and pre-freeze if desired. For powder: Blend spearmint with water. Pour measured amount onto trays and pre-freeze. Set Dry Temp to 90°F.
Freeze-Dry Time: 25-35 hours - UPDATE settings
Use: Flake or powdered seasoning, or tea.
Rehydrate: No. Add to recipes dry.

Stevia
Prep: Wash and place stevia leaves on trays and pre-freeze if desired. For powder: Blend stevia with water. Pour measured amount onto trays and pre-freeze. Set Dry Temp to 90°F.
Freeze-Dry Time: 25-35 hours - UPDATE settings
Use: Flake or powdered seasoning, or tea.
Rehydrate: No. Add to recipes dry.

Tarragon
Prep: Wash and place tarragon sprigs on trays and pre-freeze if desired. For powder: Blend tarragon with water. Pour measured amount onto trays and pre-freeze. Set Dry Temp to 90°F.
Freeze-Dry Time: 25-35 hours - UPDATE settings
Use: Flake or powdered seasoning.
Rehydrate: No. Add to recipes dry.

Thyme
Prep: Wash and place thyme sprigs on trays and pre-freeze if desired. For powder: Blend thyme with water. Pour measured amount onto trays and pre-freeze. Set Dry Temp to 90°F.
Freeze-Dry Time: 25-35 hours - UPDATE settings
Use: Flake or powdered seasoning.
Rehydrate: No. Add to recipes dry.

Turmeric
Prep: Wash, chop or shred turmeric into pieces no thicker than ½", place on trays, and pre-freeze. For powder: Blend turmeric with water. Pour measured amount onto trays and pre-freeze. Set Dry Temp to 90°F.
Freeze-Dry Time: 30-40 hours - UPDATE settings
Use: Chopped pieces or powdered seasoning.
Rehydrate: No. Add to recipes dry.

APPENDIX TWO: 147 RECIPES

The recipes in this book are suitable for freeze-drying and are relatively uncomplicated. It's important to remember that results may differ from person to person. Please exercise sound judgment and adhere to cleanliness and safety guidelines. **Always follow the weight limits for your trays.** The provided freeze-drying durations, shelf life estimates, and rehydration instructions are approximations and will be influenced by your specific ingredients, environmental conditions, packaging, and procedures.

21 BREAKFASTS

Spinach Sunrise Skillet

The Spinach Sunrise Skillet brings you a hearty and healthy breakfast packed with flavor.

| Cups: | 12 | Servings: | 12 | Serving Size: | 1 cup (176 g) | Calories: | 171 |
| Prep/Cook Time: | | 20 min | Freeze-Dry Time: | | 30-40 hrs | Shelf-Life: | 20-25 yrs |

Ingredients:

3 cups Bell Pepper, diced
12 Green Onions, sliced
6 cups Fresh Spinach
26 Eggs
2 Tbs Salt
1½ tsp Black Pepper
Optional: Tomatoes or Jalapenos

Directions:
Sauté bell pepper and green onions in a large non-stick skillet over medium heat until softened, then add spinach until it wilts. Whisk eggs, salt, and black pepper in a bowl and combine with the sautéed vegetables, cooking until soft scrambled or slightly under-done. Once cooled, place on freeze-drying trays and pre-freeze. Freeze-dry for 30-40 hours. Do a weight check and run Extra Dry Time until the weight doesn't change. Seal in 7mil mylar or a canning jar with an oxygen absorber and store in a cool, dry location.

Rehydration:
1 cup FD Spinach Sunrise Skillet (32 g)
½-⅔ cup Water (144 g)
Stir, cover, sit for 10 min, and enjoy.

Tips:
If you enjoy a bit of heat in your meals, drizzle some hot sauce or sprinkle chili flakes over your skillet after rehydration.

Savory Sausage Scramble

The Savory Sausage Scramble is an easy-to-make, satisfying breakfast dish. This recipe is loaded with protein and flavor, perfect for jump-starting your day!

| Cups: | 11 | Servings: | 11 | Serving Size: | 1 cup (178 g) | Calories: | 174 |
| Prep/Cook Time: | | 30 min | Freeze-Dry Time: | | 30-40 hrs | Shelf-Life: | 3-5 yrs |

Ingredients:

1 lb Chicken Sausage
1 med Bell Pepper, diced
1 med Onion, diced
1 lb Mushrooms, diced
16 Eggs
1 Tbs Salt
1 tsp Black Pepper

Directions:
Cook sausage in a large skillet over medium heat until browned, drain and rinse in hot water. In the same skillet, sauté bell pepper, onions, and mushroom. Whisk eggs, salt, and black pepper and add to skillet, scrambling until cooked. Cool, place on freeze-drying trays, pre-freeze, and freeze-dry for 30-40 hours. Do a weight check and run Extra Dry Time until the weight doesn't change. Seal in 7mil mylar or a canning jar with an oxygen absorber and store in a cool, dry location.

Rehydration:
1 cup FD Savory Sausage Scramble (66 g)
½-⅔ cup Water (112 g)
Stir, cover, sit for 10 min, and enjoy.

Tips:
Sprinkle some shredded cheddar or pepper jack cheese for an extra creamy texture and flavor.

Classic Ham and Egg Quiche

The Classic Ham and Egg Quiche is a traditional breakfast dish that combines the flavors of ham, eggs, and cheese baked to perfection.

Slices:	8	Servings:	8	Serving Size:	1 slice/1 cup (170 g)	Calories:	305
Prep/Cook Time:		55 min	Freeze-Dry Time:	30-40 hrs		Shelf-Life:	5-10 yrs

Ingredients:
1 premade Pie Crust
¾ lb Ham, diced
1½ cup Shredded Cheddar Cheese
8 large Eggs
1 cup 2% Milk
1 tsp Salt
½ tsp Black Pepper
Optional: Spinach

Directions:
Preheat your oven to 350°F. Layer diced ham and cheese in the bottom of the pie crust. Whisk together eggs, milk, salt, and black pepper and pour into crust. Bake for 45 minutes, cool, cut into 8 pieces or scoop and spread to make crumbles. Place on freeze-drying trays, pre-freeze, and freeze-dry for 30-40 hours. Do a weight check and run Extra Dry Time until the weight doesn't change. Seal in 7mil mylar or a canning jar with an oxygen absorber and store in a cool, dry location.

Rehydration:
1 cup FD Quiche crumbles (88 g)
¼-⅓ cup Water (82 g)
Stir, cover, sit for 10-15 min, and enjoy. For slices: hold under water until soaked, sit for 5-10 min.

Tips:
For best results, reheat the rehydrated quiche slices in the oven at 350°F for 5-10 minutes to restore the crispness of the crust.

Denver Delight Quiche

A blend of ham, bell peppers, onions, and cheese, it brings you the Denver omelet experience in a new and exciting form.

Cups:	8	Servings:	8	Serving Size:	1 slice/1 cup (175 g)	Calories:	245
Prep/Cook Time:		55 min	Freeze-Dry Time:	30-40 hrs		Shelf-Life:	5-10 yrs

Ingredients:
1 premade Pie Crust
½ lb Ham, diced
1 large Bell Pepper, diced
1 large Onion, diced
4 oz Mushrooms, chopped
1 cup Shredded Cheddar Cheese
6 large Eggs
1 cup 2% Milk
1 tsp Salt
½ tsp Black Pepper

Directions:
Preheat the oven to 350°F. Sauté diced ham, bell pepper, onion, and mushrooms in a little water, and then spread over the bottom of the pie crust. Add the shredded cheese. Whisk eggs, milk, salt, and black pepper together and pour into crust. Bake for 45 minutes, cool, cut into 8 pieces or scoop and spread to make crumbles. Place on freeze-drying trays, pre-freeze, and freeze-dry for 30-40 hours. Do a weight check and run Extra Dry Time until the weight doesn't change. Seal in 7mil mylar or a canning jar with an oxygen absorber and store in a cool, dry location.

Rehydration:
1 cup FD Quiche crumbles (84 g)
⅓-½ cup Water (91 g)
Stir, cover, sit for 10-15 min, and enjoy. For slices: hold under water until soaked, sit for 5-10 min.

Tips:
For a flavor boost, consider adding a sprinkle of fresh herbs like chives or parsley to the top of the quiche before rehydrating.

Breakfast Brunch

This is a hearty and satisfying meal that perfectly combines the flavors of sausage, eggs, cheese, and bread into a delicious casserole that's ideal for any time of day.

Cups: 12	**Servings:** 12	**Serving Size:** 1 piece/1 cup (172 g)	**Calories:** 230
Prep/Cook Time: 1hr 30 min	**Freeze-Dry Time:** 30-40 hrs		**Shelf-Life:** 3-5 yrs

Ingredients:

1 lb Chicken Sausage
12 Eggs
3 cups 2% Milk

2 tsp Mustard
1 tsp Salt
4 slices of Bread, cut in bite-size pieces
1½ cup Shredded Cheddar Cheese

Directions:
Preheat oven to 350°F. Cook sausage, drain and rinse in hot water. Whisk together eggs, milk, mustard and salt. Stir in bread, sausage, and cheese. Pour into a greased 9x13-inch pan. Bake for 1 hour and allow to cool. Cut into 12 pieces or scoop and spread to make crumbles. Place on freeze-drying trays, pre-freeze, and freeze-dry for 30-40 hours. Do a weight check and run Extra Dry Time until the weight doesn't change. Seal in 7mil mylar or a canning jar with an oxygen absorber and store in a cool, dry location.

Tips: The freeze-dried Breakfast Casserole can be enjoyed as a crunchy snack during hiking or camping trips.

Rehydration:
1 cup FD Brunch crumbles (130 g)
¼-⅓ cup Water (42 g)
Stir, cover, sit for 10-15 min, and enjoy. For slices: hold under water until soaked, sit for 5-10 min.

Or place all pieces back in dish, add 3 cups of water, cover with foil, & reheat 30 min at 350°F (175°C)

Ham Brunch

The Ham Brunch ensures a delicious and satisfying meal is always within reach, requiring minimal effort to rehydrate and enjoy.

Pieces: 12	**Servings:** 12	**Serving Size:** 1 piece/1 cup (181 g)	**Calories:** 275
Prep/Cook Time: 1hr 10 min	**Freeze-Dry Time:** 30-40 hrs		**Shelf-Life:** 5-10 yrs

Ingredients:

1 lb Ham, cubed
1 cup Cheese, grated
12 Eggs
1 small Onion
1 tsp Salt

6 slices Bread, cubed
1 cup Spinach
3 cups 2% Milk
½ tsp Mustard
½ tsp Black Pepper

Directions:
Preheat oven to 375°F. Sauté the onion until softened. In a large bowl, toss together ham, bread, cheese, sautéed onion, and spinach, and place in a greased 9x13-inch pan. In a separate bowl, whisk together eggs, milk, mustard, salt, and black pepper, and pour this mixture evenly over the bread mixture. Bake for 50 minutes, then allow to cool. Cut into 12 pieces or scoop and spread to make crumbles. Place on freeze-drying trays, pre-freeze, and freeze-dry for 30-40 hours. Do a weight check and run Extra Dry Time until the weight doesn't change. Seal in 7mil mylar or a canning jar with an oxygen absorber and store in a cool, dry location.

Rehydration:
1 cup FD Brunch crumbles (54 g)
½-⅔ cup Water (127 g)
Stir, cover, sit for 10-15 min, and enjoy. For slices: hold under water until soaked, sit for 5-10 min. Or place all pieces back in dish, add 3 cups of water, cover with foil, & reheat 30 min at 350°F (175°C)

Tips:
Try it as a satisfying dry snack while out on the trail.

Hearty Breakfast Casserole

This Hearty Breakfast Casserole recipe makes a delightful breakfast or brunch. It's packed with flavor and nutrients that make it a crowd-pleaser.

Pieces:	12	Servings:	12	Serving Size:	1 piece/1 cup (185 g)	Calories:	298
Prep/Cook Time:		1 hr 20 min	Freeze-Dry Time:	30-40 hrs		Shelf-Life:	3-5 yrs

Ingredients:

1 lb Chicken Sausage
4 Green Onions, sliced
1 large Bell Pepper, diced
12 oz Frozen Hashbrowns
15 Eggs
1 cup 2% Milk
½ cup Green Olives
1 cup Shredded Cheddar Cheese
1 cup Spinach
2 tsp Salt
½ tsp Black Pepper

Directions:

Preheat oven to 350°F. Cook sausage, rinse with hot water, and set aside. Sauté onion and pepper until softened. In a greased 9x13-inch pan, layer hashbrowns, cooked meat, and sautéed veggies. In a separate bowl, whisk together eggs, milk, olives, cheese, spinach, salt, and black pepper, and pour this mixture evenly over the layered ingredients. Bake for 45-50 minutes, then allow to cool. Cut into 12 pieces or scoop and spread to make crumbles. Place on freeze-drying trays, pre-freeze, and freeze-dry for 30-40 hours. Do a weight check and run Extra Dry Time until the weight doesn't change. Seal in 7mil mylar or a canning jar with an oxygen absorber and store in a cool, dry location.

Rehydration:

1 cup FD Casserole crumbles (127 g)
¼-⅓ cup Water (58 g)
Stir, cover, sit for 10-15 min, and enjoy. For slices: hold under water until soaked, sit for 5-10 min. Or place all pieces back in dish, add 3 cups of water, cover with foil, & reheat 30 min at 350°F (175°C)

Tips:
Try adding mushrooms, bacon, or chicken.

Berries and Cream Oatmeal

A flavorful breakfast dish that combines the tartness of berries with the smoothness of cream for a delightful balance.

Cups:	16	Servings:	16	Serving Size:	1 cup (251 g)	Calories:	239
Prep/Cook Time:		15 min	Freeze-Dry Time:	25-35 hrs		Shelf-Life:	15-20 yrs

Ingredients:

8 cups Water
8 cups Old-Fashioned Rolled Oats
4 cups 2% Milk
2 cup Mixed Berries
1 cup Sugar
2 tsp Vanilla Extract

Directions:

Boil water in a large pot, add oats and simmer 5 min. Stir in milk, mixed berries, sugar, and vanilla and simmer until berries are soft. Cool, spread on freeze-drying trays, pre-freeze, and freeze-dry for 25-35 hours. Do a weight check and run Extra Dry Time until the weight doesn't change. Seal in 7mil mylar or a canning jar with an oxygen absorber and store in a cool, dry location.

Rehydration:

1 cup FD Oatmeal crumbles (78 g)
⅔-¾ cup Water (173 g)
Stir, cover, and let it sit for about 5 minutes.

Tips:
Some berries take extra time in the freeze-dryer.

Apple Pie Oatmeal

This tasty breakfast provides a delicious and nutritious start to your day, combining the comforting flavors of apple pie with the wholesomeness of oatmeal.

Cups:	16	Servings:	16	Serving Size:	1 cup (258 g)	Calories:	248
Prep/Cook Time:	15 min	Freeze-Dry Time:	25-35 hrs			Shelf-Life:	15-20 yrs

Ingredients:
8 cups Water
8 cups Old-Fashioned Rolled Oats
2 cup 2% Milk

4 large Apples, peeled, cored, diced
1 cup Brown Sugar
2 tsp Cinnamon
½ tsp Nutmeg

Directions:
Boil water in a large pot, add oats and simmer 5 min. Stir in milk, diced apples, brown sugar, cinnamon, and nutmeg, letting it simmer until apples are soft. Cool, spread evenly on freeze-drying trays, pre-freeze, and freeze-dry for 25-35 hours. Do a weight check and run Extra Dry Time until the weight doesn't change. Seal in 7mil mylar or a canning jar with an oxygen absorber and store in a cool, dry location.

Rehydration:
1 cup FD Oatmeal crumbles (65 g)
¾-1 cup Water (193 g)
Stir, cover, and let it sit for about 5 minutes.

Tips:
For a creative twist, use your Apple Pie Oatmeal as a crunchy topping on yogurt or ice cream.

Pumpkin Pie Oatmeal

This Pumpkin Pie Oatmeal is a seasonal delight that brings the comforting taste of pumpkin to your breakfast table.

Cups:	17	Servings:	17	Serving Size:	1 cup (249 g)	Calories:	232
Prep/Cook Time:	15 min	Freeze-Dry Time:	25-35 hrs			Shelf-Life:	15-20 yrs

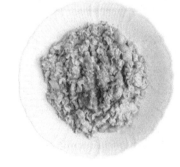

Ingredients:
8 cups Water
8 cups Old-Fashioned Rolled Oats
4 cups 2% Milk
2 cup Pumpkin Puree

1 cup Brown Sugar
2 tsp Cinnamon
½ tsp Nutmeg
½ tsp Cloves

Directions:
Boil water in a large pot, add oats and simmer 5 min. Stir in milk, pumpkin puree, brown sugar, cinnamon, nutmeg, and cloves, letting it simmer 5 min. After cooling, spread the oatmeal on freeze-drying trays, pre-freeze, and freeze-dry for 25-35 hours. Do a weight check and run Extra Dry Time until the weight doesn't change. Seal in 7mil mylar or a canning jar with an oxygen absorber and store in a cool, dry location.

Rehydration:
1 cup FD Pumpkin Pie Oatmeal (61 g)
¾ cup Water (188 g)
Stir, cover, and let it sit for about 5 minutes.

Tips:
Add Greek yogurt and a sprinkle of cinnamon on top to enhance the pumpkin pie flavor.

Blueberry Lemon Granola

Experience the perfect balance of tart and sweet with this enticing Blueberry Lemon Cobbler.

Cups:	12	Servings:	12	Serving Size:	1 cup (119g)	Calories:	123
Prep/Cook Time:	30 min	Freeze-Dry Time:	35-45 hrs			Shelf-Life:	15-20 yrs

Ingredients:
6 cups Blueberries, fresh or frozen, pierced
2 Tbs Brown Sugar
4 Tbs Lemon Juice (1 med)
2 cups Rolled Oats
Optional: Ground Flax, Chia, or Hemp Seeds

1 Tbs Ground Cinnamon
⅛ tsp Fine Salt
1 cup Applesauce
2 Tbs Maple Syrup

Directions:
Preheat oven to 350°F. In a medium bowl, mix blueberries with brown sugar, and lemon juice. Lightly mash and ensure the fruits are well coated. Mix in oats, ground seeds, cinnamon, and salt until combined. Stir in applesauce and maple syrup. Put into a 9x11 baking dish and bake for 30-35 minutes. Let cool. Spread on freeze-drying trays, pre-freeze, and freeze-dry for 35-45 hours. Do a weight check and run Extra Dry Time until the weight doesn't change. Seal in 7mil mylar or a canning jar with an oxygen absorber and store in a cool, dry location.

Rehydration:
1 cup FD Granola crumbles (35 g)
⅓-½ cup Milk (84 g)
Enjoy dry or add up to 1 cup of milk or water per 1 cup of granola for a traditional experience.

Tips:
It can also be sprinkled over yogurt or mixed into a trail mix for an added burst of flavor.

French Toast Sticks

This french toast recipe is a delicious and hearty option for breakfast or brunch, providing a good balance of macronutrients.

Sticks:	128	Servings:	16	Serving Size:	8 sticks (124 g)	Calories:	204
Prep/Cook Time:	45 min	Freeze-Dry Time:	20-30 hrs			Shelf-Life:	10-15 yrs

Ingredients:
32 slices Bread (1 lb loaf)
2 cups Milk
12 large Eggs

2 tsp Vanilla Extract
¼ tsp Cinnamon
⅛ tsp Salt

Directions:
Whisk together milk, eggs, vanilla, cinnamon, and salt in a shallow dish. Soak bread slices and fry until golden brown. Cool, and cut each slice into 4 sticks. Place them on freeze-drying trays, pre-freeze, and freeze-dry for 20-30 hours. Do a weight check and run Extra Dry Time until the weight doesn't change. Seal in 7mil mylar or a canning jar with an oxygen absorber and store in a cool, dry location.

Tips:
Can freeze-dry RAW, before cooking. Cleanliness is essential. Mark packages clearly with RAW. Rehydration process is the same. Cooking is required.

Rehydration:
FD French Toast Stick
Briefly soak in water for 30 seconds, then pan fry to rehydrate fully.

Hearty Pancakes

This wholesome pancake recipe is as nutritious as it is delicious. Made with whole grains & seeds, these hearty pancakes will keep you fueled for hours.

Pancakes:	48	Servings:	16	Serving Size:	3 pancakes (114 g)	Calories:	187
Prep/Cook Time:		30 min	Freeze-Dry Time:		20-30 hrs	Shelf-Life:	5-10 yrs

Ingredients:
4 cups Whole Wheat Flour
2 cup Rolled Oats
4 tsp Baking Powder
1 tsp Salt
Optional: Add in 2 Tbs Flax Seeds

4 large Eggs
4 cups Milk
4 Tbs Maple Syrup
2 tsp Vanilla Extract

Directions:
Mix flour, oats, baking powder, and salt in a large bowl. In another bowl, whisk eggs, milk, maple syrup, and vanilla, and combine with dry ingredients. Cook about 1 min each side. Cook pancakes on a greased griddle and cool. Stack them on freeze-drying trays, pre-freeze, and freeze-dry for 20-30 hours. Do a weight check and run Extra Dry Time until the weight doesn't change. Seal in 7mil mylar or a canning jar with an oxygen absorber and store in a cool, dry location.

Rehydration:
FD Hearty Pancake
Soak in water for 30 seconds to 1 minute, then fry on a pan until fully rehydrated.

Tips:
For an extra protein boost and a nutty flavor, spread almond, peanut, or cashew butter over your warm Hearty Pancakes before serving.

Banana Pancakes

Banana pancakes offer a sweet and satisfying twist on traditional pancakes. The bananas add natural sweetness and a delightful flavor.

Pancake:	42	Servings:	14	Serving Size:	3 pancakes (113 g)	Calories:	177
Prep/Cook Time:		30 min	Freeze-Dry Time:		20-30 hrs	Shelf-Life:	10-15 yrs

Ingredients:
3 cups All-Purpose Flour
4 tsp Baking Powder
½ tsp Salt
4 large Eggs

2 cup Milk
4 ripe Bananas, mashed
4 Tbs Honey

Directions:
Mix flour, baking powder, and salt in one bowl. Combine eggs, milk, mashed bananas, and honey in another. Combine the two, cook pancakes on a greased pan about 1 min each side and cool. Stack them on freeze-drying trays, pre-freeze, and freeze-dry for 20-30 hours. Do a weight check and run Extra Dry Time until the weight doesn't change. Seal in 7mil mylar or a canning jar with an oxygen absorber and store in a cool, dry location.

Rehydration:
FD Banana Pancake
Soak in water for 30 seconds to 1 minute, then fry on a pan until fully rehydrated.

Tips:
After rehydrating your Banana Pancakes, enhance them by topping them with fresh slices of banana and a drizzle of maple syrup or honey.

Cinnamon Roll Bites

A delightful combination of sweetness and spice, making it a delicious treat.

Piecess:	128	Servings:	16	Serving Size:	8 bites (89 g)	Calories:	315
Prep/Cook Time:		55 min		Freeze-Dry Time:	25-35 hrs	Shelf-Life:	6-12 mo

Ingredients:

4 cups Flour	1 pkg Yeast (2¼ tsp)
1 cup Granulated Sugar	2 large Eggs
1 tsp Salt	½ cup Butter, softened
1 cup Milk, warm	1 cup Brown Sugar
½ cup Butter, melted	2 Tbs Cinnamon

Directions:

Preheat oven to 350°F. In a large bowl, combine flour, sugar, and salt. In a separate bowl mix warm milk and melted butter. Whisk the yeast into the liquids, pour into the dry ingredients, add the egg, and stir well. Knead to form a smooth dough, divide in four, and roll each one into a long rectangle. Spread softened butter onto the dough and sprinkle brown sugar and cinnamon. Roll up the dough along the long edge so it is a long and skinny log. Slice each log into 8 disks. Bake 15-20 minutes and cool. Cut each cinnamon roll into four, place on trays, pre-freeze, and freeze-dry for 25-35 hours. Do a weight check and run Extra Dry Time until the weight doesn't change. Seal in 7mil mylar or a canning jar with an oxygen absorber and store in a cool, dry location.

Rehydration:

FD Cinnamon Roll Bite
Wrap in a moist paper towel, place in a zip-sealed bag and let sit for about 20 minutes.

Tips:

Best when eaten dry and crunchy.

Cornmeal Muffin Bites

Savor the comfort of cornbread in bite-sized muffins, perfect for a quick snack or side dish.

Pieces:	72	Servings:	12	Serving Size:	6 bites (67 g)	Calories:	127
Prep/Cook Time:		40 min		Freeze-Dry Time:	25-35 hrs	Shelf-Life:	5-10 yrs

Ingredients:

1½ cups Flour	1 tsp Salt
½ cup Cornmeal	2 large Eggs
¼ cup + 2 Tbs Sugar	1 cup Buttermilk
1 Tbs Baking Soda	½ cup Applesauce

Directions:

Preheat oven to 400°F and grease a mini muffin tin (12 muffins = 36 mini muffins.) In a large bowl, combine flour, cornmeal, sugar, baking soda, and salt. In a separate bowl, whisk together eggs, buttermilk, and applesauce. Pour the wet mixture into the dry ingredients and stir until just combined. Bake for 12-15 minutes and cool. Cut mini muffins in half (cut full size into 6 pieces.) Place on trays, pre-freeze, and freeze-dry for 25-35 hours. Do a weight check and run Extra Dry Time until the weight doesn't change. Seal in 7mil mylar or a canning jar with an oxygen absorber and store in a cool, dry location.

Rehydration:

FD Muffin Bite
Wrap in a moist paper towel, place in a zip-sealed bag and let sit for about 20 minutes.

Tips:

Best when eaten crunchy or dipped in soups or chili. Try adding in cheese, green onions, bacon, or chopped jalepenos.

Chocolate Muffin Bites

Enjoy the decadence of chocolate muffins in handy, bite-sized pieces.

Pieces:	72	Servings:	12	Serving Size:	6 bites (240 g)	Calories:	218
Prep/Cook Time:	40 min	Freeze-Dry Time:		25-35 hrs		Shelf-Life:	5-10 yrs

Ingredients:

2 cups Flour	2 large Eggs
1 cup Granulated Sugar	1 cup Milk
¾ cup Cocoa pwd.	½ cup Applesauce
2½ tsp Baking pwd.	1 tsp Salt

Directions:

Preheat oven to 375° and grease a mini muffin tin (12 muffins = 36 mini muffins.) In a large bowl, combine flour, sugar, cocoa powder, baking powder, and salt. In a separate bowl, whisk together the eggs, milk, and applesauce. Mix the wet ingredients into the dry ingredients, then fold in any additions. Bake for 15-20 minutes and cool. Cut each muffin into 6 bite-sized pieces or each mini muffin in half. Place on trays, pre-freeze, and freeze-dry for 25-35 hours. Do a weight check and run Extra Dry Time until the weight doesn't change. Seal in 7mil mylar or a canning jar with an oxygen absorber and store in a cool, dry location.

Rehydration:

FD Muffin Bite
Wrap in a moist paper towel, place in a zip-sealed bag and let sit for about 20 minutes.

Tips:

Best when eaten crunchy like a cracker. Try adding 1 cup Chocolate Chips, this raises the calories by 40 and lowers the shelf life to 1-2 yrs.

Cheesy Grits

This Cheesy Grits recipe provides a hearty, comforting southern dish perfect for an outdoor expedition. Loaded with cheese and a bit of spice, it's an excellent base or a fulfilling dish.

Cups:	10½	Servings:	10½	Serving Size:	1 cup (248 g)	Calories:	217
Prep/Cook Time:	15 min	Freeze-Dry Time:		25-35 hrs		Shelf-Life:	10-15 yrs

Ingredients:

4 cups Water	2 Tbs Greek Yogurt
1 cup Stone-Ground Grits	½ tsp Black Pepper
2 tsp Salt	½ tsp Paprika
1 cup Cheddar Cheese, shredded	Optional: Green Onions, Bacon Bits

Directions:

Bring water to a boil and gradually whisk in grits and salt. Simmer 15-20 minutes until thick and creamy. Stir in shredded cheese, yogurt, black pepper, and paprika. Cool, spread on freeze-drying trays, pre-freeze, and freeze-dry for 25-35 hours. Do a weight check and run Extra Dry Time until the weight doesn't change. Seal in 7mil mylar or a canning jar with an oxygen absorber and store in a cool, dry location.

Rehydration:

1 cup FD Cheesy Grits (51 g)
¾-1 cup water (197 g)
Stir, cover, and let it sit for about 3-5 minutes.

Tips:

For a variation in flavor, try different types of cheese like Monterey Jack or Gouda.

Chia Seed Puddings
Chocolate Raspberry

This rich and fruity Chocolate Raspberry Chia Seed Pudding makes a nutritious dessert or breakfast.

Cups:	10	Servings:	10	Serving Size:	1 cup (240 g)	Calories:	219
Prep/Cook Time:	15 min Set 2 hrs	Freeze-Dry Time:		35-45 hrs		Shelf-Life:	5-10 yrs

Ingredients:
6 cups Almond Milk   ½ cup Maple Syrup
1 cup Chia Seeds   4 cups Raspberries
½ cup Cocoa Powder

Rehydration:
1 cup FD Pudding (52 g)
¾ cup Water (188 g)
Stir, cover, and sit 3-5 min.

Directions:
Combine the milk, chia seeds, cocoa powder, and maple syrup in a bowl until blended well Stir in the raspberries. Refrigerate 2 hours or overnight to set. Spread on the trays and pre-freeze. Freeze-dry for 35-45 hours. Do a weight check and use Extra Dry Time as needed.

Seal in 7mil mylar or canning jars with oxygen absorbers and store in a cool, dry location.

Blueberry Vanilla

The Blueberry Vanilla Chia Seed Pudding is a great way to start your day or enjoy as a light dessert.

Cups:	10	Servings:	10	Serving Size:	1 cup (248 g)	Calories:	225
Prep/Cook Time:	15 min Set 2 hrs	Freeze-Dry Time:		35-45 hrs		Shelf-Life:	5-10 yrs

Ingredients:
6 cups Almond Milk   2 Tbs Vanilla Extract
1 cup Chia Seeds   4 cups Blueberries
½ cup Maple Syrup

Rehydration:
1 cup FD Pudding (51 g)
¾-⅞ cup Water (197 g)
Stir, cover, and sit 3-5 min.

Directions:
Combine the milk, chia seeds, maple syrup, and vanilla extract in a bowl. Add punctured blueberries. Refrigerate 2 hours or overnight to set. Spread on the trays and pre-freeze. Freeze-dry for 35-45 hours. Do a weight check and use Extra Dry Time as needed.

Seal in 7mil mylar or canning jars with oxygen absorbers and store in a cool, dry location.

Mango Coconut

The Mango Coconut Chia Seed Pudding is a delightful tropical treat to enjoy anytime.

Cups:	11	Servings:	11	Serving Size:	1 cup (246 g)	Calories:	271
Prep/Cook Time:	15 min Set 2 hrs	Freeze-Dry Time:		35-45 hrs		Shelf-Life:	3-5 yrs

Ingredients:
2 cans(13.5 oz ea)Coconut Milk   ½ cup Maple Syrup
3½ cup Almond Milk   2 Tbs Vanilla Extract
1 cup Chia Seeds   4 cups Mango, chopped

Rehydration:
1 cup FD Pudding (116 g)
½-⅔ cup Water (130 g)
Stir, cover, and sit 3-5 min.

Directions:
Combine the milks, chia seeds, maple syrup, and vanilla extract. Stir in chopped mango. Refrigerate 2 hours or overnight to set. Spread on the trays and pre-freeze. Freeze-dry for 35-45 hours. Do a weight check and use Extra Dry Time as needed.

Seal in 7mil mylar or canning jars with oxygen absorbers and store in a cool, dry location.

21 LUNCHES

Mexican Enchilada Casserole

A flavorful dish that captures the essence of Mexican cuisine.

Cups:	20	Servings:	20	Serving Size:	1 cup (242 g)	Calories:	250
Prep/Cook Time:		1 hr		Freeze-Dry Time:	25-35 hrs	Shelf-Life:	5-10 yrs

Ingredients:

2 lbs Ground Beef
1 large Onion, chopped
3 cans Enchilada Sauce (med or hot)
2 cups Black Beans, cook/drain/rinse

2 cups Corn Kernels
6 Corn Tortillas
2 cups Spinach, chopped
3 cups Cheddar Cheese, shredded

Directions:

Cook the ground beef in a large skillet and then rinse under hot water. Add onion and cook until tender. Next, stir in the enchilada sauce, black beans, and corn. Preheat oven to 350°. In a casserole dish, begin layering the tortillas, beef mixture, spinach, and cheese, repeating these layers until all ingredients are used, and finishing with a layer of cheese on top. Poke holes throughout. Bake 30min. Once cooled, put bite-sized scoops on your freeze-dryer trays, and pre-freeze. Freeze-dry the Mexican Enchilada Casserole on normal settings for 25-35 hours. Do a weight check and run Extra Dry Time until the weight doesn't change. Seal in 7mil mylar or a canning jar with an oxygen absorber and store in a cool, dry location.

Rehydration:

1 cup FD Casserole Crumbles (57 g)
¾ cup Water (185 g)
Stir, cover, and let it sit for about 15-20 minutes. Reheat in a pot for best flavor.

Tips:

Cilantro or sliced avocado make great additions.

Vegetarian Quinoa Casserole

A nutritious and tasty dish that's packed with protein and fiber.

Cups:	12	Servings:	12	Serving Size:	1 cup (246 g)	Calories:	206
Prep/Cook Time:		30 min		Freeze-Dry Time:	25-35 hrs	Shelf-Life:	15-20 yrs

Ingredients:

2 cups Quinoa
4 cups Vegetable Broth
1 large Onion, chopped
2 large Bell Peppers, chopped
3 cups Black Beans, cook/drain/rinse

2 cups Corn Kernels
1 cup Shredded Carrot (4 med)
1 tsp Marjoram
1 tsp Salt

Directions:

Cook the quinoa in vegetable broth according to the package instructions. Then, in a large skillet, sauté the onion and bell pepper until they are tender. Combine the cooked quinoa with the sautéed vegetables, black beans, corn, carrots, marjoram, and salt in a large bowl. Cool and spread this mixture out on your freeze-drying tray and pre-freeze. Freeze-dry on normal settings for 25-35 hours. Do a weight check and run Extra Dry Time until the weight doesn't change. Seal in 7mil mylar or a canning jar with an oxygen absorber and store in a cool, dry location.

Rehydration:

1 cup FD Casserole (69 g)
¾ cup Water (177 g)
Stir, cover, and let it sit for about 15-20 minutes. Reheat in a pot for best flavor.

Tips:

Add other vegetables like zucchini or squash for more variety.

Chicken, Rice, & Broccoli Casserole

A hearty casserole with a nice balance of protein, carbohydrates, and greens.

| Cups: | 13½ | Servings: | 13½ | Serving Size: | 1 cup (242 g) | Calories: | 300 |
| Prep/Cook Time: | | 1 hr 15 min | Freeze-Dry Time: | | 25-35 hrs | Shelf-Life: | 5-10 yrs |

Ingredients:
2 cups White Rice
4 cups Chicken Broth
2 cups Broccoli
1 can (10.75 oz) Cream of Chicken Soup

2 lbs Cooked Chicken, cubed
2 cups Cheddar Cheese
1 tsp Salt
½ tsp Black Pepper

Directions:
Cook the rice in chicken broth 15 min and allow to sit, covered, for 5 min. Boil broccoli for 10 min. In a large bowl, combine the cooked rice and cream of chicken soup. In a 9x13 casserole dish, start by layering the rice mixture at the bottom. Next, add cooked chicken and broccoli. Top it off with a layer of cheese. Sprinkle on salt and black pepper. Bake the casserole at 350°F for 30 minutes. Once cooled, put bite-sized scoops on your freeze-drying trays and pre-freeze. Freeze-dry on normal settings for 25-35 hours. Do a weight check and run Extra Dry Time until the weight doesn't change. Seal in 7mil mylar or a canning jar with an oxygen absorber and store in a cool, dry location.

Rehydration:
1 cup FD Casserole (73 g)
⅔-¾ cup Water (169 g)
Stir, cover, and let it sit for about 10-15 minutes. Reheat in a pot for best flavor.

Tips:
Sprinkle some extra cheese on top after rehydrating for a delicious topping. Reheat in a pot for best flavor.

Tuna Noodle Casserole & Peas

A classic comfort food dish that's easy to prepare and freeze-dry for long-term storage.

| Cups: | 12 | Servings: | 12 | Serving Size: | 1 cup (240 g) | Calories: | 337 |
| Prep/Cook Time: | | 45 min | Freeze-Dry Time: | | 25-35 hrs | Shelf-Life: | 3-5 yrs |

Ingredients:
1 lb Egg Noodles
4 cans Tuna, drained
2 cans Cream of Mushroom Soup
2 cups Milk
2 cups Peas, frozen

1 tsp Salt
1 tsp Thyme
1 tsp Black Pepper
1 tsp Onion Powder

Directions:
Cook egg noodles according to the package instructions for al dente, then drain and set aside. In a large pot, combine tuna, cream of mushroom soup, milk, peas, salt, thyme, black pepper, and onion powder. Stir in the cooked noodles until everything is well mixed. Allow to heat through, about 10 min. Once cooled, spread out on your freeze-drying trays and pre-freeze. Freeze-dry on normal settings for 25-35 hours. Do a weight check, use Extra Dry Time as needed, and seal in 7mil mylar or canning jars with oxygen absorbers, stored in a cool, dry location.

We
Rehydration:
1 cup FD Casserole (112 g)
½-⅔ cup Water (128 g)
Stir, cover, and let it sit for about 10-15 minutes. Reheat in a pot for best flavor.

Tips:
You can add a layer of shredded cheese on top before freeze-drying for extra flavor. Reheat in a pot for best flavor.

Basil Chicken Stir Fry

A quick and easy stir fry with a fresh, herbal flavor.

Cups:	16	Servings:	16	Serving Size:	1 cup (241 g)	Calories:	195
Prep/Cook Time:		50 min	Freeze-Dry Time:		25-35 hrs	Shelf-Life:	15-20 yrs

Ingredients:

2 cup Onion, chopped
6 cups Red Pepper, chopped
4 lb Chicken Breast, cooked, shredded
4 Tbs Minced Garlic
4 Tbs Minced Ginger
½ cup Soy Sauce

2 tsp Black Pepper
4 tsp Celery Seed
4 tsp Nutmeg
2 Tbs Salt
8 cups Cabbage, chopped
4 cups Basil leaves, fresh

Directions:

Sauté onion, red pepper, and chicken for about 10 minutes in a little water. Add minced garlic, minced ginger, soy sauce, black pepper, celery seed, nutmeg, and salt. Add the cabbage and basil. Cook for 10 minutes. Let it cool and spread it evenly on your freeze-dry tray. Prefreeze and freeze-dry on normal settings for 25-35 hours. Do a weight check and run Extra Dry Time until the weight doesn't change. Seal in 7mil mylar or a canning jar with an oxygen absorber and store in a cool, dry location.

Rehydration:

1 cup FD Stir Fry (46 g)
¾-⅞ cup Water (195 g)
Stir, cover, and let it sit for about 10-15 minutes. Sear in a pan for best flavor.

Tips:

Serve with rice or noodles for a complete meal.

···

Hamburger Mac

A hearty and savory dish that's perfect for any meal.

Cups:	11½	Servings:	11½	Serving Size:	1 cup (243 g)	Calories:	365
Prep/Cook Time:		30 min	Freeze-Dry Time:		25-35 hrs	Shelf-Life:	5-10 yrs

Ingredients:

2 lbs Ground Beef
2 large Onions, chopped
2 cups Water
2 cups Elbow Macaroni, uncooked

2 cans Tomato Soup
2 tsp Salt
1 tsp Black Pepper
2 cups Cheddar Cheese, shredded

Directions:

Brown the ground beef and rinse in hot water. Add onion and cook until tender. Stir in water, macaroni, tomato soup, salt, and black pepper, and simmer 5 min. Stir in cheese and simmer another 5 min, until the flavors have melded together. Once the dish has cooled, spread it evenly on your freeze-dry tray and pre-freeze. Freeze-dry on normal settings for 25-35 hours. Do a weight check and run Extra Dry Time until the weight doesn't change. Seal in 7mil mylar or a canning jar with an oxygen absorber and store in a cool, dry location.

Rehydration:

1 cup FD Hamburger Mac (83 g)
⅔ cup Water (160 g)
Stir, cover, and let it sit for about 10-15 minutes. Reheat in a pot for best flavor.

Tips:

Sprinkle fresh chives on top for a zip of flavor.

Turkey Sweet Potato Skillet

Packed with aromatic spices, it's a perfect one-pan meal for any time of the year.

Cups:	14	Servings:	14	Serving Size:	1 cup (240 g)	Calories:	163
Prep/Cook Time:		50 min	Freeze-Dry Time:		25-35 hrs	Shelf-Life:	15-20 yrs

Ingredients:
2 large Onion, finely chopped
6 cloves Garlic, minced
2 lbs ground Turkey
4 med Sweet Potatoes, peeled, diced
2 med Red Bell Pepper, diced
2 cans (14 oz each) diced Tomatoes

2 cup Chicken Broth
1 tsp Chili powder
2 tsp ground Cumin
1 tsp Paprika
2 tsp dried Oregano
4 tsp Salt
2 tsp Black Pepper

Directions:
In a large skillet, sauté the chopped onion in water for 5 minutes. Add minced garlic and ground turkey, cooking until the turkey is browned and crumbled. Stir in diced sweet potatoes, red bell pepper, diced tomatoes along with their juice, chicken broth, chili powder, cumin, paprika, oregano, salt, and black pepper. Bring the mixture to a boil, then reduce heat to low, cover, and simmer 20-25 minutes. Once the dish has cooled, spread it evenly on your freeze-dry tray and pre-freeze. Freeze-dry on normal settings for 25-35 hours. Do a weight check and run Extra Dry Time until the weight doesn't change. Seal in 7mil mylar or a canning jar with an oxygen absorber and store in a cool, dry location.

Rehydration:
1 cup FD Skillet (38 g)
¾-1 cup Water (202 g)
Stir, cover, and let it sit for about 10-15 minutes. Reheat in a pot for best flavor.

Tips: Customize this by adding additional vegetables such as corn or black beans.

- -

Chicken Salad

This Chicken Salad is perfect for sandwiches, salads, or even as a stand-alone meal. Enjoy it on the go as a quick lunch!

Cups:	10	Servings:	10	Serving Size:	1 cup (243 g)	Calories:	360
Prep/Cook Time:		30 min	Freeze-Dry Time:		25-35 hrs	Shelf-Life:	10-15 yrs

Ingredients:
2 cups Cream Cheese, 16 oz
1 tsp Salt
½ tsp Black Pepper
8 cups cooked Chicken Breast, shredded

6 large stalks Celery, finely chopped
1 cup Dill Pickle Relish
1 large Red Onion, finely chopped

Directions:
Start by mixing cream cheese, salt, and black pepper in a large bowl. Stir in shredded chicken. Stir in the celery, pickle relish, and red onion. Once the mixture is well combined, spread it evenly on your freeze-drying trays and pre-freeze. Freeze-dry on normal settings for 25-35 hours. Do a weight check and run Extra Dry Time until the weight doesn't change. Seal in 7mil mylar or a canning jar with an oxygen absorber and store in a cool, dry location.

Rehydration:
1 cup FD Chicken Salad (67 g)
⅔-¾ cup Water (176 g)
Stir, cover, and let it sit for about 10-15 minutes.

Tips:
Perfect for traveling. Mix with water and eat cold with crackers, bread, or veggies. It takes about 2½ pounds of cooked chicken to make 8 cups.

Veggie Shepherd's Pie

Packed with a variety of colorful vegetables & topped with creamy mashed potatoes, this is a delightful & satisfying dish that is sure to please everyone.

Cups:	12	Servings:	12	Serving Size:	1 cup (244 g)	Calories:	130
Prep/Cook Time:		1 hr 30 min	Freeze-Dry Time:		30-40 hrs	Shelf-Life:	5-10 yrs

Ingredients:

1 med Onion, diced
2 med Carrots, diced
2 large Celery Stalks, diced
1 large Bell Pepper, diced
1 small Zucchini, diced
1 cup Corn Kernels
1 cup Green Peas

2 cups Vegetable Broth
3 cloves Garlic, minced
1 tsp dried Thyme
1 tsp dried Rosemary
1 tsp Paprika
1 tsp Salt
½ tsp Black Pepper

Mashed Portion:
4 Large Potatoes, Peeled and Cubed
½ cup 2% Milk
2 Tbs Greek Yogurt
½ tsp Salt
¼ Black Pepper

Directions:

In a large skillet, sauté diced onion, carrots, celery, bell pepper, and zucchini in a little water until slightly softened. Add in corn, peas, vegetable broth, garlic, thyme, rosemary, paprika, salt, and black pepper. Simmer until vegetables are tender and flavors meld. Separately, boil peeled, cubed potatoes until fork-tender, drain, and mash with milk, yogurt, salt, and black pepper. Preheat the oven to 375°F and assemble the Shepherd's Pie by spreading the vegetable filling in a baking dish, topped with the mashed potatoes. Bake for 25-30 min, or until golden. Cool before putting bite-sized scoops onto freeze-drying trays and pre-freeze. Freeze-dry for 30-40 hours on normal settings.

Do a weight check and run Extra Dry Time until the weight doesn't change. Seal in 7mil mylar or a canning jar with an oxygen absorber and store in a cool, dry location.

Rehydration:

1 cups FD Shepherd's Pie Crumble (45 g)
¾-1 cup Water (199 g)
Stir, cover, and let it sit for about 15-20 minutes. Reheat in a pot for best flavor.

Tips:

Try it with a layer of 1 pound cooked ground beef (makes 14 servings at 187 calories.)

Easy Grilled Cheese Bites

Enjoy these homemade classics wherever your adventure takes you.

Pieces:	160	Servings:	10	Serving Size:	16 pieces (126 g)	Calories:	461
Prep/Cook Time:		20 min	Freeze-Dry Time:		25-35 hrs	Shelf-Life:	3-5 yrs

Ingredients:

20 slices Bread
20 slices Cheddar Cheese

Directions:

Preheat oven to 350. Toast bread in toaster and assemble sandwiches with 2 slices of cheese. Place on baking sheet and bake in oven for 10-15 minutes, or until cheese is melted. Cool, cut into 4 sticks, then cut into 4 bite-sized pieces. Arrange them on freeze-drying trays and pre-freeze. Freeze-dry for 25-35 hours. Do a weight check and run Extra Dry Time until the weight doesn't change. Seal in 7mil mylar or a canning jar with an oxygen absorber and store in a cool, dry location.

Rehydration:

Not recommended

Tips:

Try making these with lunchmeat or a mix of cheeses. These bites are perfect for on-the-go snacks or to toss in with your soups. Try them with freeze-dried tomato soup for a classic combo.

Fiesta Chicken

Packed with Mexican-inspired spices and colorful vegetables, this dish is a fiesta in your mouth!

Cups:	11	Servings:	11	Serving Size:	1 cup (242 g)	Calories:	206
Prep/Cook Time:	1 hr			Freeze-Dry Time:	30-40 hrs	Shelf-Life:	10-15 yrs

Ingredients:
2 lbs Chicken Breasts, diced
1 large Onion, diced
2 large Bell Peppers, diced
1 med Jalapeño Pepper, seeded/minced
3 cloves Garlic, minced
1 Tbs Chili powder
1 tsp Paprika
1 tsp ground Cumin
½ tsp dried Oregano
1 can (15 ounces) Black Beans, drain/rinse
1 can (15 ounces) Corn, drained
1 can (14.5 ounces) diced Tomatoes
¼ cup Cilantro, chopped
1 tsp Salt
½ tsp Black Pepper

Directions:
Sauté diced chicken and set aside. Sauté diced onion, bell peppers, jalapeño, and minced garlic in a little water. Add chili, paprika, cumin, and oregano. Add cooked chicken, black beans, corn, and diced tomatoes. Simmer for 15-20 minutes. Stir in cilantro, salt, and black pepper. Let cool, put bite-sized scoops onto freeze-drying trays, and pre-freeze. Freeze-dry for 30-40 hours. Do a weight check and run Extra Dry Time until the weight doesn't change. Seal in 7mil mylar or a canning jar with an oxygen absorber and store in a cool, dry location.

Rehydration:
1 cup FD Fiesta Chicken (84 g)
½-⅔ cup Water (158 g)
Stir, cover, and let it sit for about 15-20 minutes. Reheat in a pot for best flavor.

Tips:
Try serving the rehydrated fiesta chicken with warm tortillas, rice, or as a filling for tacos or burritos.

Egg Roll in a Bowl

Enjoy the flavors of a classic egg roll in a convenient and satisfying bowl.

Cups:	10	Servings:	10	Serving Size:	1 cup (240)	Calories:	232
Prep/Cook Time:	30 min			Freeze-Dry Time:	25-35 hrs	Shelf-Life:	5-10 yrs

Ingredients:
2 lb Ground Beef, or meat of choice
1 large sweet Onion, thinly sliced
8 cloves Garlic, minced
2 Tbs fresh Ginger, grated
½ cup Soy Sauce
2 tsp Salt
1 tsp Black Pepper
7 cups thinly slice Cabbage
2 cups grated Carrots
8 Green Onions, thinly sliced

Directions:
Brown the ground meat in a large skillet. Remove and set aside. Using the same skillet, sauté sliced onion, minced garlic, and grated ginger in a little water. Return the cooked meat to the skillet and add soy sauce, salt, and black pepper. Add sliced cabbage and grated carrots, and stir-fry mixture until tender-crisp. Sprinkle on sliced green onions. Let cool, put bite-sized scoops onto freeze-drying trays, and pre-freeze. Freeze-dry for 25-35 hours on normal settings. Do a weight check and run Extra Dry Time until the weight doesn't change. Seal in 7mil mylar or a canning jar with an oxygen absorber and store in a cool, dry location.

Rehydration:
1 cup FD Egg Roll in a Bowl (50 g)
¾-1 cup Water (190 g)
½ tsp Rice Vinegar (optional)
Stir, cover, and let it sit for about 10-15 minutes. Reheat in a pot for best flavor.

Tips: Serve over rice or noodles. Consider adding a drizzle of sriracha or a sprinkle of crushed red pepper flakes for a spicy kick.

Chicken Quesadilla Strips

Treat your taste buds to the savory goodness of Chicken Quesadilla Strips. Stuffed with juicy chicken and melty cheese, they're perfect for dipping and sharing.

Pieces:	32	**Servings:**	8	**Serving Size:**	4 pieces (177 g)	**Calories:** 434
Prep/Cook Time:	30 min	**Freeze-Dry Time:**		25-35 hrs		**Shelf-Life:** 5-10 yrs

Ingredients:

2 large (8 oz) Chicken Breasts, cooked and shredded
4 cups Shredded Cheddar Cheese
1 large Onion, diced

½ tsp Sage
1 tsp Salt
8 Large Flour Tortillas

See directions below.

Beef Quesadilla Strips

Indulge in the robust flavors of Beef Quesadilla Strips. Filled with tender beef and gooey cheese, these strips are a hearty treat that can make any meal memorable.

Pieces:	32	**Servings:**	8	**Serving Size:**	4 pieces (177 g)	**Calories:** 470
Prep/Cook Time:	30 min	**Freeze-Dry Time:**		25-35 hrs		**Shelf-Life:** 5-10 yrs

Ingredients:

1 lb Ground Beef, cooked, drained
4 cups Shredded Cheddar Cheese
1 large Onion, diced

1 tsp Rosemary
1 tsp Salt
8 Large Flour Tortillas

See directions below.

Vegetable Quesadilla Strips

Brimming with colorful veggies and melted cheese, these strips offer a tasty and wholesome option that even meat lovers will crave.

Pieces:	32	**Servings:**	8	**Serving Size:**	4 pieces (177 g)	**Calories:** 377
Prep/Cook Time:	30 min	**Freeze-Dry Time:**		25-35 hrs		**Shelf-Life:** 5-10 yrs

Ingredients:

8 oz Mushrooms
4 cups Shredded Cheddar Cheese
1 large Onion, diced
1 cup Bell Peppers, diced

½ cup Corn
½ tsp Marjoram
1 tsp Salt
8 large Flour Tortillas

Directions:

Assemble quesadillas by filling half of each tortilla with layers of cheese and your choice of filling. Cook each side in a buttered skillet on low until the cheese is melted and the tortilla is golden. Once cooled, cut each into 4 triangular strips, lay them on the freeze-drying trays and prefreeze. Freeze-dry for 25-35 hours. Do a weight check and run Extra Dry Time until the weight doesn't change. Seal in 7mil mylar or a canning jar with an oxygen absorber and store in a cool, dry location.

Rehydration:

Dip FD Quesadilla Strips in water 30 seconds and pan fry on low for about 1-5 minutes.
Best eaten as a dry snack.

Tips:

These are a fun addition tossed into soups when sliced thin prior to freeze-drying.

Vegetarian Chili

This meatless chili is packed with a variety of vegetables, beans, and aromatic spices, making it a nutritious and flavorful option for vegetarians and chili lovers alike.

Cups:	12	Servings:	12	Serving Size:	1 cup (241 g)	Calories:	285
Prep/Cook Time:		1 hr 30 min	Freeze-Dry Time:		35-45 hrs	Shelf-Life:	10-15 yrs

Ingredients:
1 med Onion, diced
2 cloves Garlic, minced
2 med Bell Peppers, diced
2 med Zucchinis, diced
2 med Carrots, diced
1 can (14 oz) diced Tomatoes
2 cans (6 oz each) Tomato Sauce
1 can (14 oz) Kidney Beans, drain/rinse
1 can (14 oz) Black Beans, drain/rinse
1 can (14 oz) Corn, drained
2 cups Vegetable Broth
2 Tbs Chili Powder
1 Tbs Cumin
1 tsp Smoked Paprika
½ tsp Cayenne Pepper
1 tsp Salt
¼ tsp Black Pepper

Dircctions:
In a large pot, sauté onion and garlic in a little water. Stir in bell peppers, zucchinis, and carrots, and sauté a few minutes. Add tomatoes, tomato sauce, kidney beans, black beans, corn, vegetable broth, and seasonings. Stir well, reduce the heat, & simmer for 1 hour, stirring occasionally. Allow to cool. Place your empty tray in the freezer, ladle chili onto your tray, and pre-freeze. Freeze-dry for 35-45 hours. Do a weight check and run Extra Dry Time until weight doesn't change. Seal in 7mil mylar or a canning jar with an oxygen absorber & store in a cool, dry location.

Rehydration:
1 cup FD Vegetarian Chili (79 g)
⅔ cup Water or vegetable broth (162 g)
Stir, cover, and let it sit for about 15-20 minutes. Reheat in a pot for best flavor.

Tips:
Add 1 lb of ground meat. (Beef: 14 servings 305 calories and shelf-life of 5-10 yrs.)

Sloppy Joe Casserole

Enjoy the classic flavors of Sloppy Joes in a convenient and delicious casserole format. It combines savory ground meat, tangy sauce, and a layer of cheesy goodness.

Cups:	17	Servings:	17	Serving Size:	1 cup (241 g)	Calories:	489
Prep/Cook Time:		50 min	Freeze-Dry Time:		30-40 hrs	Shelf-Life:	5-10 yrs

Ingredients:
2 med Onion, diced
4 cloves Garlic, minced
2 large Bell Pepper, chopped
2 lb Ground Beef
2 cans (14 oz eaxch) Tomato Sauce
1 cup Ketchup
4 Tbs Brown Sugar
2 Tbs Worcestershire Sauce
2 tsp Mustard
1 tsp Salt
½ tsp Black Pepper
8 cups cooked Elbow Macaroni
4 cups shredded Cheddar Cheese

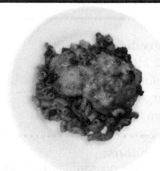

Directions:
Sauté onion, garlic, and bell pepper in a little water. Add beef, tomato sauce, ketchup, brown sugar, worcestershire sauce, mustard, salt, and black pepper and simmer 30 min. Stir in cooked macaroni and the cheddar cheese. Let cool and scoop onto Freeze-Drying trays. Pre-Freeze, then Freeze-dry for 30-40 hours. Do a weight check and run Extra Dry Time until the weight doesn't change. Seal in 7mil mylar or a canning jar with an oxygen absorber and store in a cool, dry location.

Rehydration:
1 cup FD Sloppy Joe Casserole (108 g)
½-⅔ cup Water (133 g)
Stir, cover, and let it sit for about 10-15 minutes. Reheat in a pot for best flavor.

Tips:
Add diced zucchini to enhance the nutritional content and vary the flavor.

Sweet and Sour Pork

A delightful mix of sour and sweet, perfect for a tasty lunch.

Cups:	10	Servings:	10	Serving Size:	1 cup (247 g)	Calories:	255
Prep/Cook Time:	1 hr 10 min	Freeze-Dry Time:		35-45 hrs		Shelf-Life:	5-10 yrs

Ingredients:
2 lb Pork Steak
⅔ cup Flour
¼ cup Water
2 cans (10 oz each) Pineapple & Juice
¼ cup Brown Sugar
1 cup Ketchup
2 med Onion
2 med Green Bell Pepper, sliced

Directions:
Cut pork into chunks, roll in flour and brown in a pan with the water. Retain the pineapple juice from the cans plus a small amount of water to make 3 cups of liquid. Add juice, sugar, ketchup, and onion. (Add 4 Tbs vinegar now if serving fresh.) Simmer 30 min. Add green pepper slices and pineapple. Simmer 10 min. Let cool and place in Freeze-Drying trays. Pre-Freeze, then Freeze-dry for 35-45 hours. Do a weight check and run Extra Dry Time until the weight doesn't change. Seal in 7mil mylar or a canning jar with an oxygen absorber and store in a cool, dry location.

Rehydration:
1 cup FD Sweet and Sour Pork (64 g)
¾ cup Water (183 g)
1 tsp Vinegar (optional)
Stir, cover, and let it sit for about 15-20 minutes. Reheat in a pot for best flavor.

Tips: This pairs wonderfully with a side of white rice or noodles. To serve fresh, add 4 Tbs Vinegar to the recipe at the same time as the ketchup.

Zucchini Parmesan

Zucchini Parmesan combines tender zucchini slices with a rich, creamy sauce, for a simple yet luxurious dish.

Cups:	15	Servings:	15	Serving Size:	1 cup (241 g)	Calories:	278
Prep/Cook Time:	1 hr	Freeze-Dry Time:		25-35 hrs		Shelf-Life:	1-3 yrs

Ingredients:
9 med Zucchini, sliced
4½ cups Half & Half
2½ cups Parmesan
4 cup Mozzarella Cheese
1½ Tbs Garlic powder
1½ Tbs Oregano
1½ Tbs Paprika
1½ Tbs Salt
1½ Tbs Parsley
1½ tsp Black Pepper

Directions:
Wash, peel, and slice Zucchini into rounds. Blend half & half, parmesan, mozzarella, and seasonings. Toss together until zucchini is coated and put into a 9 x 13-inch pan. Bake 45 minutes at 350°. Let cool and scoop onto Freeze-Drying trays. Pre-Freeze, then Freeze-dry for 25-35 hours. Do a weight check and run Extra Dry Time until the weight doesn't change. Seal in 7mil mylar or a canning jar with an oxygen absorber and store in a cool, dry location.

Rehydration:
1 cup FD Zucchini Parmesan (68 g)
⅔-¾ cup Water (173 g)
Stir, cover, and let it sit for about 10-15 minutes. Reheat in a pot for best flavor.

Tips: Zucchini can be diced or chopped for a different texture.

Lazy Lasagna

With a generous layer of cheddar cheese that melts into gooey perfection, every bite is a warm hug for your taste buds.

Cups:	16	Servings:	16	Serving Size:	1 cup (244 g)	Calories:	332
Prep/Cook Time:		1hr 15min	Freeze-Dry Time:		25-35 hrs	Shelf-Life:	5-10 yrs

Ingredients:
12 oz Macaroni, dry (or any Pasta)
4 cups shredded Cheddar Cheese
Cheese Mix:
2 beaten Eggs
3 cups Cottage Cheese
½ tsp Black Pepper

Meat Sauce:
1 lb Hamburger
1 med Onion, chopped
1 quart (4 cups) Tomato Sauce
2 cans (4 oz each) cooked Mushrooms
3 cloves Garlic, minced
1 tsp Salt

Directions:
Cook pasta and set aside. Brown hamburger, drain off oil, and rinse in hot water. Sauté onion. Stir in tomato sauce, mushrooms, garlic, and salt and set aside. Mix eggs, cottage cheese, and black pepper together. In a 9x13 pan assemble by laying down half the noodles, then half the meat sauce, then half the cheese mix, and then half the shredded cheese. Repeat layers. Bake at 350°F for 45 minutes. Let cool, then put bite-sized scoops onto freeze-drying trays and pre-freeze. Freeze-dry for 24-30 hours. Do a weight check and run Extra Dry Time until the weight doesn't change. Seal in 7mil mylar or a canning jar with an oxygen absorber and store in a cool, dry location.

Rehydration:
1 cup FD Lazy Lasagna (102 g)
½-⅔ cup Water (142 g)
Stir, cover, and let it sit for about 20 minutes. Reheat in a pot for best flavor.

Tips:
When at home, after rehydrating, place the lasagna under a broiler for a few minutes until the top is bubbling and slightly browned.

Beef Bulgogi

Savor the sweet and savory taste of Beef Bulgogi, a Korean classic that marries tender slices of beef with a flavorful soy and garlic marinade.

Cups:	12	Servings:	12	Serving Size:	1 cup (240 g)	Calories:	241
Prep/Cook Time:		1 hr	Freeze-Dry Time:		25-35 hrs	Shelf-Life:	1-2 yrs

Ingredients:
4 lbs Beef Sirloin, thinly sliced
½ cup Soy Sauce
2 Tbs Brown Sugar
8 cloves Garlic, minced

2 tsp Black Pepper
2 med Pear, grated
2 med Onion, sliced
4 med Green Onions, sliced
2 med Bell Pepper, sliced

Directions:
Marinate sliced beef in soy sauce, brown sugar, minced garlic, black pepper, and grated pear for at least 30 minutes. Stir-fry beef with onions, green onions, bell pepper until cooked. Let cool and scoop onto freeze-drying trays. Pre-freeze, then freeze-dry for 25-35 hours on normal settings. Do a weight check and run Extra Dry Time until the weight doesn't change. Seal in 7mil mylar or a canning jar with an oxygen absorber and store in a cool, dry location.

Rehydration:
1 cup FD Beef Bulgogi (57 g)
¾ cup Water (183 g)
Stir, cover, and let it sit for about 10-15 minutes. Reheat in a pot for best flavor.

Tips: Serve with steamed rice and kimchi for a traditional Korean meal. Adjust the sweetness by varying the amount of brown sugar up to 3 Tbs.

21 DINNERS

Chicken Korma

Enjoy the convenience of having this tasty meal ready to be rehydrated wherever your adventures take you.

Cups:	13	Servings:	13	Serving Size:	1 cup (243 g)	Calories:	213
Prep/Cook Time:	1 hr		Freeze-Dry Time:	25-35 hrs		Shelf-Life:	1-3 yrs

Ingredients:

2 med Onion, finely chopped
6 cloves Garlic, minced
2 Tbs grated Ginger
¼ cup Korma Curry Sauce
2 tsp Ground Cumin
2 tsp Ground Coriander
1 tsp Turmeric Powder
½ tsp Cinnamon Powder
3 lbs Chicken Breasts, diced
2 cups Plain Yogurt
2 cups Coconut Milk
2 cups Chicken Broth
1 Tbs Salt

Directions:

In a large skillet, sauté the onion in a little water. Add garlic and ginger, cooking until fragrant. Mix in the korma curry sauce, spices, and salt. Simmer 5 min. Add the chicken and brown it. Lower the heat, and add yogurt, coconut milk, and chicken broth. Stir and let it simmer 15-20 minutes. Let cool, ladle the mixture onto freeze-drying trays and pre-freeze. Freeze-dry for 25-35 hours on normal settings. Do a weight check and run Extra Dry Time until the weight doesn't change. Seal in 7mil mylar or a canning jar with an oxygen absorber and store in a cool, dry location.

Rehydration:

1 cup of FD Chicken Korma (47 g)
¾-1 cup of Water (196 g)
Stir, cover, and let it sit for about 10-15 minutes. Reheat in a pot for best flavor.

Tips:

Customize the chicken korma by adding vegetables such as peas, carrots, or bell peppers.

Beef Stroganoff

Savor the creamy and hearty flavors of Beef Stroganoff, perfect for satisfying your cravings in the great outdoors.

Cups:	16	Servings:	16	Serving Size:	1 cup (243 g)	Calories:	202
Prep/Cook Time:	30 min		Freeze-Dry Time:	25-35 hrs		Shelf-Life:	5-10 yrs

Ingredients:

2 lb Beef Sirloin, thinly sliced
2 med Onion, chopped
4 cloves Garlic, minced
16 oz Mushrooms, sliced
¼ cup All-Purpose Flour
2 tsp Salt
½ tsp Black Pepper
4 cups Beef Broth
2 cup Sour Cream
¼ cup Dijon Mustard
24 oz Egg Noodles, cooked

Directions:

Brown beef and set aside. In the same skillet, sauté onion and garlic in a little water. Add mushrooms and cook 5-10 minutes. Sprinkle in flour, salt, and black pepper, stir, and cook 5 minutes. Add beef broth and simmer 10 minutes. Stir in sour cream and dijon mustard. Add cooked beef and cooked noodles to the pot and simmer briefly to meld flavors. Let cool, spread on freeze-drying trays, and pre-freeze. Freeze-dry for 25-35 hours on normal settings. Do a weight check and run Extra Dry Time until the weight doesn't change. Seal in 7mil mylar or a canning jar with an oxygen absorber and store in a cool, dry location.

Rehydration:

1 cup FD Beef Stroganoff (108 g)
½-⅔ cup Water (135 g)
Stir, cover, and let it sit for about 10-15 minutes. Reheat in a pot for best flavor.

Tips:

Experiment with other starches such as rice, mashed potatoes, or even a slice of sourdough bread in place of noodles.

Pad Thai

This Pad Thai captures the essence of Thai cuisine for your on-the-go adventures. The symphony of sweet, sour, and savory makes every bite a delight.

Cups:	10	Servings:	10	Serving Size:	1 cup (241 g)	Calories:	330
Prep/Cook Time:	50 min	Freeze-Dry Time:		25-35 hrs		Shelf-Life:	10-15 yrs

Ingredients:

2 lb Chicken
16 oz Rice Noodles
2 med Onion, thinly sliced
4 cloves Garlic, minced
2 med Green Bell Pepper, thinly sliced

2 med Carrot, julienned
2 cup Bean Sprouts
½ cup Green Onions, chopped
½ cup Soy Sauce
¼ cup Sugar

Directions:

Brown chicken in a bit of water and set aside. Cook rice noodles and set aside. Sauté onion and garlic until soft. Add bell pepper, carrot, bean sprouts, and green onions and stir-fry until tender-crisp. In a bowl, whisk soy sauce and sugar, then pour over the veggie mix. Add the cooked rice noodles and chicken, toss well, and cook for 2-3 minutes. Let cool, spread on freeze-drying trays, and pre-freeze. Freeze-dry for 25-35 hours on normal settings. Do a weight check and run Extra Dry Time until the weight doesn't change. Seal in 7mil mylar or a canning jar with an oxygen absorber and store in a cool, dry location.

Rehydration:

1 cup FD Pad Thai (83 g)
⅔ cup Water (158 g)
Stir, cover, and let it sit for about 10-15 minutes. Reheat in a pot for best flavor.

Tips:

Tastes great with toppings like crushed peanuts, chopped cilantro, and lime wedges.

Loaded Veggie Goulash

This comforting dish combines a medley of colorful veggies, tender pasta, & savory spices for a satisfying meal.

Cups:	12	Servings:	12	Serving Size:	1 cup (247 g)	Calories:	226
Prep/Cook Time:	55 min	Freeze-Dry Time:		30-40 hrs		Shelf-Life:	15-20 yrs

Ingredients:

1 med Onion, diced
2 cloves Garlic, minced
2 med Bell Peppers, diced
2 small Zucchinis, diced
2 med Carrots, grated
1 can (14 oz) Diced Tomatoes
1 can (14 oz) Tomato Sauce
1 can (14 oz) Kidney Beans, drain/rinse

1 can (14 oz) Corn, drained
2 cups Vegetable Broth
2 tsp Paprika
2 tsp Dried Oregano
1 tsp Dried Basil
2 tsp Salt
½ tsp Black Pepper
3 cups Cooked Pasta

Directions:

In a large pot, sauté onion and garlic with a little water until translucent. Add bell peppers, zucchinis, and carrots, cooking for about 5 minutes. Stir in diced tomatoes, tomato sauce, kidney beans, corn, vegetable broth, tomato paste, & seasonings. Bring to a boil, then simmer for 30 minutes. Toss cooked pasta into the mixture. Simmer 5 minutes. Let cool, spread on freeze-drying trays and pre-freeze. Freeze-dry the mixture for 30-40 hours. Do a weight check and run Extra Dry Time until the weight doesn't change. Seal in 7mil mylar or a canning jar with an oxygen absorber and store in a cool, dry location.

Rehydration:

1 cup FD Loaded Veggie Goulash (62 g)
¾ cup Water or vegetable broth (185 g)
Stir, cover, and let it sit for about 15-20 minutes. Reheat in a pot for best flavor.

Tips:

Top with shredded cheese or fresh parsley. Try adding 2 lbs roast beef chunks for more protein (change servings to 16, change calories to 256, change shelf life to 5-10 yrs, and rehydrate with ½-⅔ cup water.)

Chicken Alfredo Pasta

Indulge in the creamy, rich flavors of Chicken Alfredo Pasta. A comfort food classic that's sure to impress.

Cups:	12½	**Servings:**	12½	**Serving Size:**	1 cup (243 g)	**Calories:**	385
Prep/Cook Time:	45 min	**Freeze-Dry Time:**		25-35 hrs		**Shelf-Life:**	1-3 yrs

Ingredients:

16 oz Fettuccine Pasta, cooked
4 cloves Garlic, minced
2 lb Chicken Breast, bite-sized pieces
2 tsp Salt

1 tsp Black Pepper
1 cup Half & Half
2 cups Sour Cream
2 cups Parmesan Cheese

Directions:

Cook pasta to just under-done, drain and set aside. In a large skillet, sauté minced garlic in a bit of water until soft. Add chicken, salt, and black pepper and cook 10-15 minutes. Lower the heat, add half & half and sour cream and simmer for 5 minutes. Add Parmesan cheese, stirring until smooth. Toss the cooked pasta in the sauce until well-coated. Let cool, spread the mixture on freeze-drying trays, and pre-freeze. Freeze-dry for 25-35 hours on normal settings. Do a weight check and run Extra Dry Time until the weight doesn't change. Seal in 7mil mylar or a canning jar with an oxygen absorber and store in a cool, dry location.

Rehydration:

1 cup FD Chicken Alfredo Pasta (94 g)
½-⅔ cup Water (149 g)
Stir, cover, and let it sit for about 10-15 minutes. Reheat in a pot for best flavor.

Tips:

Add additional toppings after rehydration, such as extra grated Parmesan cheese, fresh chives, ground black pepper, or red pepper flakes for a hint of heat.

Herbed Mushroom Risotto

With its rich and aromatic blend of herbs, this dish is a satisfying and flavorful option for a hearty outdoor meal.

Cups:	12	**Servings:**	12	**Serving Size:**	1 cup (248 g)	**Calories:**	167
Prep/Cook Time:	40 min	**Freeze-Dry Time:**		25-35 hrs		**Shelf-Life:**	5-10 yrs

Ingredients:

2 medium Onions, finely chopped
4 cloves Garlic, minced
16 oz Mushrooms, sliced
2 cups Arborio Rice
8 cups Vegetable Broth

½ cup Parmesan Cheese
¼ cup Greek Yogurt
2 Tbs Fresh Thyme, chopped
1 Tbs Fresh Parsley, chopped
1 tsp Salt
½ tsp Black Pepper

Directions:

In a large skillet, sauté onions in a little water until translucent. Add minced garlic and sliced mushrooms and cook 10 minutes, or until tender. Stir in Arborio rice and vegetable broth, stirring frequently for 15 minutes or until absorbed. Stir in Parmesan cheese, yogurt, fresh herbs, and spices. Let cool, spread on the freeze-drying trays and pre-freeze. Freeze-dry for 25-35 hours on normal settings. Do a weight check and run Extra Dry Time until the weight doesn't change. Seal in 7mil mylar or a canning jar with an oxygen absorber and store in a cool, dry location.

Rehydration:

1 cup FD Herbed Mushroom Risotto (47 g)
¾-1 cup Water (201 g)
Stir, cover, and let it sit for about 10-15 minutes. Reheat in a pot for best flavor.

Tips:

Try adding 2 lbs of chicken chunks for more protein (change servings to 16, calories to 275, and rehydrate with ½-⅔ cup water.)

Classic Chili

This Chili recipe offers a hearty and flavorful option for outdoor meals. Packed with protein and a blend of spices, it's a satisfying dish that will warm you up even in the great outdoors.

Cups:	12½	Servings:	12½	Serving Size:	1 cup (246 g)	Calories:	319
Prep/Cook Time:		1 hr		Freeze-Dry Time:	30-40 hrs	Shelf-Life:	5-10 yrs

Ingredients:

2 lb Ground Beef
1 med Onion, chopped
2 cloves Garlic, minced
1 med Red Bell Pepper, chopped
2 cups Beef Broth
1 can (6 oz) Tomato Paste
1 can (14 oz) diced Tomatoes
1 can (15 oz) Kidney Beans, drain/rinse
1 can (15 oz) Black Beans, drain/rinse
2 Tbs Chili Powder
1 Tbs Ground Cumin
1 tsp Paprika
1 tsp Salt
½ tsp Black Pepper
½ tsp Dried Oregano

Directions:

In a large skillet, brown the beef and drain off fat. Add the onion, garlic, and bell pepper, sautéing until tender. Stir in broth and tomato paste. Add diced tomatoes, beans, and spices. Bring to a boil before lowering the heat to simmer for 30 min. Let cool, ladle on the freeze-drying trays and pre-freeze. Freeze-dry for 30-40 hours on normal settings. Do a weight check and run Extra Dry Time until the weight doesn't change. Seal in 7mil mylar or a canning jar with an oxygen absorber and store in a cool, dry location.

Rehydration:

1 cup FD Classic Chili (158 g)
⅓-½ cup Water (88 g)
Stir, cover, and let it sit for about 10-15 minutes. Reheat in a pot for best flavor.

Tips:

Try adding vegetables, such as corn or zucchini, before freeze-drying. Add toppings like shredded cheese or chopped green onions after rehydrating.

Meat Lovers Chili

Indulge in the robust flavors of this meat lovers chili, packed with a combination of ground beef, stew meat, and sausage. This hearty and comforting dish is perfect for chilly days.

Cups:	16	Servings:	16	Serving Size:	1 cup (240 g)	Calories:	407
Prep/Cook Time:		1 hr 30 min	Freeze-Dry Time:		30-40 hrs	Shelf-Life:	3-5 yrs

Ingredients:

1 lb Ground Beef
1 lb Chicken Sausage
1 lb Stew Meat
1 large Onion, finely chopped
4 cloves Garlic, minced
1 med Green Bell Pepper, diced
1 med Red Bell Pepper, diced
2 Tbs Tomato Paste
1 can (14 oz) Tomato Sauce
1 can (14 oz) Kidney Beans, drain/rinse
1 can (14 oz) Black Beans, drain/rinse
1 can (14 oz) Pinto Beans, drain/rinse
1 can (14 oz) Diced Tomatoes
2 Tbs Worcestershire Sauce
2 Tbs Chili Powder
1 tsp Ground Cumin
1 tsp Paprika
2 tsp Salt
½ tsp Black Pepper

Directions:

In a large pot, cook ground beef, stew meat, and sausage, drain, and rinse in hot water. Add the onion, garlic, and bell peppers, sautéing until soft. Stir in tomato paste and sauce. Add the beans, diced tomatoes, worcestershire sauce, and spices. Bring to a boil, reduce heat, and simmer 1 hour. Let cool, ladle on the freeze-drying trays and pre-freeze. Freeze-dry for 30-40 hours on normal settings. Do a weight check and run Extra Dry Time until the weight doesn't change. Seal in 7mil mylar or a canning jar with an oxygen absorber and store in a cool, dry location.

Rehydration:

1 cup FD Meat Lovers Chili (120 g)
½-⅔ cup Water (120 g)
Stir, cover, and let it sit for about 10-15 minutes. Reheat in a pot for best flavor.

Tips:

Add additional heat & spice with diced jalapeños or a dash of hot sauce.

Rice and Vegetable Medley

Packed with a variety of vegetables and fluffy rice, this medley is a convenient and satisfying dish that can accompany any main course.

Cups:	11	Servings:	11	Serving Size:	1 cup (176 g)	Calories:	158
Prep/Cook Time:		50 min	Freeze-Dry Time:		25-35 hrs	Shelf-Life:	15-20 yrs

Ingredients:
4 cups Vegetable Broth
2 cups Long-Grain White Rice
1 med Onion, diced
2 cloves Garlic, minced
1 med Orange Bell Pepper, diced
1 med Yellow Bell Pepper, diced
1 small Zucchini, diced
1 cup Corn
1 cup Green Peas
1 tsp Salt
½ tsp Black Pepper

Directions:
In a medium pot, cook vegetable broth and rice, reduce heat and simmer 15 minutes. In a separate skillet, sauté the onion and garlic in a little water. Add bell peppers, zucchini, corn, peas, and seasonings, cooking until tender-crisp. Combine with the cooked rice. After cooling, spread the mixture on freeze-drying trays and pre-freeze. Freeze-dry for 25-35 hours on normal settings. Do a weight check and run Extra Dry Time until the weight doesn't change. Seal in 7mil mylar or a canning jar with an oxygen absorber and store in a cool, dry location.

Rehydration:
1 cup FD Rice and Vegetable Medley (41 g)
½-⅔ cup Water (135 g)
Stir, cover, and let it sit for about 15-20 minutes. Reheat in a pot for best flavor.

Tips:
Add 1 lb chicken chunks for more protein (change servings to 14, calories to 200, and rehydrate with ⅓-½ cup water.)

Yellow Chicken Curry

This Yellow Chicken Curry recipe combines aromatic spices, tender chicken, and vibrant vegetables to create a flavorful and convenient meal.

Cups:	16	Servings:	16	Serving Size:	1 cup (245 g)	Calories:	242
Prep/Cook Time:		1 hr	Freeze-Dry Time:		25-35 hrs	Shelf-Life:	1-3 yrs

Ingredients:
2 med Onion, thinly sliced
4 cloves Garlic, minced
2 Tbs Grated Ginger
4 Tbs Yellow Curry Paste
2 cup Chicken Broth
2 cans (14 oz each) Coconut Milk
4 lbs Chicken Breast, bite-sized pieces
2 med Green Bell Pepper
2 small Zucchini, sliced, sliced
2 cup Green Peas
1 tsp Salt
¼ tsp Black Pepper

Directions:
In a large skillet, sauté onions in a bit of water until soft. Add garlic, ginger, and yellow curry paste, stir, and cook 2 minutes. Stir in broth and coconut milk. Add chicken, bell pepper, zucchini, peas, and seasonings. Bring to a simmer, and let it cook covered for 45 minutes. Cool the curry, then evenly spread it on freeze-drying trays. Freeze-dry for 25-35 hours on normal settings. Do a weight check and run Extra Dry Time until the weight doesn't change. Seal in 7mil mylar or a canning jar with an oxygen absorber and store in a cool, dry location.

Rehydration:
1 cup FD Yellow Chicken Curry (91 g)
⅔ cup Water (154 g)
Stir, cover, and let it sit for about 10-15 minutes. Reheat in a pot for best flavor.

Tips:
Experiment with different protein options, such as tofu or shrimp.

Beef & Barley Stew

This hearty and comforting Stew is a classic dish with robust flavors. The easy rehydration, makes it perfect for camping trips.

Cups:	12	Servings:	12	Serving Size:	1 cup (247 g)	Calories:	176
Prep/Cook Time:		1 hr 30 min	Freeze-Dry Time:		25-35 hrs	Shelf-Life:	5-10 yrs

Ingredients:

1½ lbs Beef Stew Meat, bite-sized pieces
1 med Onion, diced
2 cloves Garlic, minced
1 Tbs Tomato Paste
1 can (14.5 oz) Tomato Sauce
4 cups Beef Broth
1 tsp Dried Thyme
1 Bay Leaf
2 tsp Salt
½ tsp Black Pepper
1 cup Pearled Barley
2 med Carrots, diced
2 large Celery Stalks, diced
1 cup Green Peas
1 cup Sweet Corn

Directions:

In a large pot, brown stew meat in a little water and set aside. In the same pot, sauté diced onion and garlic until soft. Add tomato paste, tomato sauce, broth, and seasonings, stirring well. Add the pearled barley, carrots, and celery and simmer 10 minutes. Add the meat back in, along with the peas, and corn. Stir and simmer on low, covered, for 1 hour. After cooling, ladle the stew on freeze-drying trays and pre-freeze. Freeze-dry for 25-35 hours on normal settings. Do a weight check and run Extra Dry Time until the weight doesn't change. Seal in 7mil mylar or a canning jar with an oxygen absorber and store in a cool, dry location.

Rehydration:

1 cup FD Beef & Barley Stew (126 g)
½ cup Water (121 g)
Stir, cover, and let it sit for about 15-20 minutes. Reheat in a pot for best flavor.

Tips:

If desired, you can use a mix of beef broth and red wine for added depth of flavor. Adjust the ratio according to your preference.

Chickpea Curry

This Curry offers a delightful blend of aromatic spices, tender chickpeas, and a rich tomato-based sauce.

Cups:	16	Servings:	16	Serving Size:	1 cup (241 g)	Calories:	126
Prep/Cook Time:		1 hr	Freeze-Dry Time:		30-40 hrs	Shelf-Life:	1-2 yrs

Ingredients:

2 large Onion, finely chopped
4 cloves Garlic, minced
2 Tbs grated Ginger
4 Tbs Red Curry Paste
2 cup Vegetable Broth
2 cans (14 oz each) Coconut Milk
4 cups cooked Chickpeas
½ cup Green Peas
4 large Bell Peppers, diced
2 cans (14 oz each) crushed Tomatoes
2 Tbs Lime Juice
2 Tbs Soy Sauce
2 tsp Brown Sugar
2 tsp Salt
1 tsp Black Pepper

Directions:

In a large pot over medium heat, sauté onions in a little water. Add garlic, ginger, and red curry paste. Stir and cook for 2 minutes. Stir in broth and coconut milk. Add chickpeas, green peas, bell peppers, and crushed tomatoes. Add the rest of the ingredients. Stir, simmer on low for 45 minutes. Allow to cool. Spread onto freeze-drying trays and pre-freeze. Freeze-dry for 30-40 hours. Do a weight check and run Extra Dry Time until the weight doesn't change. Seal in 7mil mylar or a canning jar with an oxygen absorber and store in a cool, dry location.

Rehydration:

1 cup FD Red Chickpea Curry (34 g)
¾-1 cup Water (207 g)
Stir, cover, and let it sit for about 10-15 minutes. Reheat in a pot for best flavor.

Tips:

Top with fresh cilantro. Experiment with different types of curry paste, such as green curry or yellow curry, to create variations.

Cheesy Macaroni

Whether you're exploring the great outdoors or looking for a quick and satisfying meal at home, this freeze-dried version of a beloved favorite will not disappoint.

Cups:	16	**Servings:**	16	**Serving Size:**	1 cup (200 g)	**Calories:**	380
Prep/Cook Time:	30 min	**Freeze-Dry Time:**	25-35 hrs	**Shelf-Life:**	3-5 yrs

Ingredients:

2 lbs Macaroni Pasta, cooked
1 cup Sour Cream
¼ cup All-Purpose Flour
1 tsp Mustard Powder

4 oz Cream Cheese
1 cup Milk
4 cups Shredded Cheddar Cheese
1 tsp Salt
½ tsp Black Pepper

Directions:

Cook macaroni until just under done. In a saucepan, heat sour cream and stir in flour and mustard powder to form a roux. Gradually whisk in cream cheese and milk until thickened. On low heat, melt shredded cheddar cheese and add seasonings into the sauce. Combine with cooked macaroni. Let cool, spread the mixture on freeze-drying trays and pre-freeze. Freeze-dry for 25-35 hours on normal settings. Do a weight check and run Extra Dry Time until the weight doesn't change. Seal in 7mil mylar or a canning jar with an oxygen absorber and store in a cool, dry location.

Rehydration:

1 cup FD Cheesy Macaroni (117 g)
⅓-½ cup Water (83 g)
Stir, cover, and let it sit for about 10-15 minutes. Reheat in a pot for best flavor.

Tips:

For a touch of spice, incorporate a pinch of cayenne pepper or a few dashes of hot sauce into the cheese sauce before freeze-drying.

Steak Strips and Vegetables

Hearty steak strips paired with vibrant vegetables for a satisfying and convenient meal.

Cups:	16	**Servings:**	16	**Serving Size:**	1 cup (240 g)	**Calories:**	327
Prep/Cook Time:	30 min	**Freeze-Dry Time:**	25-35 hrs	**Shelf-Life:**	5-10 yrs

Ingredients:

6 lbs Strip Steak, cut in strips
4 Tbs Steak Seasoning
2 large Onions, sliced

4 large Bell Peppers, sliced
5 med Carrots, cut in sticks
2 cups Broccoli Florets

Directions:

Season strip steak with steak seasoning and let it sit for 20 minutes. Sauté sliced onions, bell peppers, carrots, and broccoli in water, seasoning lightly if desired. Sear the steak strips over medium heat. Combine with the veggies. Let cool, spread on freeze-drying trays, and pre-freeze. Freeze-dry for 25-35 hours on normal settings. Do a weight check and run Extra Dry Time until the weight doesn't change. Seal in 7mil mylar or a canning jar with an oxygen absorber and store in a cool, dry location.

Rehydration:

1 cup FD Steak Strips and Vegetables (197 g)
¼ cup Water (43 g)
Stir, cover, and let it sit for about 10-15 minutes. Sear in a pan for best flavor.

Tips:

Try adding different vegetables or seasoning variations to the mix to explore flavors.

Fried Rice

Enjoy this freeze-dried version of a beloved Asian dish while camping, hiking, or as a quick and delicious meal at home.

Cups:	14	Servings:	14	Serving Size:	1 cup (173 g)	Calories:	190
Prep/Cook Time:		30 min	Freeze-Dry Time:		20-30 hrs	Shelf-Life:	1-2 yrs

Ingredients:
2 large Onion, diced
4 cloves Garlic, minced
4 Eggs, beaten
2 cup frozen Mixed Vegetables

¼ cup Soy Sauce
2 Tbs Oyster Sauce
1 tsp Salt
¼ tsp Black Pepper
8 cups Cooked Rice

Directions:
Sauté diced onion and garlic in a little water. Scramble beaten eggs, then mix with the onions and garlic. Stir-fry frozen mixed veggies until thawed. Stir in soy sauce, oyster sauce, salt, and black pepper. Combine eggs, veggies, and cooked rice, breaking up any clumps. Allow to cool, spread the mixture on freeze-drying trays, and pre-freeze. Freeze-dry for 20-30 hours. Do a weight check and run Extra Dry Time until the weight doesn't change. Seal in 7mil mylar or a canning jar with an oxygen absorber and store in a cool, dry location.

Rehydration:
1 cup FD Fried Rice (65 g)
⅓-½ cup Water (108 g)
Stir, cover, and let it sit for about 1-5 minutes. Reheat in a pot for best flavor.

Tips:
4 cups raw rice = 8 cups cooked. Customize your Fried Rice by adding protein options, such as chicken chunks or shrimp. Add chopped green onions or sesame seeds for garnish.

Beef Stew

A hearty Hungarian-style stew with beef, potatoes, and paprika.

Cups:	16	Servings:	16	Serving Size:	1 cup (244 g)	Calories:	184
Prep/Cook Time:		1 hr 30 min	Freeze-Dry Time:		25-35 hrs	Shelf-Life:	5-10 yrs

Ingredients:
2 lb Beef Stew Meat
1 large Onion, chopped
2 cloves Garlic, minced
2 qts Beef Broth
4 cups Potatoes, cubed

2 med Carrots, chopped
2 large Celery Stalks, chopped
2 Tbs Paprika
2 tsp Salt
1 tsp Black Pepper

Directions:
In a large pot, sauté beef, onion, and garlic until the beef is browned and the onions are soft. Add broth, potatoes, carrots, celery, paprika, salt, and black pepper. Allow the mixture to simmer 1+ hour until the beef is tender and the flavors meld. Cool, transfer onto freeze-drying trays, and pre-freeze. Freeze-dry for 25-35 hours. Do a weight check and run Extra Dry Time until the weight doesn't change. Seal in 7mil mylar or a canning jar with an oxygen absorber and store in a cool, dry location.

Rehydration:
1 cup FD Beef Stew (160 g)
⅓-½ cup Water (84 g)
Stir, cover, and let it sit for about 10-15 minutes. Reheat in a pot for best flavor.

Tips:
For optimal rehydration and flavor, ensure beef cubes are uniformly cut ½"-¾".

Pork Carnitas

These Pork Carnitas are ideal for adventurers, busy families, or anyone in need of a quick and delicious meal.

Cups:	11	Servings:	11	Serving Size:	1 cup (248 g)	Calories:	269
Prep/Cook Time:	1 hr 30 min	Freeze-Dry Time:		25-35 hrs		Shelf-Life:	5-10 yrs

Ingredients:
4 lbs Pork Shoulder, cut into chunks
2 med Onion, thinly sliced
6 cloves Garlic, minced
2 Tbs Ground Cumin

2 cup Chicken Broth
⅔ cup Orange Juice
2 tsp Salt
1 tsp Black Pepper

Directions:
Brown the pork in a small amount of water over medium heat. Add the chopped onion and minced garlic, cooking until softened. Stir in cumin, broth, orange juice, salt and black pepper. Simmer 1+ hour, until the pork is tender and easily shredded. Cool and shred the pork. Spread it evenly on trays and pre-freeze. Freeze-dry for 25-35 hours on normal settings. Do a weight check and run Extra Dry Time until the weight doesn't change. Seal in 7mil mylar or a canning jar with an oxygen absorber and store in a cool, dry location.

Rehydration:
1 cup FD Pork Carnitas (55 g)
¾ cup Water (193 g)
Stir, cover, and let it sit for about 10-15 minutes. Sear in a pan for best flavor.

Tips:
If you enjoy a bit of spice, consider adding a teaspoon of chipotle powder or diced jalapeños to the mix before cooking.

Pork Lo Mein

Bring the vibrant flavors of your favorite Asian cuisine to your kitchen or campsite with our Pork Lo Mein.

Cups:	12	Servings:	12	Serving Size:	1 cup (245 g)	Calories:	388
Prep/Cook Time:	45 min	Freeze-Dry Time:		25-35 hrs		Shelf-Life:	1-2 yrs

Ingredients:
2 lb Lo Mein Noodles
2 lb Pork Tenderloin, thinly sliced
4 Tbs Soy Sauce
2 Tbs Oyster Sauce

1 lb Mushrooms, sliced
2 large Onions, sliced
2 med Bell Peppers, sliced
4 cloves Garlic, minced
2 tsp Ginger, grated

Directions:
Cook the noodles slightly under-done and set aside. In a large skillet, stir-fry the pork, sauces, vegetables, and seasonings until the pork is cooked through and the vegetables are tender. Add the cooked noodles to the skillet and mix everything together until well combined. Allow to cool, place on freeze-dry trays, and pre-freeze. Freeze-dry for 25-35 hours on normal settings. Do a weight check and run Extra Dry Time until the weight doesn't change. Seal in 7mil mylar or a canning jar with an oxygen absorber and store in a cool, dry location.

Rehydration:
1 cup FD Pork Lo Mein (106 g)
½-⅔ cup Water (139 g)
Stir, cover, and let it sit for about 10-15 minutes. Sear in a pan for best flavor.

Tips:
Avoid overcooking noodles before freeze-drying. By cooking al dente, or just under-done, it ensures they rehydrate perfectly without becoming mushy.

Spicy Pork Chili

A hearty and warming dish that combines the robust flavors of ground pork with the rich textures of beans and corn, all simmered in a smoky, spicy tomato broth.

Cups:	12½	Servings:	12½	Serving Size:	1 cup (240 g)	Calories:	359
Prep/Cook Time:	1 hr	Freeze-Dry Time:		30-40 hrs		Shelf-Life:	5-10 yrs

Ingredients:

2 lbs Ground Pork
1 large Onion, chopped
3 cloves Garlic, minced
2 cans (14 oz each) Diced Tomatoes
1 can (15 oz) Corn, drained
1 can (15 oz) Black Beans, drain/rinse

1 cup Beef Broth
2 Tbs Chili Powder
1 Tbs Cumin
1 tsp Smoked Paprika
2 tsp Salt
½ tsp Black Pepper

Directions:

Brown pork in a small amount of water over medium heat. Add the onions and garlic, cooking until softened. Stir in the tomatoes, corn, beans, broth, and seasonings. Reduce heat to low and let it simmer 30 minutes, or until all the flavors are well combined. Let cool, ladle onto trays, and pre-freeze. Freeze-dry for 30-40 hours on normal settings. Do a weight check and run Extra Dry Time until the weight doesn't change. Seal in 7mil mylar or a canning jar with an oxygen absorber and store in a cool, dry location.

Rehydration:

1 cup FD Spicy Pork Chili (95 g)
½-⅔ cup Water (145 g)
Stir, cover, and let it sit for about 15-20 minutes. Reheat in a pot for best flavor.

Tips:

Using water to brown the pork helps to cook it evenly without adding extra fat.

Lemon Herb Chicken

Each bite of the tender chicken breast is infused with the perfect balance of citrus and garlic, creating a delightfully light yet satisfying meal.

Cups:	14	Servings:	14	Serving Size:	1 cup (247 g)	Calories:	243
Prep/Cook Time:	1 hr	Freeze-Dry Time:		25-35 hrs		Shelf-Life:	15-20 yrs

Ingredients:

6 lbs Chicken Breast, diced
Juice and Zest of 4 Lemons (½ cup)
12 cloves Garlic, minced
4 tsp fresh Rosemary, chopped

4 tsp fresh Thyme, chopped
1 tsp Salt
½ tsp Black Pepper
2 cup Chicken Broth

Directions:

Marinate the diced chicken in lemon juice, garlic, rosemary, thyme, salt, and black pepper for 20 minutes or overnight in the fridge. After marinating, cook the chicken in a small amount of juices until it begins to brown. Add broth and let it simmer on low heat 30 minutes or until the chicken is fully cooked and tender. Allow to cool, place on trays, and pre-freeze. Freeze-dry for 25-35 hours on normal settings. Do a weight check and run Extra Dry Time until the weight doesn't change. Seal in 7mil mylar or a canning jar with an oxygen absorber and store in a cool, dry location.

Rehydration:

1 cup FD Lemon Herb Chicken (55 g)
¾-1 cup Water (192 g)
Stir, cover, and let it sit for about 10-15 minutes. Sear in a pan for best flavor.

Tips:

Try serving with roasted potatoes and carrots, sprinkled with some parsley.

Beef Vegetable Stew

Warm up with a bowl of our comforting Beef Vegetable Stew, where every spoonful is a blend of hearty beef, tender vegetables, and a savory broth seasoned with thyme.

| Cups: | 14½ | Servings: | 14½ | Serving Size: | 1 cup (242 g) | Calories: | 219 |
| Prep/Cook Time: | | 1 hr 20 min | | Freeze-Dry Time: | 30-40 hrs | Shelf-Life: | 5-10 yrs |

Ingredients:

2 lb Beef Stew Meat, cubed
1 lb Red Potatoes, cubed
2 large Onions, chopped
4 cloves Garlic, minced
4 large Carrots, diced
4 large Celery stalks, diced
4 cups Beef Broth
2 cup Green Peas
2 tsp Thyme
2 tsp Salt
½ tsp Black Pepper

Directions:
Brown the beef in a little water, then sauté the potatoes, onions, garlic, carrots, and celery 10 minutes, or until softened. Add the broth, peas, thyme, salt, and black pepper, stirring well. Let it simmer on low for 20-30 minutes until the flavors meld. Allow it to cool, ladel on trays, and pre-freeze. Freeze-dry for 30-40 hours on normal settings. Do a weight check and run Extra Dry Time until the weight doesn't change. Seal in 7mil mylar or a canning jar with an oxygen absorber and store in a cool, dry location.

Rehydration:
1 cup FD Beef Vegetable Stew (114 g)
½-⅔ cup Water (128 g)
Stir, cover, and let it sit for about 10-15 minutes. Reheat in a pot for best flavor.

Tips:
Cut the beef into uniform ½"-¾" cubes to ensure even cooking and easier rehydration.

21 SOUPS

Tomato Soup

Experience the essence of comfort with our Tomato Soup. Made from ripe tomatoes and a dash of spices, it's a hug in a bowl that will warm your soul and satisfy your hunger.

| Cups: | 14 | Servings: | 14 | Serving Size: | 1 cup (240 g) | Calories: | 49 |
| Prep/Cook Time: | | 1 hr | | Freeze-Dry Time: | 30-40 hrs | Shelf-Life: | 15-20 yrs |

Ingredients:

10 cups Tomatoes, diced
2 med Onions, diced
4 cloves Garlic, minced
3 cups Vegetable Broth
2 tsp Salt
1 tsp Black Pepper
2 Tbs Sugar

Directions:
Combine diced tomatoes, onions, garlic, vegetable broth, salt, black pepper, and sugar in a large pot. Bring to a boil and simmer for 30 minutes. Blend soup until smooth and cool. Place your empty tray in the freezer, pour soup onto your tray, and pre-freeze. Freeze-dry for 30-40 hours. Do a weight check and run Extra Dry Time until the weight doesn't change. Seal in 7mil mylar or a canning jar with an oxygen absorber and store in a cool, dry location.

Rehydration:
⅓-½ cup FD Tomato Soup Powder (15 g)
¾-1 cup Water (226 g)
Stir, cover, and let it sit for about 3-5 minutes. Adjust as needed. Reheat in a pot for best flavor.

Tips:
Tomato soup can bubble up when freeze-drying due to the natural sugars. It's completely normal and will not affect the quality or taste.

Vegetable Medley Soup

This convenient and flavorsome stew is perfect for outdoor adventures or quick and nourishing meals at home.

Cups:	16	Servings:	16	Serving Size:	1 cup (240 g)	Calories:	107
Prep/Cook Time:		1 hr 30 min	Freeze-Dry Time:		30-40 hrs	Shelf-Life:	5-10 yrs

Ingredients:
2 large Onion, diced
4 cloves Garlic, minced
4 med Carrots, diced
4 large Celery Stalks, diced
2 cup fresh or frozen Corn
2 cup fresh or frozen Green Beans
4 cups Tomatoes, diced

4 cups Vegetable Broth
4 cups cooked Chicken (2 lbs)
4 tsp dried Oregano
4 tsp dried Basil
2 tsp Paprika
2 tsp Salt
½ tsp Black Pepper

Directions:
In a large skillet, sauté diced onion and garlic in water. Add carrots, celery, corn, green beans, diced tomatoes, and vegetable broth. Stir in your choice of cooked protein, and season with herbs and spices. Simmer on low, covered, for 1 hour, stirring occasionally. Cool. Place your empty tray in the freezer, pour soup onto your tray, and pre-freeze. Freeze-dry for 30-40 hours. Do a weight check and run Extra Dry Time until the weight doesn't change. Seal in 7mil mylar or a canning jar with an oxygen absorber and store in a cool, dry location.

Rehydration:
1 cup FD Vegetable Medley Soup Crumbles (68 g)
⅔-¾ cup Water (172 g)
Stir, cover, and let it sit for about 15-20 minutes. Adjust as needed. Reheat in a pot for best flavor.

Tips:
Protein can be meat such as beef, chicken, shellfish, and pork or plant-based like tofu, tempeh, peas, beans, and lentils.

....

Potato Leek Soup

A creamy and comforting soup with hearty potatoes and the subtle flavor of leeks.

Cups:	15	Servings:	15	Serving Size:	1 cup (249 g)	Calories:	141
Prep/Cook Time:		1 hr	Freeze-Dry Time:		25-35 hrs	Shelf-Life:	5-10 yrs

Ingredients:
8 cups Vegetable Broth
8 cups Potatoes, cubed
2 cups Leeks, sliced

2 tsp Salt
1 tsp Black Pepper
2 cup Sour Cream

Directions:
In a large pot, combine the vegetable broth, cubed potatoes, sliced leeks, salt, and black pepper. Bring to a simmer and cook 30 min, or until the potatoes are tender. Stir in the sour cream and simmer 10 minutes. Allow the soup to cool. Place your empty tray in the freezer, pour soup onto your tray, and pre-freeze. Freeze-dry for 25-35 hours on normal settings. Do a weight check and run Extra Dry Time until the weight doesn't change. Seal in 7mil mylar or a canning jar with an oxygen absorber and store in a cool, dry location.

Rehydration:
1 cup FD Potato Leek Soup Crumbles (55 g)
¾-1 cup Water (194 g)
Stir, cover, and let it sit for about 10-15 minutes. Adjust as needed. Reheat in a pot for best flavor.

Tips:
Try adding bacon, cheese, celery, mushrooms, or jalepenos.

Minestrone Soup

A hearty Italian vegetable soup with pasta and beans.

Cups:	14	Servings:	14	Serving Size:	1 cup (247 g)	Calories:	153
Prep/Cook Time:		1hr 10 min	Freeze-Dry Time:		30-40 hrs	Shelf-Life:	10-15 yrs

Ingredients:

2 qts Vegetable Broth
2 cups Chopped Tomatoes
2 large Carrots, diced
2 large Celery Stalks, chopped
1 large Onion, chopped
3 cloves Garlic, minced

2 tsp Salt
1 tsp Black Pepper
2 tsp dried Basil
2 tsp dried Oregano
2 cups Cannellini Beans
2 cups Pasta Shells

Directions:

In a large pot, combine the vegetable broth, chopped tomatoes, diced carrots, chopped celery, chopped onion, minced garlic, salt, black pepper, basil, and oregano. Bring to a simmer and cook for 30 minutes. Add the pasta and cannellini beans, and continue cooking for an additional 10 minutes until the pasta is tender. Allow the soup to cool. Place your empty tray in the freezer, pour soup onto your tray, and pre-freeze. Freeze-dry for 30-40 hours on normal settings. Do a weight check and run Extra Dry Time until the weight doesn't change. Seal in 7mil mylar or a canning jar with an oxygen absorber and store in a cool, dry location.

Rehydration:

1 cup FD Minestrone Soup Crumbles (64 g)
¾ cup Water (183 g)
Stir, cover, and let it sit for about 10-15 minutes.
Adjust as needed. Reheat in a pot for best flavor.

Tips: You can add other vegetables such as zucchini or green beans if desired.

Lentil Soup

A nourishing and hearty soup, perfect for vegetarians and meat-eaters alike.

Cups:	12½	Servings:	12½	Serving Size:	1 cup (241 g)	Calories:	187
Prep/Cook Time:		1hr 15 min	Freeze-Dry Time:		25-35 hrs	Shelf-Life:	10-15 yrs

Ingredients:

2 qts Vegetable Broth
3 cups Lentils
3 large Carrots, chopped
3 large Celery Stalks, chopped
1 large Onion, chopped

2 cloves Garlic, minced
2 tsp Salt
1 tsp Black Pepper
1 tsp Cumin
1 tsp Turmeric

Directions:

In a large pot, combine vegetable broth, lentils, chopped carrots, celery, onion, minced garlic, salt, black pepper, cumin, and turmeric. Bring to a boil, then reduce the heat and simmer for an hour, or until the lentils and vegetables are tender. Allow the soup to cool. Place your empty tray in the freezer, pour soup onto your tray, and pre-freeze. Freeze-dry for 25-35 hours on normal settings. Do a weight check and run Extra Dry Time until the weight doesn't change. Seal in 7mil mylar or a canning jar with an oxygen absorber and store in a cool, dry location.

Rehydration:

1 cup FD Lentil Soup Crumbles (51 g)
¾-1 cup Water (190 g)
Stir, cover, and let it sit for about 10-15 minutes.
Adjust as needed. Reheat in a pot for best flavor.

Tips:

Try adding 2 cups chopped ham. Top with a squeeze of lemon and fresh parsley.

Seafood Chowder

A creamy and hearty chowder packed with a variety of seafood and potatoes.

| Cups: | 11 | Servings: | 11 | Serving Size: | 1 cup (249 g) | Calories: | 195 |
| Prep/Cook Time: | | 50 min | Freeze-Dry Time: | | 25-35 hrs | Shelf-Life: | 5-10 yrs |

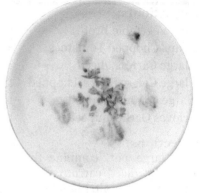

Ingredients:
½ cup Onion, diced
1 cups Celery, diced
1 clove Garlic, minced
1 qts Fish or Seafood Stock
1½ cups Potatoes, diced

1 tsp Salt
½ tsp White Pepper
2 cups Sour Cream
1 lb Shrimp
1 lb Fish (Salmon, Tilapia)

Directions:
In a large pot, sauté onion, celery, and garlic in a little water until soft. Add seafood stock, potatoes, and seasonings and simmer 20 minutes or until the potatoes are tender. Add sour cream and seafood and simmer briefly until heated, about 5 min. Allow to cool. Place your empty tray in the freezer, pour soup onto your tray, and pre-freeze. Freeze-dry for 25-35 hours on normal settings. Do a weight check and run Extra Dry Time until the weight doesn't change. Seal in 7mil mylar or a canning jar with an oxygen absorber and store in a cool, dry location.

Rehydration:
1 cup FD Seafood Chowder Crumbles (104 g)
½-⅔ cup Water (145 g)
Stir, cover, and let it sit for about 10-15 minutes. Adjust as needed. Reheat in a pot for best flavor.

Tips:
Add croutons or chopped fresh parsley or dill for a flavor boost.

Spicy Chicken Tortilla Soup

A vibrant Mexican-style soup that's brimming with chicken, beans, and spices.

| Cups: | 15 | Servings: | 15 | Serving Size: | 1 cup (245 g) | Calories: | 137 |
| Prep/Cook Time: | | 45 min | Freeze-Dry Time: | | 25-35 hrs | Shelf-Life: | 10-15 yrs |

Ingredients:
2 qts Chicken Broth
2 lbs Shredded Cooked Chicken
2 cups cooked Black Beans
1 cup Corn
1 large Onion, chopped

2 cloves Garlic, minced
1 cup Salsa Verde
1 tsp Cumin
1 tsp Chili Powder
2 tsp Salt

Directions:
In a large pot, combine chicken broth, shredded cooked chicken, black beans, corn, chopped onion, minced garlic, salsa verde, cumin, chili powder, and salt. Simmer for about 30 minutes, until everything is heated through. Allow to cool. Place your empty tray in the freezer, pour soup onto your tray, and pre-freeze. Freeze-dry on normal settings for 25-35 hours on normal settings. Do a weight check and run Extra Dry Time until the weight doesn't change. Seal in 7mil mylar or a canning jar with an oxygen absorber and store in a cool, dry location.

Rehydration:
1 cup FD SCT Soup Crumbles (82 g)
⅔-¾ cup Water (163 g)
Stir, cover, and let it sit for about 15-20 minutes. Adjust as needed. Reheat in a pot for best flavor.

Tips:
Top with avocado slices, tortilla strips, and fresh cilantro.

Broccoli Cheddar Soup

A rich, creamy soup that's perfect for any cheese lover.

| Cups: | 14 | Servings: | 14 | Serving Size: | 1 cup (240 g) | Calories: | 163 |
| Prep/Cook Time: | 30 min | Freeze-Dry Time: | 25-35 hrs | | | Shelf-Life: | 1-5 yrs |

Ingredients:

1 large Onion, diced
2 cloves Garlic, minced
2 qts Chicken Broth
4 cups Broccoli Florets, chopped

2 cups Half & Half
3 cups Cheddar Cheese, shredded
2 tsp Salt
1 tsp Black Pepper

Directions:

In a large pot, sauté the onion and garlic in water until soft. Add chicken broth and broccoli and simmer 10-15 minutes. Stir in the half & half, cheese, salt, and black pepper. Simmer until the cheese melts, about 5 minutes. Allow to cool. Place your empty tray in the freezer, pour soup onto your tray, and pre-freeze. Freeze-dry on normal settings for 25-35 hours on normal settings. Do a weight check and run Extra Dry Time until the weight doesn't change. Seal in 7mil mylar or a canning jar with an oxygen absorber and store in a cool, dry location.

Rehydration:

¾ cup FD Broccoli Cheddar Soup Crumbles (68 g)
⅔-¾ cup Water (172 g)
Stir, cover, and let it sit for about 10-15 minutes. Adjust as needed. Reheat in a pot for best flavor.

Tips:

Top with extra shredded cheddar and black pepper.

Tuscan White Bean Soup

A hearty soup with robust flavors inspired by the Tuscany region of Italy.

| Cups: | 10 | Servings: | 10 | Serving Size: | 1 cup (242 g) | Calories: | 225 |
| Prep/Cook Time: | 55 min | Freeze-Dry Time: | 25-35 hrs | | | Shelf-Life: | 10-15 yrs |

Ingredients:

1 large Onion, finely chopped
4 cloves Garlic, minced
1 large Celery Stalk, diced
2 large Carrots, peeled and chopped
3 cans (15 oz each) Cannellini Beans, drain/rinse
3 cups Vegetable or Chicken Broth
2 cups finely chopped Kale

1 tsp Salt
1 tsp Dried Thyme
2 Bay Leaves
½ tsp Dried Oregano
¼ tsp Red Pepper Flakes
¼ tsp Black Pepper
¼ tsp Italian Seasoning

Directions:

In a large pot, sauté the finely chopped onion, minced garlic, diced celery, and chopped carrots in water until softened. Add the drained and rinsed cannellini beans, broth, kale, and spices and stir well. Let it simmer for about an hour, or until the vegetables and beans are tender. Allow to cool. Place your empty tray in the freezer, pour soup onto your tray, and pre-freeze. Freeze-dry for 25-35 hours on normal settings. Do a weight check and run Extra Dry Time until the weight doesn't change. Seal in 7mil mylar or a canning jar with an oxygen absorber and store in a cool, dry location.

Rehydration:

1 cup FD TWB Soup Crumbles (105 g)
½-⅔ cup Water (137 g)
Stir, cover, and let it sit for about 10-15 minutes. Adjust as needed. Reheat in a pot for best flavor.

Tips:

Mix in some cooked Italian sausage, ham, or shrimp for a heartier dish.

Italian Wedding Soup

A deliciously warming soup with meatballs, hearty vegetables, and tiny pasta.

Cups:	12	Servings:	12	Serving Size:	1 cup (241 g)	Calories:	136
Prep/Cook Time:		55 min	Freeze-Dry Time:		30-40 hrs	Shelf-Life:	10-15 yrs

Ingredients:

½ cup Onion, chopped
½ cup Bell Pepper, chopped
2 large Celery Stalks
24 Meatballs (Quartered)
½ cup Tomatoes, diced
2 qts Chicken Broth

2 tsp Oregano
1 tsp Salt
½ tsp Black Pepper
½ cup Ziti Pasta
2 cups Spinach

Directions:

In a large pot, sauté onion, bell pepper, and celery in water. Add meatballs, diced tomatoes, broth, oregano, salt, and black pepper. Simmer for 20 minutes. Add the pasta and cook 10 minutes. Stir in spinach. Allow to cool. Place your empty tray in the freezer, pour soup onto your tray, and pre-freeze. Freeze-dry for 30-40 hours on normal settings. Do a weight check and run Extra Dry Time until the weight doesn't change. Seal in 7mil mylar or a canning jar with an oxygen absorber and store in a cool, dry location.

Rehydration:

1 cup FD Italian Wedding Soup Crumbles (56 g)
¾-1 cup Water (185 g)
Stir, cover, and let it sit for about 10-15 minutes. Adjust as needed. Reheat in a pot for best flavor.

Tips:

Use small meatballs or cut into bite-sized pieces for optimal freeze-drying.

Creamy Tomato Basil Soup

This soup is packed full of flavor with a combination of ripe tomatoes and sweet basil.

Cups:	14	Servings:	14	Serving Size:	1 cup (249 g)	Calories:	125
Prep/Cook Time:		40 min	Freeze-Dry Time:		30-40 hrs	Shelf-Life:	5-10 yrs

Ingredients:

8 cups Tomato Puree
4 cups Water
2 cups Fresh Basil, chopped
2 cloves Garlic, minced

1 tsp Salt
1 tsp Black Pepper, ground
2 cups Sour Cream

Directions:

In a large pot, combine tomato puree, water, chopped basil, garlic, salt, and ground black pepper. Simmer for 20 minutes. Add in the sour cream and simmer 10 min. Use an immersion blender to blend until smooth. Allow to cool. Place your empty tray in the freezer, pour soup onto your tray, and pre-freeze. Freeze-dry for 30-40 hours. Do a weight check and run Extra Dry Time until the weight doesn't change. Seal in 7mil mylar or a canning jar with an oxygen absorber and store in a cool, dry location.

Rehydration:

¼-½ cup FD Tomato Basil Soup Powder (53 g)
¾-1 cup Water (196 g)
Stir, cover, and let it sit for about 5-10 minutes. Adjust as needed. Reheat in a pot for best flavor.

Tips:

You can replace the tomato puree with diced tomatoes for a chunkier variety.

Lentil, Sausage & Potato Soup

Enjoy this delicious and filling dish on your outdoor adventures or whenever you crave a hearty and satisfying meal.

Cups:	16	Servings:	16	Serving Size:	1 cup (247 g)	Calories:	227
Prep/Cook Time:		1 hr 10 min	Freeze-Dry Time:		25-35 hrs	Shelf-Life:	1-2 yrs

Ingredients:

2 med Onion, Diced	2 qts Vegetable or Chicken Broth
4 med Carrots, Diced	4 cups diced Potatoes
4 large Celery Stalks, Diced	2 tsp dried Thyme
6 cloves Garlic, Minced	1 tsp Smoked Paprika
1 lb Beef Sausage, Sliced	2 tsp Salt
2 cup Dried Lentils	1 tsp Black Pepper

Directions:

In a large pot, sauté diced onion, carrots, celery, and garlic with a little water until soft. Cook the sliced sausage until browned and rinse in hot water. Rinse lentils in cold water. Combine ingredients and add broth, diced potatoes, thyme, paprika, salt and black pepper to the pot, stirring well. Bring to a boil, then reduce the heat to low and simmer for 30 minutes, or until the potatoes are tender. Allow to cool. Place your empty tray in the freezer, pour soup onto your tray, and pre-freeze. Freeze-dry for 25-35 hours. Do a weight check and run Extra Dry Time until the weight doesn't change. Seal in 7mil mylar or a canning jar with an oxygen absorber and store in a cool, dry location.

Rehydration:

1 cup FD LSP Soup Crumbles (51 g)
¾-1 cup Water (196 g)
Stir, cover, and let it sit for about 10-15 minutes. Adjust as needed. Reheat in a pot for best flavor.

Tips: For an extra kick of spice, sprinkle some red pepper flakes into the soup while it simmers. Use fresh Parsley for garnish.

Pumpkin Soup

A creamy and delicious soup that is perfect for the fall season.

Cups:	12	Servings:	12	Serving Size:	1 cup (240 g)	Calories:	106
Prep/Cook Time:		50 min	Freeze-Dry Time:		30-40 hrs	Shelf-Life:	5-10 yrs

Ingredients:

2 qts Vegetable Broth	2 tsp Salt
4 cups Pumpkin Puree	1 tsp Black Pepper, ground
1 large Onion, chopped	1 tsp Nutmeg
2 cloves Garlic, minced	2 cups Sour Cream

Directions:

In a large pot, combine the vegetable broth, pumpkin puree, chopped onion, minced garlic, salt, ground black pepper, and nutmeg. Simmer for 30 minutes, stirring regularly. Stir in the sour cream and cook for an additional 10 minutes. Allow to cool. Place empty tray in the freezer, pour soup onto your tray, and pre-freeze. Freeze-dry on normal settings for 30-40 hours on normal settings. Do a weight check and run Extra Dry Time until the weight doesn't change. Seal in 7mil mylar or a canning jar with an oxygen absorber and store in a cool, dry location.

Rehydration:

¼-½ cup FD Pumpkin Soup Powder (50 g)
¾-1 cup Water (190 g)
Stir, cover, and let it sit for about 5-10 minutes. Adjust as needed. Reheat in a pot for best flavor.

Tips:

Serve this soup with a dollop of cream or a sprinkle of cinnamon on top.

Vegetable Barley Soup

This hearty and healthy soup is loaded with vegetables and barley.

Cups:	17	Servings:	17	Serving Size:	1 cup (241 g)	Calories:	119
Prep/Cook Time:	1 hr	Freeze-Dry Time:		25-35 hrs		Shelf-Life:	10-15 yrs

Ingredients:
3 qts Vegetable Broth
2 cups Pearled Barley
3 large Carrots, chopped
2 large Celery Stalks, chopped
1 large Onion, chopped

2 cup Peas
1 cup Green Beans, chopped
2 tsp Salt
1 tsp Dried Thyme
1 tsp Dried Rosemary
½ tsp Black Pepper, ground

Directions:
In a large pot, combine the vegetable broth, pearled barley, chopped carrots, chopped celery, chopped onion, green beans, peas, thyme, rosemary, salt, and ground black pepper. Bring to a simmer and cook for 40 minutes, stirring regularly. Allow to cool. Place your empty tray in the freezer, pour soup onto your tray, and pre-freeze. Freeze-dry on normal settings for 25-35 hours on normal settings. Do a weight check and run Extra Dry Time until the weight doesn't change. Seal in 7mil mylar or a canning jar with an oxygen absorber & store in a cool, dry location.

Rehydration:
1 cup FD Vegetable Barley Soup Crumbles (33 g)
¾-1 cup Water (208 g)
Stir, cover, and let it sit for about 10-15 minutes. Adjust as needed. Reheat in a pot for best flavor.

Tips:
Try adding 1-2 cups of chopped chicken, beef, ham or seafood to turn this meal more hearty.

Beef Noodle Soup

A classic and comforting soup with tender beef and hearty noodles.

Cups:	15	Servings:	15	Serving Size:	1 cup (247 g)	Calories:	120
Prep/Cook Time:	50 min	Freeze-Dry Time:		25-35 hrs		Shelf-Life:	5-10 yrs

Ingredients:
1½ qts Beef Broth
1 large Carrots, diced
1 large Celery Stalks, chopped
1 small Onion, chopped
½ tsp dried Parsley

½ tsp Dried Thyme
1 tsp Salt
¼ tsp Black Pepper, ground
2 cups cooked Beef, chopped
8 oz Egg Noodles

Directions:
In a large pot, combine the beef broth, diced carrots, chopped celery, chopped onion, parsley, thyme, salt, and ground black pepper. Bring to a simmer and cook for 20 minutes. Add the cooked beef and egg noodles, and continue cooking for an additional 10 minutes until the noodles are al dente (just under-done). Allow to cool. Place your empty tray in the freezer, pour soup onto your tray, and pre-freeze. Freeze-dry for 25-35 hours on normal settings. Do a weight check and run Extra Dry Time until the weight doesn't change. Seal in 7mil mylar or a canning jar with an oxygen absorber & store in a cool, dry location.

Rehydration:
1 cup FD Beef Noodle Soup Crumbles (83 g)
⅔-¾ cup Water (164 g)
Stir, cover, and let it sit for about 10-15 minutes. Adjust as needed. Reheat in a pot for best flavor.

Tips: You can replace the egg noodles with other types of pasta if preferred. It takes just under a pound of beef to get a cup of chopped.

Creamy Mushroom Soup

The rich flavors of this velvety smooth soup create a satisfying & delicious dish for any occasion.

Cups:	15	Servings:	15	Serving Size:	1 cup (245 g)	Calories:	160
Prep/Cook Time:		50 min	Freeze-Dry Time:		25-35 hrs	Shelf-Life:	5-10 yrs

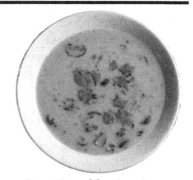

Ingredients:

2 lb Mushrooms, sliced
2 medium Onion, diced
4 cloves Garlic, minced
2 qts Chicken Broth

2 tsp dried Thyme
1 tsp dried Rosemary
2 tsp Salt
1 tsp Black Pepper
2 cups Sour Cream

Directions:
In a large pot, over medium heat, add mushrooms and onions to sauté until soft and translucent. Stir in garlic for a minute, followed by the broth, thyme, rosemary, salt and black pepper. Bring to a boil before simmering for 20 minutes. Carefully puree the soup with an immersion blender. Stir in the sour cream and simmer for 5 minutes. Allow to cool. Place your empty tray in the freezer, pour soup onto your tray, and pre-freeze. Freeze-dry for 25-35 hours on normal settings. Do a weight check and run Extra Dry Time until the weight doesn't change. Seal in 7mil mylar or a canning jar with an oxygen absorber and store in a cool, dry location.

Rehydration:
¾ cup FD Mushroom Soup Crumbles (52 g)
¾-1 cup Water (193 g)
Stir, cover, and let it sit for about 5-10 minutes. Adjust as needed. Reheat in a pot for best flavor.

Tips: For a more textured soup, reserve a small portion of sautéed mushrooms before blending the soup and stir in. Use fresh parsley for garnish.

Chicken Noodle Soup

This chicken noodle soup is a comforting classic, making it a heartwarming dish.

Cups:	13	Servings:	13	Serving Size:	1 cup (246 g)	Calories:	129
Prep/Cook Time:		45 min	Freeze-Dry Time:		25-35 hrs	Shelf-Life:	15-20 yrs

Ingredients:

2 qts Chicken Broth
2 large Carrots, chopped
1 large Celery Stalks, chopped
1 small Onion, chopped
1 cloves Garlic, minced

1 tsp Salt
1 tsp dried Parsley
½ tsp Black Pepper, ground
¼ tsp Dried Thyme
2 cups Egg Noodles
2 lbs cooked Chicken, shredded or cubed

Directions:
In a large pot, combine chicken broth, carrots, celery, onion, garlic, salt, dried parsley, black pepper, and dried thyme. Bring to a simmer and cook for 20 minutes. Add the egg noodles and continue simmering for an additional 5 minutes, or until the noodles are al dente (just under-done). Stir in the cooked chicken and heat through for about 5 minutes. Allow to cool. Place your empty tray in the freezer, pour soup onto your tray, and pre-freeze. Freeze-dry on normal settings for 25-35 hours on normal settings. Do a weight check and run Extra Dry Time until the weight doesn't change. Seal in 7mil mylar or a canning jar with an oxygen absorber & store in a cool, dry location.

Rehydration:
1 cup FD Chicken Noodle Soup Crumbles (85 g)
⅔-¾ cup Water (161 g)
Stir, cover, and let it sit for about 10-15 minutes. Adjust as needed. Reheat in a pot for best flavor.

Tips:
For a variation, consider adding chopped potatoes or a mix of your favorite vegetables. A single chicken can provide both the meat and broth needed for this recipe when cooked and deboned.

Creamy Salmon & Dill Soup

This luxurious soup is especially suited for replenishing energy after outdoor activities.

Cups:	17	Servings:	17	Serving Size:	1 cup (241 g)	Calories:	173
Prep/Cook Time:		50 min	Freeze-Dry Time:		30-40 hrs	Shelf-Life:	2-5 yrs

Ingredients:
2 lb Salmon Fillet, diced
2 med Onion, finely chopped
4 cloves Garlic, minced
4 cups Potatoes, diced
2 qts Fish Stock
2 tsp Salt
1 tsp Black Pepper
2 cup Sour Cream
¼ cup Fresh Dill, chopped

Directions:
Sear salmon in a pan with a little water. Sauté onion and garlic until translucent. Add potatoes, fish stock, salt, and black pepper to pot and simmer 20 min. Add cooked salmon to the pot and simmer 10 minutes. Stir in sour cream and dill. Allow to cool. Place your empty tray in the freezer, pour soup onto your tray, and pre-freeze. Freeze-dry for 30-40 hours. Do a weight check and run Extra Dry Time until the weight doesn't change. Seal in 7mil mylar or a canning jar with an oxygen absorber and store in a cool, dry location.

Rehydration:
¾ cup FD Salmon & Dill Soup Crumbles (54 g)
¾ cup Water (187 g)
Stir, cover, and let it sit for about 10-15 minutes. Adjust as needed. Reheat in a pot for best flavor.

Tips: Opt for wild-caught salmon for a richer flavor. Garnish with extra dill and a squeeze of lemon juice upon serving.

Spicy Shrimp & Corn Chowder

A spicy chowder filled with juicy shrimp and corn, perfect for warming up on cold days.

Cups:	18	Servings:	18	Serving Size:	1 cup (244 g)	Calories:	131
Prep/Cook Time:		45 min	Freeze-Dry Time:		25-35 hrs	Shelf-Life:	5-10 yrs

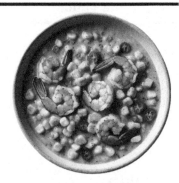

Ingredients:
2 large Onion, diced
4 cloves Garlic, minced
2 qts Seafood Broth
4 cups Corn, fresh or frozen
2 large Bell Pepper, diced
2 tsp Smoked Paprika
1 tsp Cayenne Pepper
2 tsp Salt
1 tsp Black Pepper
2 lb Shrimp, peeled and deveined
2 cup Sour Cream

Directions:
In a large pot sauté the diced onion and minced garlic with water until softened. Add the broth, corn, bell pepper, smoked paprika, cayenne pepper, salt, and black pepper. Bring to a simmer and cook for about 10 minutes. Add the shrimp and cook 5 minutes, or until they turn pink. Stir in the sour cream. Allow to cool. Place your empty tray in the freezer, pour soup onto your tray, and pre-freeze. Freeze-dry for 25-35 hours on normal settings. Do a weight check and run Extra Dry Time until the weight doesn't change. Seal in 7mil mylar or a canning jar with an oxygen absorber and store in a cool, dry location.

Rehydration:
1 cup FD SS&C Chowder Crumbles (88 g)
½-⅔ cup Water (156 g)
Stir, cover, and let it sit for about 15-20 minutes. Adjust as needed. Reheat in a pot for best flavor.

Tips: Adjust the amount of cayenne to control the spice level. Serve with chopped green onions for added freshness.

Thai Coconut Curry Soup

A vibrant and spicy soup with exotic flavors of Thai curry and creamy coconut milk with a bounty of vegetables. It's a taste adventure that's both comforting and exhilarating.

Cups:	14	Servings:	14	Serving Size:	1 cup (248 g)	Calories:	151
Prep/Cook Time:		30 min	Freeze-Dry Time:		25-35 hrs	Shelf-Life:	1-3 yrs

Ingredients:

2 lb Chicken Breast, thinly sliced
4 Tbs Red Curry Paste
2 can (14 oz each) Coconut Milk
1 qt Chicken Broth
2 med Bell Pepper, sliced

2 cup Bamboo Shoots
2 Tbs Fish Sauce
2 Tbs Sugar
4 tsp Lime Juice

Directions:
Sauté the thinly sliced chicken with the red curry paste in a large pot until the chicken is cooked through. Add the coconut milk, chicken broth, bell pepper, and bamboo shoots, then bring to a simmer. Stir in the fish sauce, sugar, and lime juice, and let it cook for 5 minutes. Allow to cool. Place your empty tray in the freezer, pour soup onto your tray, and pre-freeze. Freeze-dry for 25-35 hours on normal settings. Do a weight check and run Extra Dry Time until the weight doesn't change. Seal in 7mil mylar or a canning jar with an oxygen absorber and store in a cool, dry location.

Rehydration:
1 cup FD TCC Soup Crumbles (51 g)
¾-1 cup Water (197 g)
Stir, cover, and let it sit for about 10-15 minutes. Adjust as needed. Reheat in a pot for best flavor.

Tips:
The soup can be blended for a smooth, creamy curry soup.

· ·

Southwest Black Bean Soup

A robust and zesty dish featuring black beans, corn, and spices, simmered together to create a deeply flavorful and nutritious meal.

Cups:	18	Servings:	18	Serving Size:	1 cup (244 g)	Calories:	354
Prep/Cook Time:		45 min	Freeze-Dry Time:		30-40 hrs	Shelf-Life:	10-15 yrs

Ingredients:

2 large Onion, chopped
2 large Red Bell Pepper, diced
4 cloves Garlic, minced
4 cans (15 oz each) Black Beans, drain/rinse
2 cup Corn Kernels, fresh or frozen

2 qts Vegetable Broth
2 tsp Ground Cumin
2 tsp Chili Powder
1 tsp Smoked Paprika
1 tsp Salt
½ tsp Black Pepper

Directions:
In a large pot, sauté onion, red bell pepper, and garlic in water until soft. Add black beans, corn, vegetable broth, cumin, chili powder, paprika, salt, and black pepper. Bring to a boil and simmer for 30 minutes. Use an immersion blender to partially blend the soup for a thicker consistency, if desired. Allow to cool. Place your empty tray in the freezer, pour soup onto your tray, and pre-freeze. Freeze-dry for 30-40 hours. Do a weight check and run Extra Dry Time until the weight doesn't change. Seal in 7mil mylar or a canning jar with an oxygen absorber and store in a cool, dry location.

Rehydration:
1 cup FD SBB Soup Crumbles (95 g)
⅔ cup Water (149 g)
Stir, cover, and let it sit for about 15-20 minutes. Adjust as needed. Reheat in a pot for best flavor.

Tips: For added heat, include diced jalapeño while sautéing the vegetables.

21 SNACKS

Berry S'mores Trail Mix

A fruity twist on the classic S'mores blend, with freeze-dried berries for an added pop of flavor.

| Cups: | 3 | Servings: | 12 | Serving Size: | ¼ cup (29 g) | Calories: | 84 |
| Prep Time: | 10 min | Freeze-Dry Time: | n/a | | | Shelf-Life: | 6-12 mo |

Ingredients:

1 cup Freeze-Dried Mixed Berries (like strawberries, blueberries, raspberries)
1½ cup Golden Grahams Cereal
½ cup Freeze-Dried Mini Marshmallows
½ cup Milk Chocolate Chips

Directions:

In a large mixing bowl, combine freeze-dried mixed berries, Golden Grahams, freeze-dried mini marshmallows, and milk chocolate chips. Gently mix and package in airtight containers to preserve their shelf life. No oxygen absorber.

Tips:
For a richer flavor, consider using dark chocolate chips instead of milk chocolate.

Tropical Bliss Trail Mix

This trail mix brings the islands to you with a blend of freeze-dried mango, coconut, and cashews.

| Cups: | 3 | Servings: | 12 | Serving Size: | ¼ cup (41 g) | Calories: | 106 |
| Prep Time: | 10 min | Freeze-Dry Time: | n/a | | | Shelf-Life: | 6-12 mo |

Ingredients:

1 cup Freeze-Dried Mango pieces
1 cup Freeze-Dried Pineapple
½ cup Raw Cashews
½ cup Flaked Coconut

Directions:

In a large mixing bowl, combine freeze-dried mango slices, freeze-dried pineapple, cashews, and coconut. Gently mix and package in airtight containers to preserve their shelf life. No oxygen absorber.

Tips:
Toast the shredded coconut for a more intense flavor.

Berry Nutty Trail Mix

The perfect sweet and nutty blend for any snack time, featuring freeze-dried strawberries and blueberries.

| Cups: | 3 | Servings: | 12 | Serving Size: | ¼ cup (44 g) | Calories: | 118 |
| Prep Time: | 10 min | Freeze-Dry Time: | n/a | | | Shelf-Life: | 6-12 mo |

Ingredients:

1 cup Freeze-Dried Strawberry Slices
1 cup Freeze-Dried Blueberries
1 cup Almonds
½ cup Dark Chocolate Chips

Directions:

In a large mixing bowl, combine freeze-dried strawberry slices, freeze-dried blueberries, almonds, and dark chocolate chips. Gently mix and package in airtight containers to preserve their shelf life. No oxygen absorber.

Tips:
Use unsalted almonds to balance the sweetness of the berries and chocolate.

Spicy Fiesta Trail Mix

A savory mix with a kick, featuring freeze-dried corn, spicy peanuts, and pumpkin seeds.

Cups:	3	Servings:	12	Serving Size:	¼ cup (35 g)	Calories:	138
Prep Time:	10 min	Freeze-Dry Time:	n/a			Shelf-Life:	6-12 mo

Ingredients:

1 cup Freeze-Dried Corn
1 cup Spicy Peanuts
½ cup Pepitas Seeds
½ cup Sunflower Seeds

Directions:

In a large mixing bowl, combine freeze-dried corn, spicy peanuts, pepitas, and sunflower seeds. Gently mix and package in airtight containers to preserve their shelf life. No oxygen absorber.

Tips:
Add a sprinkle of chili powder for an extra kick.

Apple Pie Trail Mix

Experience the flavors of a classic dessert in this delightful trail mix featuring freeze-dried apple slices.

Cups:	3	Servings:	12	Serving Size:	¼ cup (25 g)	Calories:	58
Prep Time:	10 min	Freeze-Dry Time:	n/a			Shelf-Life:	6-12 mo

Ingredients:

2 cups Freeze-Dried Apples, slices or pieces
40 Mini Nilla Wafers (or 16 regular, cut in fourths)
½ cup Walnuts

Directions:

In a large mixing bowl, combine freeze-dried apple slices, Mini Nilla Wafers, and walnuts. Gently mix and package in airtight containers to preserve their shelf life. No oxygen absorber.

Tips:
Try using pecans for a variation in texture and flavor.

Choco-Raspberry Trail Mix

A decadent blend that features the tartness of raspberries with the richness of chocolate & almonds.

Cups:	3	Servings:	12	Serving Size:	¼ cup (38 g)	Calories:	98
Prep Time:	10 min	Freeze-Dry Time:	n/a			Shelf-Life:	6-12 mo

Ingredients:

2 cup Freeze-Dried Raspberries
½ cup Dark Chocolate Chips or Chunks
1 cup Sliced Almonds

Directions:

In a large mixing bowl, combine freeze-dried raspberries, dark chocolate chunks, and sliced almonds. Gently mix and package in airtight containers to preserve their shelf life. No oxygen absorber.

Tips:
Works great to replace the raspberries with cherries, too.

Garden Herb Trail Mix

A savory mix featuring freeze-dried veggies and herbed croutons. Perfect for when you want something less sweet.

Cups:	3	Servings:	12	Serving Size:	¼ cup (41 g)	Calories:	89
Prep Time:	10 min	Freeze-Dry Time:	n/a			Shelf-Life:	6-12 mo

Ingredients:
1 cup Freeze-Dried Peas
1 cup Freeze-Dried Corn
½ cup Freeze-Dried Asparagus
1 cup Sunflower Seeds

Directions:
In a large mixing bowl, combine freeze-dried peas, freeze-dried corn, freeze-dried asparagus, and sunflower seeds. Gently mix and package in airtight containers to preserve their shelf life. No oxygen absorber.

Tips:
Try adding seasoning powder, such as ranch, barbeque, or cajun.

Peachy Keen Trail Mix

The ultimate summer trail mix featuring freeze-dried peaches, pecans, and white chocolate chips.

Cups:	3	Servings:	12	Serving Size:	¼ cup (41 g)	Calories:	108
Prep Time:	10 min	Freeze-Dry Time:	n/a			Shelf-Life:	6-12 mo

Ingredients:
2 cup Freeze-Dried Peaches, slices or pieces
1 cup Pecan Halves
½ cup White Chocolate Chips

Directions:
In a large mixing bowl, combine freeze-dried peach slices, pecan halves, and white chocolate chips. Gently mix and package in airtight containers to preserve their shelf life. No oxygen absorber.

Tips:
For a little extra flavor, you can add a pinch of cinnamon to the mix.

Nutty Nanners Trail Mix

Recreate the comfort of banana bread in a handy format with this freeze-dried banana and walnut trail mix.

Cups:	3	Servings:	12	Serving Size:	¼ cup (35 g)	Calories:	89
Prep Time:	10 min	Freeze-Dry Time:	n/a			Shelf-Life:	6-12 mo

Ingredients:
2 cups Freeze-Dried Banana Slices, sprinkled with Cinnamon
1 cup Walnuts

Directions:
In a large mixing bowl, combine freeze-dried cinnamon banana slices and walnuts. Gently mix and package in airtight containers to preserve their shelf life. No oxygen absorber.

Tips:
Add a dash of nutmeg for a banana bread flavor.

Blueberry Applesauce

This fruity fusion of apples and blueberries makes for a flavorful and nutritious snack or dessert.

Cups:	9	Servings:	18	Serving Size:	½ cup (131 g)	Calories:	74
Prep/Cook Time:		1hr 30 min	Freeze-Dry Time:		25-35 hrs	Shelf-Life:	20-25 yrs

Ingredients:
3 lbs (9 med) Apples, peeled, cored, chopped
3 cups Blueberries
1½ cups Water
½ cup Sugar
1 Tbs Lemon Juice

Directions:
Peel, core, and chop apples. Combine apples, blueberries, water, sugar, and lemon juice in a saucepan. Cook until tender, about 20 minutes. Cool, puree, spread ½" on trays, and pre-freeze. Freeze-dry for 25-35 hours. Do a weight check and run Extra Dry Time until the weight doesn't change. Seal in 7mil mylar or a canning jar with an oxygen absorber and store in a cool, dry location.

Rehydration:
1 cup FD Applesauce Powder (20 g)
¾ cup Water (111 g)
Mix powder with water and stir well.
Add more or less for consistency.

Tips:
The recipe can be made with strawberries or blackberries to try out different flavors.

Pineapple Applesauce

This tropical twist on applesauce is a sweet and tangy treat.

Cups:	9	Servings:	18	Serving Size:	½ cup (130 g)	Calories:	72
Prep/Cook Time:		1hr 30 min	Freeze-Dry Time:		30-40 hrs+	Shelf-Life:	20-25 yrs

Ingredients:
3 lbs (9 med) Apples, peeled, cored, chopped
3 cups Pineapple, chopped
1½ cups Water
½ cup Sugar
1 Tbs Lemon Juice

Directions:
Peel, core, and chop apples and pineapple. Combine apples, pineapple, water, sugar, and lemon juice in a saucepan. Cook until tender, about 20 minutes. Cool, puree, spread ½" on trays, and pre-freeze. Freeze-dry for 30-40 hours. Do a weight check and run Extra Dry Time until the weight doesn't change. Seal in 7mil mylar or a canning jar with an oxygen absorber and store in a cool, dry location.

Rehydration:
1 cup FD Applesauce Powder (40 g)
¾ cup Water (90 g)
Mix powder with water and stir well.
Add more or less for consistency.

Tips:
Try other fruit flavors by substituting mangos or peaches for the pineapple.

Pear Sauce

This sweet and smooth pear sauce is a tasty alternative to traditional applesauce.

| Cups: | 9½ | Servings: | 19 | Serving Size: | ½ cup (130 g) | Calories: | 80 |
| Prep/Cook Time: | 1hr | Freeze-Dry Time: | 25-35 hrs | | | Shelf-Life: | 20-25 yrs |

Ingredients:
9 large Pears, peeled, cored, chopped
1½ cups Water
½ cup Sugar
1 Tbs Lemon Juice

Directions:
Peel, core, and chop pears. Combine pears, water, sugar, and lemon juice in a saucepan. Cook until tender, about 20 minutes. Cool, puree, spread ½" on trays, and pre-freeze. Freeze-dry for 25-35 hours. Do a weight check and run Extra Dry Time until the weight doesn't change. Seal in 7mil mylar or a canning jar with an oxygen absorber and store in a cool, dry location.

Rehydration:
1 cup FD Applesauce Powder (22 g)
¾ cup Water (108 g)
Mix powder with water and stir well.
Add more or less for consistency.

Tips:
To add a cinnamon flavor, add 1 Tbs Cinnamon.

Strawberry Yogurt Drops

These delicious and nutritious yogurt drops are quick, healthy, and loved by all!

| Drops: | 360 | Servings: | 10 | Serving Size: | ¾ c or 36 drops (184 g) | Calories: | 160 |
| Prep Time: | 20 min | Freeze-Dry Time: | 20-30 hrs | | | Shelf-Life: | 10-15 yrs |

Ingredients:
64 oz Strawberry Greek Yogurt
3 Tbs Arrowroot flour

Variations:
Mix in diced fruit or puree for a burst of flavor
Stir in granola, muesli, chia seeds, or crushed nuts for crunch
Blend in cookie crumbles & diced peaches for a peach cobbler taste
Incorporate flavored protein powders for an extra nutrition boost!

Directions:
Prepare trays with non-stick liners. Combine the arrowroot powder thoroughly with the yogurt. Integrate any chosen fruits, cereals, or flavor enhancers. Transfer the mixture into a pastry bag (or a plastic bag with a corner snipped off,) gently squeeze out small yogurt dots (1 tsp) onto the trays, and pre-freeze. Set Dry Temp to 90°F and freeze-dry the Yogurt Drops for 20-30 hours. Do a weight check and run Extra Dry Time until the weight doesn't change. Seal in 7mil mylar or a canning jar with an oxygen absorber and store in a cool, dry location.

Rehydration:
36 Yogurt Drops (41 g)
½ cup Water (143 g)
For a ¾ cup serving of smooth, creamy yogurt, mix ½ cup of water with 36 Yogurt Bites (or ¾ cup powder.) Adjust water for desired consistency.

Tips:
Experiment with various yogurt types and flavors. Each 8oz cup of yogurt yields roughly 45 drops (1 tsp each).

Ranch Dip

This smooth dip is excellent for pairing with vegetables, chips, crackers, and other snacks.

Cups:	12	Servings:	48	Serving Size:	4 Tbs (59 g)	Calories:	117
Prep Time:		30 min		Freeze-Dry Time:	30-40 hrs	Shelf-Life:	10-15 yrs

Ingredients:
96 oz Sour Cream (12 cups)
4 Tbs Italian Seasoning
4 tsp Onion Powder
4 tsp Garlic Powder
4 tsp Salt

*To make Italian Seasoning
Mix 1 Tbs each of Marjoram, Basil, Oregano, and Parsley and 1 tsp each of Rosemary, Thyme, and Sage.

Directions:
Mix the Italian seasoning, onion powder, garlic powder, and salt into the sour cream until well blended. Spread the mixture evenly onto freeze-drying trays, making sure not to exceed the weight limits and pre-freeze. Freeze-dry the dip for 30-40 hours on normal settings. Do a weight check and run Extra Dry Time until the weight doesn't change. Seal in 7mil mylar or a canning jar with an oxygen absorber and store in a cool, dry location.

Rehydration:
1 cup FD Ranch Powder (17 g)
¾ cup Water (42 g)
Mix the Ranch Powder with the water & whip well.

Tips:
Add ¼ cup extra water to use it as a dressing. To make a more robust ranch salad, add diced ham, crab, chicken, bacon, black olives, or scallions.

Salsa

This tasty salsa can be prepared as a fresh or roasted version; it is a versatile snack for backpacking meals.

Cups:	12	Servings:	24	Serving Size:	½ cup (134 g)	Calories:	44
Prep/Cook Time:		40 min		Freeze-Dry Time:	30-40 hrs	Shelf-Life:	20-25 yrs

Ingredients:
8 cups Tomatoes, peeled, seeded, quartered (7lbs, 8 large)
2½ cups Onions, cut in quarters (3 large)
1½ cups Bell Pepper, seeded & cut in half (3 large)
½ cup Jalapeno Pepper, seeded & cut in half (6 large)
¼ cup Fresh Parsley or Cilantro, chopped

2 Tbs Garlic, minced (12 large cloves)
2 cups Tomato Paste (32 oz)
2 cups Tomato Sauce (32 oz)
2 tsp Black Pepper
2 tsp Cumin powder
2 Tbs Salt

Directions:
Clean and chop the vegetables. For enhanced flavor, roast tomatoes, onions, and peppers on a baking sheet at 400°F for 20 minutes. Let them cool for 10 minutes, then process with all the other ingredients in a food processor. Spread on trays and pre-freeze. Freeze-dry on normal settings for 30-40 hours. Do a weight check and run Extra Dry Time until the weight doesn't change. Seal in 7mil mylar or a canning jar with an oxygen absorber and store in a cool, dry location.

Rehydration:
1 cup FD Salsa (17 g)
½ cup Water (117 g)
1 tsp Vinegar
Combine water and vinegar and stir into the freeze-dried salsa. Adjust the quantity as needed to achieve your preferred consistency.

Tips: Shorten freeze-dry time by removing seeds.

Cauliflower Nibbles

Enjoy these as a crunchy, flavorful snack without any need for rehydration.

Cups:	16	Servings:	16	Serving Size:	1 cup (162 g)	Calories:	43
Prep/Cook Time:		25 min		Freeze-Dry Time:	30-40 hrs	Shelf-Life:	1-2 yrs

Ingredients:
3 large heads Cauliflower (6 lbs)
¼ cup Soy Sauce
1 tsp Salt
½ tsp Black Pepper

Directions:
Preheat oven to 400°F. Clean and cut cauliflower. Toss cauliflower florets with soy sauce, salt, and black pepper. Place on a baking sheet and roast for 15 minutes. Increase oven to broil (or 500°F) and broil for 5 minutes until done. Cool. Spread on freeze-drying trays and pre-freeze. Freeze-dry for 30-40 hours on normal settings. Do a weight check and run Extra Dry Time until the weight doesn't change. Seal in 7mil mylar or a canning jar with an oxygen absorber and store in a cool, dry location.

Rehydration:
Best enjoyed dry as a crunchy snack.

Optional Flavors:

Garlic Parmesan
1 cup finely shredded Parmesan cheese
¾ cup Panko bread crumbs
1½ teaspoon dried thyme, crushed
4 cloves garlic, minced (1 tsp pwd)

Lemon Herb
1 cup Fincly Grated Asiago cheese
¾ cup Almond Flour for a gluten-free option
1½ teaspoon Dried Rosemary, crushed
Zest of 1 Lemon
4 cloves Garlic, minced (or 1 tsp garlic powder)

Tips:
The Lemon Herb variation offers a lighter, zestier option that pairs wonderfully with summer salads or as a standalone snack.

Sweet Potato Cubes

A sweet and savory snack that is perfect for on-the-go.

Cups:	8	Servings:	16	Serving Size:	½ cup (68 g)	Calories:	64
Prep/Cook Time:		45 min		Freeze-Dry Time:	25-35 hrs	Shelf-Life:	5-10 yrs

Ingredients:
8 large Sweet Potatoes (5")
2 Tbs Onion pwd
2 Tbs Garlic pwd
2 tsp Salt
2 tsp Black Pepper

Directions:
Preheat the oven to 400°F. Wash, peel, and cube sweet potatoes. Toss the cubes with seasonings. Place on a baking sheet and roast for for 30 minutes or until golden. Cool. Spread on freeze-drying trays and pre-freeze. Freeze-dry for 25-35 hours on normal settings. Do a weight check and run Extra Dry Time until the weight doesn't change. Seal in 7mil mylar or a canning jar with an oxygen absorber and store in a cool, dry location.

Rehydration:
Best enjoyed dry as a crunchy snack.

Tips:
Sweet Potato Cubes are perfect as a snack on their own or added to a salad for a sweet crunch. Add 1 Tbs Cumin or Paprika for a new flavor.

Mixed Fruit Medley

Energize your hiking adventures with this Trail-Ready Fruit Medley! It's the perfect snack to fuel your journey.

Cups:	25	Servings:	25	Serving Size:	1 cup (179 g)	Calories:	100
Prep Time:		25 min	Freeze-Dry Time:		50-60 + hrs	Shelf-Life:	20-25 yrs

Ingredients:
6 cups Mangoes, (5 med) peeled and diced
4 cups Strawberries, (2 lbs) hulled and halved
4 cups Mandarin Oranges, (5 small) peeled and segmented
4 cups Blueberries, (1½ lbs) halved or pricked
4 cups Seedless Grapes, (2lbs) halved
3 cups Golden Kiwi, (6) peeled and sliced
3 cups Pineapple, (1 large) peeled, cored, and cubed

Directions:
Wash and chop large fruits. Pierce or cut oranges, blueberries, and grapes. Combine all fruits together in a large bowl. Gently toss to mix. Spread evenly across the freeze-drying trays, ensuring not to overload them, and pre-freeze. Freeze-dry on normal settings for 50-60 hours. The pineapple as well as the seeds in the berries will take a very long time. Do a weight check and run Extra Dry Time until the weight doesn't change. Seal in 7mil mylar or a canning jar with an oxygen absorber and store in a cool, dry location.

Rehydration:
1 cup FD Fruit Salad (42 g)
½-⅔ cup Water (137 g)
½ tsp Lime Juice
½ tsp Honey
Mix Water, Lime Juice, & Honey. Stir in the freeze-dried Fruit Salad. Adjust for taste & texture.

Tips:
If concerned about the kiwi's tartness, switch it out with 3 cups of pear slices to maintain the medley's sweetness.

Fruit Crisps

Delight in these light and nutritious fruit crisps, an ideal pick-me-up for your outdoor excursions.

Pieces:	300	Servings:	15	Serving Size:	20 crisps (159 g)	Calories:	84
Prep Time:		30 min	Freeze-Dry Time:		30-40 hrs	Shelf-Life:	20-25 yrs

Ingredients:
3 med Apples
3 med Pears
3 med Peaches
3 med Plums
3 med Mangos

Dip: 1 Tbs Lemon Juice + 1 cup Water

Directions:
Cut fruits in half, removing cores, and slice them into thin ¼-inch strips. To prevent discoloration, dip them in a lemon juice mixture. Arrange the slices on your freeze-dryer trays, season by misting with water and sprinkling on flavors, and pre-freeze. Freeze-dry for 30-40 hours. Do a weight check and run Extra Dry Time until the weight doesn't change. Seal in 7mil mylar or a canning jar with an oxygen absorber and store in a cool, dry location.

Variations:
Sprinkle with Cinnamon & Sugar
Sprinkle with Brown Sugar & Oats
Drizzle with Caramel Sauce
Sprinkle with freeze-dried Fruit Powders
Try spices like Ginger, Clove, & Nutmeg

Rehydration:
Best enjoyed dry as a crunchy snack. To rehydrate for a pie, soak for 10 min.

Tips:
The variety of flavors options lets you create your own unique trail mix combinations. Try slicing up canteloupe or honcydew to add to the mix.

Vegetable Crisps

Transform your favorite veggies into crunchy, savory crisps. Homemade spice mixes can elevate their taste for a delightful flavor experience.

Crisps: 360	**Servings:**	12	**Serving Size:**	30 crisps (80 g)	**Calories:** 49
Prep Time: 30 min	**Freeze-Dry Time:**		25-35 hrs		**Shelf-Life:** 20-25 yrs

Ingredients:

2 medium Sweet Potatoes, 5"
2 medium Beets, 2"
2 small Turnips, 2"
3 small Carrots, 1" x 5"
3 small Parsnips, 1" x 5"

Seasoning Varieties:

Herbal Blend
1 cup Dried Basil
1 cup Dried Oregano
½ cup Fine Salt
½ cup Ground Black Pepper
½ cup Onion Powder
¼ cup Dried Thyme
¼ cup Ground Sage

Zesty Lemon Pepper
1 cup Lemon Zest (dried & ground)
½ cup Black Pepper
½ cup Fine Sea Salt
¼ cup Garlic Powder

Spicy Taco Mix
1 cup Ground Chili
1 cup Dried Minced Onion
½ cup Ground Paprika
½ cup Dried Cilantro
¼ cup Fine Salt
¼ cup Garlic Powder
¼ cup Crushed Red Pepper Flakes

Smoky Cajun Spice
1 cup Smoked Paprika
¾ cup Dried Oregano
½ cup Ground Cayenne
½ cup Onion Powder
¼ cup Ground Thyme
¼ cup Fine Salt

Directions:
Slice the vegetables into ⅛" thin rounds (or ½" strips.) Arrange the slices on your freeze-dryer trays, season by misting with water and evenly sprinkling on the flavors, and pre-freeze. Freeze-dry on normal settings for 25-35 hours. Do a weight check and run Extra Dry Time until the weight doesn't change. Seal in 7mil mylar or a canning jar with an oxygen absorber and store in a cool, dry location.

Rehydration:
Best enjoyed dry as a crunchy snack.

Tips:
These versatile spice mixes can also be applied to zucchini, yellow squash, kale, broccoli, carrots, and green beans. Combine them with dips or as a garnish on salads for extra flavor and crunch.

Cheese Crisps

Savor the spicy kick of Pepper Jack and the smooth melt of Monterey Jack cheese crisps.

Pieces: 384	**Servings:**	32	**Serving Size:**	12 crisps (28 g)	**Calories:** 106
Prep Time: 20 min	**Freeze-Dry Time:**		20-30 hrs		**Shelf-Life:** 10-15 yrs

Ingredients:
1 lb Pepper Jack Cheese (16 oz)
1 lb Monterey Jack Cheese (16 oz)

Directions:
Cut each type of cheese into 48 slices. Cut these slices into quarters for small, bite-sized pieces. Place paper towels on the freeze-drying trays to absorb oils. Arrange the cheese pieces on top and pre-freeze. Freeze-dry on normal settings for 20-30 hours. Do a weight check and run Extra Dry Time until the weight doesn't change. Seal in 7mil mylar or a canning jar with an oxygen absorber and store in a cool, dry location.

Rehydration:
Best enjoyed dry as a crunchy snack.

Tips:
Choose any sliceable cheese variety to craft your own custom cheese crisps.

21 TREATS

Colorful Candy Orbs

Perfect for snacking, these candies offer a melt-in-your-mouth experience that's both familiar and excitingly different.

Ounces: 50	**Servings:** 50	**Serving Size:** 1 oz or 29 pieces (30 g)	**Calories:** 120
Prep/Cook Time: 5 min	**Freeze-Dry Time:** 4-6 hrs		**Shelf-Life:** 1-2 yrs

Ingredients:
50 oz Party Bag of Skittles®

Directions:
Spread Skittles® in a single layer on the freeze-dryer trays. This gives them enough space to swell. Load the trays into your freeze-dryer. Freeze-dry on CANDY MODE at 145°F for 4-6 hours. Check to ensure they are crunchy and fully dried. Package in airtight containers to preserve their shelf life. No oxygen absorber.

Rehydration:
Best enjoyed dry.

Tips:
These make a nice addition to trail mixes. Experiment with different flavors for a fun variety.

Popped Caramel Spheres

An irresistibly crunchy snack perfect for those who love a sweet treat with a twist.

Pieces: 374	**Servings:** 34	**Serving Size:** 11 pieces (28 g)	**Calories:** 130
Prep/Cook Time: 5 min	**Freeze-Dry Time:** 4-6 hrs		**Shelf-Life:** 6-12 mo

Ingredients:
34 oz Party Bag of Caramel M&M's®

Directions:
Spread Caramel M&M's® loosely on the freeze-dryer trays, using pre-cut parchment paper for less mess. Space them out so there is room to swell. Load the trays into your freeze-dryer. Freeze-dry on CANDY MODE at 145°F for 4-6 hours. Check to ensure they are crunchy. Place back in the freeze-dryer for 30-60 minutes to allow the chocolate to set. The parchment will be oily. Package in airtight containers to preserve their shelf life. No oxygen absorber.

Rehydration:
Best enjoyed dry.

Tips:
Enjoy as a unique snack, add to trail mixes, or use as a fun topping for ice cream. This recipe also works for the Caramel Cold Brew flavor.

Taffy Puffs

Perfect for a novel snacking experience that revisits a cherished seaside treat with a twist.

Pieces: 180	**Servings:** 30	**Serving Size:** 5 pieces (30 g)	**Calories:** 110
Prep/Cook Time: 30 min	**Freeze-Dry Time:** 4-6 hrs		**Shelf-Life:** 1-2 yrs

Ingredients:
2 lb bag of Salt Water Taffy (assorted flavors)

Directions:
Unwrap and cut the taffy into four equal pieces. Roll into a ball and place on freeze-dryer trays lined with parchment paper, ensuring they're spaced apart. Use dividers to keep them from touching. After arranging the taffy pieces, load the trays into your freeze-dryer. Freeze-dry the taffy on CANDY MODE at 145°F for 4-6 hours. Check to ensure they've fully dried and are crunchy. Package in airtight containers to preserve their shelf life. No oxygen absorber.

Rehydration:
Best enjoyed dry.

Tips:
Prior to rolling into a ball, the taffy can be mixed for unique color pairings. This recipe works for all brands and types of taffy.

Marshmallows

Try them in hot cocoa for a melt-in-your-mouth experience!

Cups:	12	Servings:	18	Serving Size:	⅔ cup (30 g)	Calories:	90
Prep Time:	5 min	Freeze-Dry Time:	6-8 hrs			Shelf-Life:	1-2 yrs

Ingredients:
2 bags (10 oz each) Mini Marshmallows

Directions:
Spread marshmallows out evenly on the trays. For uniform drying, ensure they do not stick together. Freeze-dry the marshmallows on CANDY MODE at 145°F for 6-8 hours. Check to ensure they've fully dried and are crunchy. Package in airtight containers to preserve their shelf life. No oxygen absorber.

Rehydration:
Best enjoyed dry.

Tips:
These make the perfect addition to camping treats and trail mixes.

S'mores Bites

Recreate the magic of campfires and starry nights with freeze-dried S'mores Bites.

Cups:	9	Servings:	18	Serving Size:	½ cup (44 g)	Calories:	197
Prep Time:	10 min	Freeze-Dry Time:	n/a			Shelf-Life:	6-12 mo

Ingredients:
4 cups Teddy Grahams
3 cups Freeze-dried Mini Marshmallows
2 cup M&M's Candies

Directions:
In a large mixing bowl, combine Teddy Grahams, freeze-dried mini marshmallows, and M&M's candies. Gently toss to ensure an even mix. Package in airtight containers to preserve their shelf life. No oxygen absorber.

Rehydration:
Best enjoyed dry.

Tips:
These bites are a quick and satisfying treat, perfect for on-the-go.

Ice Cream Sandwich Sticks

Experience the joy in a shelf-stable form that you can savor whenever the craving hits.

Piecess:	24	Servings:	12	Serving Size:	2 pieces (56 g)	Calories:	150
Prep Time:	15 min	Freeze-Dry Time:	20-25 hrs			Shelf-Life:	10-15 yrs

Ingredients:
Pack of 12 ice cream sandwiches

Directions:
Unwrap the ice cream sandwiches and cut in half lengthwise to make sticks or cut into smaller pieces. Place on a cold tray. Pre-freeze for 12+ hours. Adjust initial freeze to -25°F. Allow the Chamber to cool 60-90 minutes after pressing Start. Freeze-dry for 20-24 hours. Do a weight check and run Extra Dry Time until the weight doesn't change. Seal in 7mil mylar or a canning jar with an oxygen absorber and store in a cool, dry location.

Rehydration:
Best enjoyed dry.

Tips:
They're a fun and easy treat, great for camping and hiking trips.

Mini Ice Cream Cones

These tiny treats pack all the flavor and fun of traditional ice cream cones, but in a form that's perfect for on-the-go.

Cones:	12	Servings:	12	Serving Size:	1 cone (44 g)	Calories:	100+
Prep Time:	15 min	Freeze-Dry Time:		20-25 hrs		Shelf-Life:	10-15 yrs

Ingredients:
12 Mini Ice Cream Cones, any brand or flavor

Directions:
Place the mini ice cream cones on a cold tray. You may need to slice them in half lengthwise. Pre-freeze 12+ hours. Adjust initial freeze to -25°F. Allow the Chamber to cool 60-90 minutes after pressing Start. Freeze-dry on normal settings for 20-24 hours. Do a weight check and run Extra Dry Time until the weight doesn't change. Seal in 7mil mylar or a canning jar with an oxygen absorber and store in a cool, dry location.

Rehydration:
Best enjoyed dry.

Tips:
These freeze-dried mini ice cream cones are perfect as a lightweight, mess-free snack for hiking, camping, or simply as a novel treat.

Creamy Ice Cream

Dive into the delight of homemade ice cream, a creamy concoction that is delicious & fun.

Cups:	8½	Servings:	8½	Serving Size:	1 cup (133 g)	Calories:	187
Prep Time:	40 min	Freeze-Dry Time:		25-35 hrs		Shelf-Life:	1-3 yrs

Ingredients:
1½ cups 2% Milk
2½ cups Half & Half
¾ cup Granulated Sugar
1 Tbs Pure Vanilla Extract

Items Needed:
3 cups Rock Salt
12 cups Crushed Ice
2 ea 2-Gallon Zip Bag
1 ea 4-Gallon Zip Bag

Directions:
Stir together milk, cream, sugar, and vanilla in a 2-gallon zip-sealed bag. Double bag it to ensure a secure seal.
In the 4-gallon zip-sealed bag, mix the rock salt with the crushed ice. Nestle the bag of cream mixture into the larger bag filled with ice, ensuring it's fully covered and the 4-gallon bag is tightly sealed. Shake energetically for about 20 minutes or until the mixture thickens. Carefully remove the ice cream bag, wiping off any salt before opening to remove second bag. Open the inner bag and scoop the ice cream onto the trays or put into molds. Pre-freeze 12+ hours. Adjust initial freeze to -25°F. Allow the Chamber to cool 60-90 minutes after pressing Start. Freeze-dry for 25-35 hours. Do a weight check and run Extra Dry Time until the weight doesn't change. Seal in 7mil mylar or a canning jar with an oxygen absorber and store in a cool, dry location.

Rehydration:
Best enjoyed dry.

Tips:
Blend in pureed berries, favorite fruits, caramel sauce, or some other fun options. For a creamier flavor substitute Heavy Cream for the H&H.

Drizzled Banana Crisps

Light, crunchy, and drizzled with decadence, these banana crisps are a guilt-free pleasure.

Cups:	4	Servings:	12	Serving Size:	⅓ cup (73 g)	Calories:	116
Prep Time:		30 min +2 hrs	Freeze-Dry Time:		30-40 hrs	Shelf-Life:	5-10 yrs

Ingredients:
6 Bananas
6 oz Chocolate Chips, melted

Directions:
Slice bananas into ½-inch thick slices and place them on a baking sheet lined with parchment paper. Melt and then drizzle the chocolate over the banana slices. Place the baking sheet in the freezer for 2 hours until the bananas and chocolate are frozen. Transfer the slices to the freeze-dry tray. Freeze-dry on normal settings for 30-40 hours. Do a weight check and run Extra Dry Time until the weight doesn't change. Place back in the freeze-dryer for 30-60 minutes to allow the chocolate to set. Seal in 7mil mylar or a canning jar with an oxygen absorber and store in a cool, dry location.

Rehydration:
Best enjoyed dry.

Tips: These drizzled banana crisps make an excellent topping for ice cream, yogurt, or to enjoy on their own as a sweet, crunchy snack.

Lemon Tea Bread Bites

A tangy and sweet lemon bread that's perfect for breakfast, snack time, or a treat with tea.

Pieces:	96	Servings:	24	Serving Size:	4 pieces (56 g)	Calories:	204
Prep/Cook Time:		1½ - 2 hrs	Freeze-Dry Time:		25-35 hrs	Shelf-Life:	15-20 yrs

Ingredients:
4 cups Flour
2 tsp Baking Soda
1 tsp Salt
Zest of 2 Lemons
1½ cup Granulated Sugar
4 large Eggs
2 tsp Vanilla Extract
½ cup Lemon Juice
1 cup Applesauce, unsweetened

Directions:
Preheat oven to 350°F and butter loaf pans. Mix dry and wet ingredients separately before incorporating together. Pour into 2 loaf pans and bake for 50-60 minutes. Cool completely, cut each loaf into 12 thin slices and then cut each slice into 4 pieces to make bites. Place on tray and pre-freeze. Freeze-dry for 25-35 hours. Do a weight check and run Extra Dry Time until the weight doesn't change. Seal in 7mil mylar or a canning jar with an oxygen absorber and store in a cool, dry location.

Rehydration:
Best enjoyed dry. To rehydrate, place in a zip-sealed bag with a damp paper towel for 20 minutes.

Tips:
Cut extra thin for a biscotti-like bite.

Zucchini Cake Bites

This sweet and slightly spiced zucchini bread is transformed into handy bite-sized pieces for an easy snack or breakfast.

Pieces:	72	Servings:	24	Serving Size:	3 pieces (66 g)	Calories:	192
Prep/Cook Time:	1½ - 2 hrs	Freeze-Dry Time:		25-35 hrs		Shelf-Life:	15-20 yrs

Ingredients:

3 cups Flour
2 tsp Baking Pwd
½ tsp Salt
1½ tsp Cinnamon
3 cups Granulated Sugar

4 large Eggs
1 tsp Baking Soda
1 cup Applesauce, unsweetened
1 cup Brown Sugar
3 cups shredded Zucchini, (2 med)

Directions:

Preheat oven to 350°F and butter a 9x13 cake pan. Mix dry and wet ingredients separately before combining together, folding in the shredded zucchini last. Bake 60-70 minutes. Cool completely, slice into strips ½" x 3" or smaller, bite-sized pieces, and pre-freeze. Freeze-dry for 25-35 hours, perform a weight check and use Extra Dry Time. Store in 7mil mylar or canning jars with oxygen absorbers, in a cool, dry location.

Rehydration:

Best enjoyed dry. To rehydrate, place in a zip-sealed bag with a damp paper towel for 20 minutes.

Tips:

Delicious as a biscotti-like bite. Try adding chocolate chips!

Oil-Free Brownie Bites

Enjoy the rich, chocolaty goodness of these brownie bites, made without any oil for a lighter treat.

Pieces:	32	Servings:	16	Serving Size:	2 pieces (43 g)	Calories:	91
Prep/Cook Time:		30 min		Freeze-Dry Time:	25-35 hrs	Shelf-Life:	15-20 yrs

Ingredients:

1 cup Unsweetened Applesauce
2 large Eggs
1 cup Granulated Sugar
1 teaspoon Vanilla Extract

¾ cup All-Purpose Flour
½ cup Unsweetened Cocoa Powder
½ teaspoon Baking Powder
½ teaspoon Salt

Directions:

Preheat oven to 350°F. In a large bowl, mix together the applesauce, eggs, sugar, and vanilla. In a separate bowl, sift together the flour, cocoa powder, baking powder, and salt. Gradually stir the dry ingredients into the wet ingredients until just combined. Pour the batter into a buttered 8x8 inch baking pan. Bake for 20-25 minutes. Allow the brownies to cool completely before cutting into pieces measuring 1" x 2". Place the brownie bites on trays and freeze-dry on normal settings for 25-35 hours. Do a weight check and run Extra Dry Time until the weight doesn't change. Seal in 7mil mylar or a canning jar with an oxygen absorber and store in a cool, dry location.

Rehydration:

Best enjoyed dry.

Tips:

Sprinkle sea salt on top before baking for a sweet and salty flavor contrast. Also try adding in ½ cup of Chocolate Chips. Brownie mixes can be used, but will have a shelf-life of 6-12 months and will have about 160 calories.

Mini Cookies

Perfectly preserved and irresistibly crunchy! A delightful snack that's as fun as it is flavorful.

Cookies:	60	Servings:	30	Serving Size:	2 cookies (28 g)	Calories:	110-150
Prep/Cook Time:		30 min	Freeze-Dry Time:		20-30 hrs	Shelf-Life:	1-2 yrs

Ingredients:
30 oz Cookie Dough (store-bought or homemade)

Directions:
Purchase or make Cookie Dough. Roll dough into ½-inch balls (1 Tbs dough.) Place on a baking sheet, spacing them about 1 inch apart. Bake according to package (or about 6-10 minutes.) Cool completely. Place the cookies on trays and pre-freeze. Freeze-dry on normal settings for 20-30 hours. Do a weight check and run Extra Dry Time until the weight doesn't change. Seal in 7mil mylar or a canning jar with an oxygen absorber and store in a cool, dry location.

Rehydration:
Best enjoyed dry.

Tips:
Any type of cookie dough will work. The less oil, the longer the shelf-life.

Lemon Burst Cookies

Infused with fresh lemon zest and a hint of vanilla, these cookies transform into an irresistibly crisp snack once freeze-dried, capturing the essence of lemon in every bite.

Cookies:	72	Servings:	36	Serving Size:	2 cookies (28 g)	Calories:	116
Prep/Cook Time:		35 min	Freeze-Dry Time:		20-30 hrs	Shelf-Life:	1-2 yrs

Ingredients:
2¾ cups All-purpose Flour
1 tsp Baking Powder
½ tsp Baking Soda
¼ tsp Salt
Zest of 2 Lemons

1 cup Greek Yogurt
1½ cups Granulated Sugar
2 Large Eggs
2 tsp Vanilla Extract
2 Tbs Fresh Lemon Juice

Directions:
Preheat oven to 350°F. In a large bowl, mix together the yogurt and sugar until fluffy. Beat in eggs, one at a time, then stir in vanilla extract, lemon zest, and lemon juice until well combined. In a separate bowl, sift together the flour, baking powder, baking soda, and salt. Gradually add to the wet ingredients until mixed. Roll dough into ½-inch balls (1 Tbs dough.) Place on a baking sheet, spacing them about 1 inch apart. Bake for 6-8 minutes, or until golden around the edges. The cookies should still be a bit soft in the center. Cool on the baking sheet for 2 minutes before transferring to a wire rack to cool completely. Place the cookies on trays and pre-freeze. Freeze-dry on normal settings for 20-30 hours. Do a weight check and run Extra Dry Time until the weight doesn't change. Seal in 7mil mylar or a canning jar with an oxygen absorber and store in a cool, dry location.

Rehydration:
Best enjoyed dry.

Tips:
Adjust the amount of lemon zest and juice according to taste for a stronger or more subtle lemon flavor.

Simple Cherry Cobbler

This delightful Cherry Cobbler is the perfect sweet and tart dessert that's sure to please.

Pieces: 27	Servings: 9	Serving Size: 3 pieces (128 g)	Calories: 171
Prep/Cook Time: 90 min	Freeze-Dry Time: 35-45 hrs		Shelf-Life: 15-20 yrs

Ingredients:
1 cup All-Purpose Flour
¾ cup Granulated Sugar
1 tsp Baking Powder
¼ tsp Fine Salt
1 cup 2% Milk
2 Tbs Lemon Juice
1 tsp Vanilla Extract
¼ tsp Almond Extract
4 cups Sweet Cherries, pitted

Directions:
Preheat oven to 350°F. In a large bowl, whisk together the flour, sugar, baking powder, and salt. Add in the milk, lemon juice, vanilla, and almond extract and mix until the batter is smooth. Spread the cherries in the bottom of a 9x9 baking dish, lightly mashing to ensure the cherries have released juices. Pour the batter over the cherries. Bake for 55-60 minutes. Cool completely. Cut into 1" x 3" pieces or scoop onto freeze-dryer trays, and pre-freeze. Freeze-dry on normal settings for 35-45 hours. Do a weight check and run Extra Dry Time until the weight doesn't change. Seal in 7mil mylar or a canning jar with an oxygen absorber and store in a cool, dry location.

Rehydration:
3 FD Cherry Cobbler Pieces (46 g)
⅓ cup Water (82 g)
Enjoy dry for a crunchy treat or rehydrate with a light mist of water to revive a more traditional cobbler texture.

Tips:
Frozen cherries will also work well for this recipe. Try the same recipe with berries substituted for some or all of the cherries. Any type of milk can be substituted.

Quick 'n' Easy Peach Cobbler

This mouthwatering Peach Cobbler captures the essence of summer in every bite.

Pieces: 27	Servings: 9	Serving Size: 3 pieces (130 g)	Calories: 184
Prep/Cook Time: 30 min	Freeze-Dry Time: 35-45 hrs		Shelf-Life: 15-20 yrs

Ingredients:
1¼ cups Flour
1 cup Granulated Sugar
1 tablespoon Baking Powder
½ tsp Salt
1 cup 2% Milk
4 cups Sliced Peaches (8 med)
Cinnamon, to sprinkle

Directions:
Preheat oven to 350°F. In a large bowl, whisk together the flour, sugar, baking powder, and salt. Add in the milk and mix until smooth. Add the peaches and stir. Pour the mixture into a 9x9 baking dish and sprinkle cinnamon on top. Bake for 35-45 minutes. Cool completely. Cut into 1" x 3" pieces or scoop onto freeze-dryer trays, and pre-freeze. Freeze-dry on normal settings for 35-45 hours. Do a weight check and run Extra Dry Time until the weight doesn't change. Seal in 7mil mylar or a canning jar with an oxygen absorber and store in a cool, dry location.

Rehydration:
3 FD Cherry Cobbler Pieces (50 g)
⅓ cup Water (80 g)
Enjoy dry for a crunchy treat or rehydrate by lightly misting with water to revive a more traditional cobbler texture.

Tips:
You can use canned peaches, just be sure to drain them well before adding to the cobbler.

Strawberry Pudding

This fruity Strawberry Pudding is a great way to enjoy a light and creamy dessert.

Cups:	6	Servings:	12	Serving Size:	½ cup (125 g)	Calories:	138
Prep/Cook Time:	30 min	Freeze-Dry Time:	25-35 hrs			Shelf-Life:	2-5 yrs

Ingredients:

4 cups Whole Strawberries (1 lb)
4 Tbs Cornstarch
¼ cup 2% Milk
2¾ cups 2% Milk

1 cup Granulated Sugar
Pinch of salt
4 Egg Yolks
2 tsp Vanilla Extract

Directions:

Wash and remove tops from strawberries and puree in a blender. In a small bowl, whisk cornstarch & ¼ cup milk & set aside. In a medium saucepan, warm the puree, sugar, 2¾ cup milk, and salt for 5-10 minutes or until just at a simmer and remove from heat. In a medium bowl beat egg yolks and whisk in half of the warm milk mixture. Pour this back into the saucepan and slowly stir in the cornstarch mixture. Heat, while whisking constantly, for 4-6 minutes. Remove from heat, stir in vanilla extract, and cool. Chill in fridge before serving. Spread a ½" layer onto freeze-dryer trays, and pre-freeze. Freeze-dry on normal settings for 25-35 hours. Do a weight check and run Extra Dry Time until the weight doesn't change. Seal in 7mil mylar or a canning jar with an oxygen absorber and store in a cool, dry location.

Rehydration:

1 cup Powder (33 g)
⅓-½ cup Water (92 g)
Mix powder with water and stir well.
Add more or less for consistency.

Tips: You can use 2 cups of strawberry puree in place of the whole strawberries.

Butterscotch Pudding

This velvety Butterscotch Pudding is sure to satisfy your sweet tooth.

Cups:	4	Servings:	8	Serving Size:	½ cup (126 g)	Calories:	223
Prep/Cook Time:	35 min	Freeze-Dry Time:	25-35 hrs			Shelf-Life:	6-12 mo

Ingredients:

1½ cups 2% Milk
1 cup Half & Half
4 large Egg Yolks
¼ cup Cornstarch

¾ cup Brown Sugar, packed
3 Tbs Water
½ tsp Salt
3 Tbs Unsalted Butter
1 tsp Vanilla Extract

Directions:

In a medium bowl, whisk milk and half & half together and set aside. In a medium, heavy-duty saucepan, stir together the brown sugar, water, and salt. Heat for 5-6 minutes until caramelized. Carefully add in the milk mixture, whisking and cooking until just boiling, and then turn heat to low. In a medium bowl, beat the egg yolks, add the cornstarch, and whisk in about ½ cup of the warm milk. Pour this into the saucepan and stir the mixture well. Whisk constantly and cook for 1-2 minutes. Remove from heat and stir in the butter until smooth. Stir in the vanilla extract, and cool. Chill in fridge before serving. Spread a ½" layer onto freeze-dryer trays, & pre-freeze. Freeze-dry on normal settings for 25-35 hours. Do a weight check & run Extra Dry Time until the weight doesn't change. Seal in 7mil mylar or a canning jar with an oxygen absorber & store in a cool, dry location.

Rehydration:

1 cup Powder (45 g)
¼-⅓ cup Water (81 g)
Mix powder with water and stir well.
Add more or less for consistency.

Tips:

When serving fresh, add in 1 Tbs Rum, Scotch, or Bourbon for an adult version.

Mixed-Berry Smoothie Cubes

Rich in flavor and packed with nutrients, cubes make it easy to enjoy your favorite smoothie.

| Cups: | 8 | Servings: | 8 | Serving Size: | 10 cubes (239 g) | Calories: | 131 |
| Prep Time: | | 15 min | Freeze-Dry Time: | 25-35 hrs | | Shelf-Life: | 10-15 yrs |

Ingredients:

2 cups Strawberries
2 cups Blueberries
2 cups Blackberries
2 cups Baby Spinach

2 cups Kale
2 large Banana
1 cup of Greek Yogurt
1½ cup of Water

3 cups needed for tray size Small
4 cups needed for tray size Medium

5 cups needed for tray size Large
10 cups needed for tray size X-Large

Directions:

Combine all ingredients in a blender and blend until smooth. Place your empty tray in the freezer and pour your smoothie onto your tray. Pre-freeze until solid. Alternatively, pour into ice cube trays or silicone molds and after pre-freezing, transfer to a tray. Freeze-dry on normal settings for 25-35 hours. Do a weight check and run Extra Dry Time until the weight doesn't change. With a sharp knife, cut into bite size cubes. Seal the smoothie cubes in 7mil mylar or a canning jar with an oxygen absorber. Store in a cool, dry location.

Rehydration:

1 cup Powder (43 g)
¾-1 cup Water or juice (196 g)
Best as a crunchy snack. To rehydrate to a smoothie, crush cubes into a powder and blend with water or juice until smooth.

Tips: For an extra protein kick, add a scoop of your favorite protein powder before blending. Try using juice instead of water. Try adding 2 Tbs honey for a sweeter flavor.

Tropical Mango Smoothie Cubes

Now you can carry a tropical smoothie in your pocket with these delicious cubes.

| Cups: | 8 | Servings: | 8 | Serving Size: | 10 cubes (239 g) | Calories: | 130 |
| Prep Time: | | 15 min | Freeze-Dry Time: | 35-45 hrs | | Shelf-Life: | 10-15 yrs |

Ingredients:

4½ cups Diced Mango
3 cup Pineapple Chunks
2 large Banana

1 cup Coconut Yogurt
2 cup Coconut Water
1 tsp Ground Ginger

3 cups needed for tray size Small
4 cups needed for tray size Medium

5 cups needed for tray size Large
10 cups needed for tray size X-Large

Directions:

Combine all ingredients in a blender and blend until smooth. Place your empty tray in the freezer and pour your smoothie onto your tray. Pre-freeze until solid. Alternatively, pour into ice cube trays or silicone molds and after pre-freezing, transfer to a tray. Freeze-dry on normal settings for 25-35 hours. Do a weight check and run Extra Dry Time until the weight doesn't change. With a sharp knife, cut into bite size cubes. Seal the smoothie cubes in 7mil mylar or a canning jar with an oxygen absorber. Store in a cool, dry location.

Rehydration:

1 cup Powder (44 g)
¾-1 cup Water or juice (195 g)
Best as a crunchy snack. To rehydrate to a smoothie, crush cubes into a powder and blend with water or juice until smooth.

Tips: Add a bit of lime zest before blending to bring an extra zing. Substitute coconut milk for the coconut water for a creamier smoothie.

Creamsicle Cubes

Indulge in this perfect blend of sweet and tangy, with a hint of vanilla and the richness of cashews to mimic that beloved creamsicle taste.

Cups: 9	**Servings:** 9	**Serving Size:** 10 cubes (242 g)		**Calories:** 334
Prep Time: 4 hrs + 15 min	**Freeze-Dry Time:** 30-40 hrs			**Shelf-Life:** 1-2 yrs

Ingredients:
2 cup Raw Cashews
8 Oranges, peeled and sectioned

2 medium Bananas, very ripe
14 Medjool Dates, pitted
1 cup Almond Milk

3 cups needed for tray size Small
4 cups needed for tray size Medium

5 cups needed for tray size Large
10 cups needed for tray size X-Large

Directions:
Soak cashews in water 4-12 hours and drain. Combine all ingredients in a blender and blend until smooth and creamy. Place your empty tray in the freezer and pour the mixture onto your tray. Pre-freeze until solid. Alternatively, pour into ice cube trays or silicone molds and after pre-freezing, transfer to a tray. Freeze-dry on normal settings for 30-40 hours. Do a weight check and run Extra Dry Time until the weight doesn't change. With a sharp knife, cut into bite size cubes. Seal the cubes in 7mil mylar or a canning jar with an oxygen absorber. Store in a cool, dry location.

Rehydration:
1 cup Powder (82 g)
⅔-¾ Water or juice (160 g)
Best as a crunchy snack. To rehydrate to a smoothie, crush cubes into a powder and blend with water or juice until smooth.

Tips:
To enhance the creamsicle flavor, add a teaspoon of vanilla extract to the blend. Soy and dairy milk also work well with this recipe.

··

21 DRINKS

Fruit Juices

Enjoy your favorite fruit juices anytime, anywhere with this convenient freeze-dried fruit juice powder.

Cups: 3, 4, 5, 10	**Servings:** varies	**Serving Size:** 1 cup (240 g)		**Calories:** 90-110
Prep Time: 10-20 min	**Freeze-Dry Time:** 25-35 hrs			**Shelf-Life:** 15-20 yrs

Ingredients:
Top 12: Apples, Blueberries, Cherries, Cranberries, Grapes, Grapefruits, Lemons, Mangoes, Oranges, Peaches, Pineapples, Pomegranates.
Others: Acai Berries, Apricots, Blackberries, Cantaloupe, Kiwi, Limes, Pears, Prunes, Raspberries, Strawberries, Tangerines, Watermelon.

3 cups Juice needed for tray size Small
4 cups Juice needed for tray size Medium

5 cups Juice needed for tray size Large
10 cups Juice needed for tray size X-Large

Directions:
Purchase juice or run fruits through a juicer. Dilute with an equal amount of water. Place your empty tray in the freezer and pour your chosen fruit juice onto your tray. Pre-freeze until solid. Freeze-dry on normal settings for 25-35 hours or until completely dry and crumbly. Pulverize into a fine powder using a food processor or blender. Store in airtight containers or mylar bags with oxygen absorbers in a cool, dry place.

Rehydration:
2-4 Tbs Juice Powder
1 cup Water
Mix powder with water and shake well. Add more or less for taste.

Tips:
Use the powder as a natural flavor enhancer in baking or cooking. Sprinkle powder on desserts for a flavorful addition.

Citrus Juices

Capture the zest and tang of citrus fruits in a versatile powder form. Ideal for adding a burst of flavor to drinks, desserts, and savory dishes.

Cups: 3, 4, 5, 10	**Servings:** varies	**Serving Size:** 1 cup (240 g)	**Calories:** 90-120
Prep Time: 10-20 min	**Freeze-Dry Time:** 25-35 hrs		**Shelf-Life:** 15-20 yrs

Ingredients:
Select from: Citron, Grapefruit, Kumquats, Lemons, Limes, Mandarins, Oranges, Pomelos, Tangerines

3 cups Juice needed for tray size Small
4 cups Juice needed for tray size Medium

5 cups Juice needed for tray size Large
10 cups Juice needed for tray size X-Large

Directions:
Purchase citrus juice or peel off rind and pith and run any variety of citrus fruits through a juicer. Dilute with an equal amount of water. Place your empty tray in the freezer and pour your citrus juice onto your tray. Pre-freeze until solid. Freeze-dry on normal settings for 25-35 hours or until completely dry and crumbly. Pulverize into a fine powder using a food processor or blender. Store in airtight containers or mylar bags with oxygen absorbers in a cool, dry place.

Rehydration:
4 Tbs Juice Powder
1 cup Water
Mix powder with water and shake well. Add more or less for taste.

Tips: Powder can be a natural flavor enhancer in baking, cooking, or as a cocktail glass rimming salt. It is also excellent for making homemade flavor enhancers, seasoning blends, or for a quick vitamin C boost.

Pineapple Juice

Capture the tropical essence of pineapple in a powder form, perfect for adding a punch of flavor to beverages, desserts, and marinades, providing a sweet and tangy twist.

Cups: 3, 4, 5, 10	**Servings:** varies	**Serving Size:** 1 cup (240 g)	**Calories:** 131
Prep Time: 10-20 min	**Freeze-Dry Time:** 25-35 hrs		**Shelf-Life:** 15-20 yrs

Ingredients:
Pineapples (2 pounds will yield 1 cup)

3 cups Juice needed for tray size Small
4 cups Juice needed for tray size Medium

5 cups Juice needed for tray size Large
10 cups Juice needed for tray size X-Large

Directions:
Purchase unsweetened pineapple juice or run pineaple chunks through a juicer. Dilute with an equal amount of water. Place your empty tray in the freezer and pour your chosen pineapple juice onto your tray. Pre-freeze until solid. Freeze-dry on normal settings for 25-35 hours or until completely dry and crumbly. Pulverize into a fine powder using a food processor or blender. Store in airtight containers or mylar bags with oxygen absorbers in a cool, dry place.

Rehydration:
3-4 Tbs Juice Powder
1 cup Water
Mix powder with water and shake well. Add more or less for taste.

Tips:
Pineapple juice powder works wonderfully as a natural meat tenderizer. It's a great addition to homemade dry rubs and seasoning mixes. Add to desserts for a tropical flavor.

Vegetable Juices

A nutritious and easy way to enjoy the benefits of vegetables. This freeze-dried vegetable juice powder is also great for boosting the nutritional content of meals and snacks.

Cups:	3, 4, 5, 10	Servings:	varies	Serving Size:	1 cup (240 g)	Calories:	50-70
Prep Time:	10-20 min	Freeze-Dry Time:	25-35 hrs			Shelf-Life:	15-20 yrs

Ingredients:

Top 12: Beets, Cabbage, Carrots, Celery, Cucumbers, Kale, Parsley, Spinach, Swiss Chard, Tomatoes, Wheatgrass, Zucchini.

Others: Asparagus, Bok Choy, Broccoli, Cilantro, Collard Greens, Dandelion Greens, Fennel, Ginger, Mint, Sweet Potato, Romaine, Tatsoi.

3 cups Juice needed for tray size Small

4 cups Juice needed for tray size Medium

5 cups Juice needed for tray size Large

10 cups Juice needed for tray size X-Large

Directions:

Purchase juice or run vegetables through a juicer. Place your empty tray in the freezer and pour your chosen vegetable juice onto your tray. Pre-freeze until solid. Freeze-dry on normal settings for 25-35 hours or until completely dry and crumbly. Pulverize into a fine powder using a food processor or blender. Store in airtight containers or mylar bags with oxygen absorbers in a cool, dry place.a cool, dry place.

Rehydration:

2-3 Tbs Juice Powder

1 cup Water

Mix powder with water and shake well. Add more or less for taste.

Tips:

Incorporate into soups, stews, and sauces for an added nutrient boost. The powder can also be used as a natural coloring agent in dishes.

Greens Juices

Boost your daily intake of greens with this easy-to-make, freeze-dried greens juice powder. Perfect for adding to smoothies, juices, or even sprinkling over salads for a nutritional punch.

Cups:	3, 4, 5, 10	Servings:	varies	Serving Size:	1 cup (240 g)	Calories:	50-80
Prep Time:	10-20 min	Freeze-Dry Time:	25-35 hrs			Shelf-Life:	15-20 yrs

Ingredients:

Bases: Cucumbers, Zucchinis

Greens: Asparagus, Bok Choy, Broccoli, Cabbage, Celery, Cilantro, Collard Greens, Dandelion Greens, Fennel, Kale, Mint, Parsley, Spinach, Swiss Chard, Romaine, Tatsoi, Wheatgrass.

Sweeteners: Apples, Ginger, Grapes, Grapefruit, Kiwis, Oranges, Pears, Pineapple, Strawberries.

3 cups Juice needed for tray size Small

4 cups Juice needed for tray size Medium

5 cups Juice needed for tray size Large

10 cups Juice needed for tray size X-Large

Directions:

Purchase a greens juice or run ingredients through a juicer. A balanced greens juice will have a base vegetable, a handful of selected greens, and a sweetener or two. Place your empty tray in the freezer and pour your chosen greens juice onto your tray. Pre-freeze until solid. Freeze-dry on normal settings for 25-35 hours or until completely dry and crumbly. Pulverize into a fine powder using a food processor or blender. Store in airtight containers or mylar bags with oxygen absorbers in a cool, dry place.

Rehydration:

2 Tbs Juice Powder

1 cup Water

Mix powder with water and shake well. Add more or less for taste.

Tips:

Greens powder is a great way to increase your vegetable intake without altering the taste of your meals significantly. Powder can be added to smoothies for an extra health boost.

Carrot Juice

Transform nutritious carrot juice into a versatile powder form, perfect for boosting the nutritional content of smoothies, baked goods, and savory dishes with a subtle sweetness and a dose of essential vitamins.

| **Cups:** | 3, 4, 5, 10 | **Servings:** | varies | **Serving Size:** | 1 cup (240 g) | **Calories:** | 96 |
| **Prep Time:** | | 10-20 min | **Freeze-Dry Time:** | | 25-35 hrs | **Shelf-Life:** | 15-20 yrs |

Ingredients:
Carrots (1 pound will yield 1 cup)

3 cups Juice needed for tray size Small
4 cups Juice needed for tray size Medium

5 cups Juice needed for tray size Large
10 cups Juice needed for tray size X-Large

Directions:
Purchase carrot juice or wash and run carrots through a juicer. Place your empty tray in the freezer and pour your chosen carrot juice onto your tray. Pre-freeze until solid. Freeze-dry on normal settings for 25-35 hours or until completely dry and crumbly. Pulverize into a fine powder using a food processor or blender. Store in airtight containers or mylar bags with oxygen absorbers in a cool, dry place.

Rehydration:
2 Tbs Juice Powder
1 cup Water
Mix powder with water and shake well. Add more or less for taste.

Tips:
Carrot juice powder can be used to naturally sweeten and color dishes. Great for adding to foods for an extra vitamin boost.

Dairy Milk

Preserve the nutritional benefits and convenience of milk in powder form, ideal for baking, cooking, or even direct consumption when mixed with water.

| **Cups:** | 3, 4, 5, 10 | **Servings:** | varies | **Serving Size:** | 1 cup (240 g) | **Calories:** | 80-150 |
| **Prep Time:** | | 5-10 min | **Freeze-Dry Time:** | | 25-35 hrs | **Shelf-Life:** | 10-20 yrs |

Ingredients:
Cow, goat, or sheep milk
Skim, 1%, 2%, or Whole

3 cups Milk needed for tray size Small
4 cups Milk needed for tray size Medium

5 cups Milk needed for tray size Large
10 cups Milk needed for tray size X-Large

Directions:
Purchase any variety of dairy milk. Keep in mind that the higher the fat content, the lower the shelf-life. Place your empty tray in the freezer and pour your milk onto your tray. Pre-freeze until solid. Freeze-dry on normal settings for 25-35 hours or until completely dry and crumbly. Pulverize into a fine powder using a food processor or blender. Store in airtight containers or mylar bags with oxygen absorbers in a cool, dry place.

Rehydration:
¼ cup Milk Powder
1 cup Water
Mix powder with water and shake well. Add more or less for consistency.

Tips:
Use the powder in coffee, tea, or for making homemade yogurt. It's a convenient option for camping trips or emergency food storage.

Chocolate Milk

Enjoy the creamy, comforting taste of chocolate milk in a portable, easy-to-store powder form, perfect for a quick chocolatey drink or as a flavor booster for desserts.

Cups: 6	Servings: 6	Serving Size: 1 cup (240 g)	Calories: 180
Prep Time: 10-20 min	Freeze-Dry Time: 25-35 hrs		Shelf-Life: 10-15 yrs

Ingredients:
6 cups Milk
1 tsp Vanilla
¼ cup Cocoa Powder
⅓ cup Confectioners (Powdered) Sugar

3 cups mixture needed for tray size Small
4 cups mixture needed for tray size Medium
5 cups mixture needed for tray size Large
10 cups mixture needed for tray size X-Large

Directions:
Purchase pre-made chocolate milk or prepare in a blender. Add all ingredients and blend until smooth. Place your empty tray in the freezer and pour your milk mixture onto your tray. Pre-freeze until solid. Freeze-dry on normal settings for 25-35 hours or until completely dry and crumbly. Pulverize into a fine powder using a food processor or blender. Store in airtight containers or mylar bags with oxygen absorbers in a cool, dry place.

Rehydration:
¼ cup Powder
1 cup Water
Mix powder with water and shake well. Add more or less for consistency.

Tips:
Sprinkle chocolate milk powder over ice cream or use it in baking for an extra chocolate flavor. Mix with water for an instant hot chocolate.

Strawberry Milk

Capture the sweet and fruity flavor of strawberry milk in powder form, offering a fun and tasty way to enjoy this beloved beverage anytime, anywhere.

Cups: 6	Servings: 6	Serving Size: 1 cup (240 g)	Calories: 240
Prep Time: 10-20 min	Freeze-Dry Time: 25-35 hrs		Shelf-Life: 10-15 yrs

Ingredients:
5 cups Milk
¾ cup Water
3 cups fresh strawberries, halved
¾ cup Sugar

3 cups mixture needed for tray size Small
4 cups mixture needed for tray size Medium
5 cups mixture needed for tray size Large
10 cups mixture needed for tray size X-Large

Directions:
Purchase pre-made strawberry milk or prepare your own. In a saucepan, heat strawberries, water, and sugar and simmer for 20 minutes. Strain syrup and discard solids. There should be about 1 cup of syrup. Stir syrup into milk until well blended. Place your empty tray in the freezer and pour your milk mixture onto your tray. Pre-freeze until solid. Freeze-dry on normal settings for 25-35 hours or until completely dry and crumbly. Pulverize into a fine powder using a food processor or blender. Store in airtight containers or mylar bags with oxygen absorbers in a cool, dry place.

Rehydration:
¼ cup Powder
1 cup Water
Mix powder with water and shake well. Add more or less for consistency.

Tips:
Use the powder to flavor milkshakes, smoothies, or desserts for a burst of strawberry flavor. A perfect addition to oatmeal, cereal, or desserts for a fruity twist.

Oat Milk

Create your own oat milk from scratch and transform it into a convenient, versatile powder form. Perfect for vegans or those with dairy sensitivities, this oat milk powder can be used in coffees, teas, baking, and cooking.

Cups:	6	**Servings:**	6	**Serving Size:**	1 cup (240 g)	**Calories:**	130
Prep Time:	30 min	**Freeze-Dry Time:**	25-35 hrs	**Shelf-Life:**	20-25 yrs

Ingredients:
2 cup Rolled Oats
6 cups Water

Optional Additions:
⅛ tsp Salt   1 tsp Vanilla
4 Dates   ¼ cup Cocoa Powder

3 cups mixture needed for tray size Small
4 cups mixture needed for tray size Medium

5 cups mixture needed for tray size Large
10 cups mixture needed for tray size X-Large

Directions:
Purchase or make oat milk. Soak rolled oats in water for 30 minutes. Drain and rinse to remove excess starch. Add oats, water, and any additions to a blender and blend on high 1 minute. Strain the mixture using a fine mesh strainer or cotton towel to obtain smooth oat milk and discard the solids. Place your empty tray in the freezer and pour your milk onto your tray. Pre-freeze until solid. Freeze-dry on normal settings for 25-35 hours or until completely dry and crumbly. Pulverize into a fine powder using a food processor or blender. Store in airtight containers or mylar bags with oxygen absorbers in a cool, dry place.

Rehydration:
2 Tbs Powder
1 cup Water
Mix powder with water and shake well. Add more or less for consistency.

Tips:
Enhance your oat milk by adding vanilla extract or cocoa powder before freezing for flavored milk powders. The powder is also an excellent dairy-free alternative for coffee creamer.

- -

Rice Milk

Homemade rice milk can easily be turned into a dairy-free milk powder, offering a hypoallergenic and vegan alternative to traditional milk powders. Use it in beverages, cooking, and baking for a mild, sweet flavor.

Cups:	6	**Servings:**	6	**Serving Size:**	1 cup (240 g)	**Calories:**	110
Prep Time:	2 hrs	**Freeze-Dry Time:**	25-35 hrs	**Shelf-Life:**	20-25 yrs

Ingredients:
2 cup Cooked White Rice
6 cups Water

Optional Additions:
⅛ tsp Salt   2 Tbs Maple Syrup
2 tsp Nutmeg   ½ - 1 cup Berries

3 cups mixture needed for tray size Small
4 cups mixture needed for tray size Medium

5 cups mixture needed for tray size Large
10 cups mixture needed for tray size X-Large

Directions:
Purchase or make rice milk. Add cooked rice (make it with 1 cup raw rice and 2 cups water), water, and any additions to a blender and blend on high 1-2 minutes. Strain the mixture using a fine mesh strainer or cotton towel to obtain creamy rice milk and discard the solids. Place your empty tray in the freezer and pour your milk onto your tray. Pre-freeze until solid. Freeze-dry on normal settings for 25-35 hours or until completely dry and crumbly. Pulverize into a fine powder using a food processor or blender. Store in airtight containers or mylar bags with oxygen absorbers in a cool, dry place.

Rehydration:
2 Tbs Powder
1 cup Water
Mix powder with water and shake well. Add more or less for consistency.

Tips:
Rice milk powder is naturally sweet and light, making it an excellent addition to tea or coffee.

Smoothies

Transform your favorite smoothies into convenient freeze-dried powders, preserving the nutrients, flavors, and colors. Perfect for a quick and healthy drink on the go, simply by adding water.

Cups: 3, 4, 5, 10	**Servings:** varies	**Serving Size:** 1 cup (240 g)	**Calories:** 160-300
Prep Time: 10-20 min	**Freeze-Dry Time:** 25-35 hrs		**Shelf-Life:** 1-5 yrs

Ingredients: Bases: Avocados, Bananas, Coconut milk, Cottage Cheese, Dairy Milk, Juice, Kefir, Nut Milks, Oats, Yogurt. **Fruits:** Apples, Apricots, Blueberries, Blackberries, Cherries, Grapes, Mangoes, Peaches, Pears, Pineapples, Raspberries, Strawberries, Watermelon. **Optional Additions:** Seeds- Chia, Flax, Hemp, Sunflower. Nuts & Butters - Peanut, Almond, Cashew. Greens- Kale, Mint, Parsley, Spinach, Swiss Chard, Romaine, Tatsoi, Wheatgrass. Sweeteners- Agave, Honey, Maple Syrup, Stevia, Sugar, Medjool Dates. Spices- Cinnamon, Cloves, Ginger, Nutmeg, Turmeric, Vanilla.

3 cups mixture needed for tray size Small
4 cups mixture needed for tray size Medium

5 cups mixture needed for tray size Large
10 cups mixture needed for tray size X-Large

Directions:
Purchase or prepare your smoothie. Smoothies have a base, with liquids & creamy foods, loads of fruits, & sometimes fats, greens, sweeteners, & spices. Blend bases & greens until creamy, add fruits & pulverize, add anything else, & blend 30-60 seconds until smooth. Dilute with an equal amount of water. Place your empty tray in the freezer & pour your smoothie mixture onto your tray. Pre-freeze until solid. Freeze-dry on normal settings for 25-35 hours or until completely dry & crumbly. Pulverize into a fine powder using a food processor or blender. (Or cut into bites.) Store in airtight containers or mylar bags with oxygen absorbers in a cool, dry place.

Rehydration:
2-4 Tbs Powder
1 cup Water
Mix powder with water and shake well. Add more or less for consistency.

Tips: Experiment with different smoothie recipes to create a variety of flavors. Freeze-dried smoothie powder is also great for adding to oatmeal, yogurt, or baked goods for an extra nutritional boost. Adding fats, nuts, or seeds raises the calories and lowers the shelf-life.

Protein Shakes

Preserve the protein-packed goodness of your favorite homemade protein shakes in powder form for a quick and convenient post-workout recovery drink or a protein boost anytime, anywhere.

Cups: 3, 4, 5, 10	**Servings:** varies	**Serving Size:** 1 cup (240 g)	**Calories:** 150-200
Prep Time: 5-15 min	**Freeze-Dry Time:** 25-35 hrs		**Shelf-Life:** 1-5 yrs

Ingredients: Bases: Coconut milk, Dairy Milk, Grain Milk, Kefir, Nut Milk. **Protein Powder:** Whey, Hemp, Pea, Rice. **Other Additions:** Fruits- Apricots, Avocados, Bananas, Blueberries, Blackberries, Cherries, Mangoes, Peaches, Raspberries, Strawberries. Seeds- Chia, Flax, Hemp, Sunflower. Nuts & Butters - Peanut, Almond, Cashew. Greens- Bok Choy, Kale, Spinach, Tatsoi. Sweeteners- Agave, Dates, Honey, Maple Syrup, Stevia.

3 cups mixture needed for tray size Small
4 cups mixture needed for tray size Medium

5 cups mixture needed for tray size Large
10 cups mixture needed for tray size X-Large

Directions:
Purchase or prepare your protein shake. Shakes have a milk base, with protein powder & additions such as fruits, seeds, nuts, greens, & sweeteners. Blend base with powder & greens. Add other ingredients & blend 30-60 seconds until smooth. Dilute with an equal amount of water. Place your empty tray in the freezer & pour your shake mixture onto your tray. Pre-freeze until solid. Freeze-dry on normal settings for 25-35 hours or until completely dry & crumbly. Pulverize into a fine powder using a food processor or blender. Store in airtight containers or mylar bags with oxygen absorbers in a cool, dry place.

Rehydration:
2-3 Tbs Powder
1 cup Water
Mix powder with water and shake well. Add more or less for consistency.

Tips:
Customize your protein shake powder with different flavors and supplements according to your dietary needs and preferences. A great way to ensure you always have your post-workout nutrition ready to go.

Cold Brew Coffee

This simple coffee recipe is ideal for outdoor excursions, ensuring you can savor a flavorful, freshly brewed cup wherever your travels lead.

Cups:	8	Servings:	8	Serving Size:	1 cup (240 g)	Calories:	3
Prep Time:	12 hrs + 20 min	Freeze-Dry Time:		25-35 hrs		Shelf-Life:	20-25 yrs

Ingredients:
2 cups Ground Coffee Beans
8 cups Cold Water

Other Items:
Pitcher or Jar
Cheesecloth or Coffee Filter

3 cups coffee needed for tray size Small
4 cups coffee needed for tray size Medium

5 cups coffee needed for tray size Large
10 cups coffee needed for tray size X-Large

Directions:

In a pitcher or jar, mix ground coffee with cold water thoroughly. Cover and steep in the fridge for 12 to 24 hours. Strain through a cheesecloth or coffee filter to remove the grounds. Place your empty tray in the freezer and pour your coffee onto your tray. Pre-freeze until solid. Freeze-dry on normal settings for 25-35 hours or until completely dry and crumbly. Pulverize into a fine powder using a food processor or blender. Store in airtight containers or mylar bags with oxygen absorbers in a cool, dry place.

Rehydration:
1-3 tsp Powder
1 cup Boiling Water for hot coffee.
For iced coffee use ¾ cup of cold water, stir, and add ½ cup of ice.

Tips: After rehydrating, you have the option to include milk, sweeteners, or flavors according to your preference. For maximum yield, ensure the brew is strong.

Spiced Cold Brew Coffee

Wake up to a glass of invigorating Spiced Cold Brew Coffee. With the subtle infusion of cinnamon and nutmeg, this drink offers a refreshing twist to your morning routine.

Cups:	8	Servings:	8	Serving Size:	1 cup (240 g)	Calories:	5
Prep Time:	12 hrs + 20 min	Freeze-Dry Time:		25-35 hrs		Shelf-Life:	20-25 yrs

Ingredients:
2 cups Ground Coffee Beans
8 cups Cold Water
½ tsp Nutmeg
1 tsp Cinnamon

Other Items:
Pitcher or Jar
Cheesecloth or Coffee Filter

3 cups coffee needed for tray size Small
4 cups coffee needed for tray size Medium

5 cups coffee needed for tray size Large
10 cups coffee needed for tray size X-Large

Directions:

In a pitcher or jar, mix ground coffee with cinnamon, nutmeg, and cold water. Cover and steep in the fridge for 12 to 24 hours. Strain through a cheesecloth or coffee filter to remove the grounds. Place your empty tray in the freezer and pour your coffee onto your tray. Pre-freeze until solid. Freeze-dry on normal settings for 25-35 hours or until completely dry and crumbly. Pulverize into a fine powder using a food processor or blender. Store in airtight containers or mylar bags with oxygen absorbers in a cool, dry place.

Rehydration:
1-3 tsp Powder
1 cup Boiling Water for hot coffee.
For iced coffee use ¾ cup of cold water, stir, and add ½ cup of ice.

Tips:
Adding a little brown sugar could enhance the spiced flavors when rehydrating.

Vanilla Cold Brew Coffee

Indulge in the comforting notes of Vanilla Cold Brew Coffee. Smooth, aromatic, and easy to make, it's the perfect sip for those who crave a little luxury in their daily grind.

Cups:	8	Servings:	8	Serving Size:	1 cup (240 g)	Calories:	5
Prep Time:		12 hrs + 20 min	Freeze-Dry Time:		25-35 hrs	Shelf-Life:	20-25 yrs

Ingredients:
2 cups Ground Coffee Beans
8 cups Cold Water
2 Vanilla Beans, split lengthwise

Other Items:
Pitcher or Jar
Cheesecloth or Coffee Filter

3 cups coffee needed for tray size Small
4 cups coffee needed for tray size Medium

5 cups coffee needed for tray size Large
10 cups coffee needed for tray size X-Large

Directions:
In a pitcher or jar, mix ground coffee with vanilla beans and cold water. Cover and steep in the fridge for 12 to 24 hours. Strain through a cheesecloth or coffee filter to remove the grounds. Place your empty tray in the freezer and pour your coffee onto your tray. Pre-freeze until solid. Freeze-dry on normal settings for 25-35 hours or until completely dry and crumbly. Pulverize into a fine powder using a food processor or blender. Store in airtight containers or mylar bags with oxygen absorbers in a cool, dry place.

Rehydration:
1-3 tsp Powder
1 cup Boiling Water for hot coffee.
For iced coffee use ¾ cup of cold water, stir, and add ½ cup of ice.

Tips:
Vanilla offers a naturally sweet undertone to the coffee. You may not need to add any sweetener, or perhaps less than usual. Also, try adding a splash of cream or milk when rehydrating for a smoother, richer flavor.

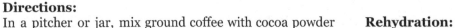

Mocha Cold Brew Coffee

Unveil a layer of indulgence with each sip. A harmonious blend of coffee and chocolate makes it the ideal pick-me-up for any time of day.

Cups:	8	Servings:	8	Serving Size:	1 cup (240 g)	Calories:	15
Prep Time:		12 hrs + 20 min	Freeze-Dry Time:		25-35 hrs	Shelf-Life:	10-15 yrs

Ingredients:
2 cups Ground Coffee Beans
8 cups Cold Water
⅓ cup Unsweetened Cocoa Powder

Other Items:
Pitcher or Jar
Cheesecloth or Coffee Filter

3 cups coffee needed for tray size Small
4 cups coffee needed for tray size Medium

5 cups coffee needed for tray size Large
10 cups coffee needed for tray size X-Large

Directions:
In a pitcher or jar, mix ground coffee with cocoa powder and cold water. Cover and steep in the fridge for 12 to 24 hours. Strain through a cheesecloth or coffee filter to remove the grounds. Place your empty tray in the freezer and pour your coffee onto your tray. Pre-freeze until solid. Freeze-dry on normal settings for 25-35 hours or until completely dry and crumbly. Pulverize into a fine powder using a food processor or blender. Store in airtight containers or mylar bags with oxygen absorbers in a cool, dry place.

Rehydration:
1-3 tsp Powder
1 cup Boiling Water for hot coffee.
For iced coffee use ¾ cup of cold water, stir, and add ½ cup of ice.

Tips:
Add a bit of honey or stevia to sweeten the rich, cocoa flavor.

Bone Broth

Transform nutritious homemade bone broth into a convenient and versatile powder, perfect for adding depth and flavor to soups, stews, and sauces, or simply rehydrating for a warm, comforting drink.

Cups:	8	**Servings:**	8	**Serving Size:**	1 cup (240 g)	**Calories:**	45
Prep/Cook Time:	24 hrs + 40 min	**Freeze-Dry Time:**		25-35 hrs		**Shelf-Life:**	10-15 yrs

Ingredients:

2 lbs Mixed Bones (chicken, beef, or turkey)
2 large Carrots, roughly chopped
2 large Celery Stalks, roughly chopped
½ tsp Black Peppercorns
2 Tbs Apple Cider Vinegar

1 large Onion, quartered
2 cloves Garlic, smashed
1 tsp Salt
2 Bay Leaves
12 cups Water

3 cups broth needed for tray size Small
4 cups broth needed for tray size Medium

5 cups broth needed for tray size Large
10 cups broth needed for tray size X-Large

Directions:

Roast bones at 400°F for 30 minutes. Place in a large pot and add all other ingredients. Bring to a boil, then reduce heat and simmer on low for 24-48 hours, adding water as needed to keep bones submerged. Strain broth through a fine mesh sieve, discarding solids, and allow the broth to cool. Place your empty tray in the freezer and pour the broth onto your tray. Pre-freeze until solid. Freeze-dry on normal settings for 25-35 hours or until completely dry and crumbly. Pulverize into a fine powder using a food processor or blender. Store in airtight containers or mylar bags with oxygen absorbers in a cool, dry place.

Rehydration:

4 Tbs Powder
1 cup Water
Mix powder with water and stir. Add more or less for consistency and flavor.

Tips:

Bone broth powder is a great source of protein and collagen, perfect for dietary supplements. Opt for organic, grass-fed beef bones and organic, pasture-raised poultry.

Vegetable Broth

Create your own vegetable broth powder from scratch, ideal for vegans and vegetarians looking to add a quick and easy flavor boost to their meals without the hassle of liquid broth.

Cups:	8	**Servings:**	8	**Serving Size:**	1 cup (240 g)	**Calories:**	20
Prep/Cook Time:	2 hrs + 30 min	**Freeze-Dry Time:**		25-35 hrs		**Shelf-Life:**	20-25 yrs

Ingredients:

4 large Carrots, chopped
4 large Celery Stalks, chopped
2 large Onions, chopped
4 cloves Garlic, smashed

1 cup Mushrooms, chopped (optional)
½ tsp Black Peppercorns
2 Bay Leaves
1 tsp Salt
12 cups Water

3 cups broth needed for tray size Small
4 cups broth needed for tray size Medium

5 cups broth needed for tray size Large
10 cups broth needed for tray size X-Large

Directions:

Combine all ingredients in a large pot. Bring to a boil, then reduce heat and simmer for 1-2 hours, or until the broth is flavorful. Strain broth through a fine mesh sieve, discarding solids, and allow the broth to cool. Place your empty tray in the freezer and pour the broth onto your tray. Pre-freeze until solid. Freeze-dry on normal settings for 25-35 hours or until completely dry and crumbly. Pulverize into a fine powder using a food processor or blender. Store in airtight containers or mylar bags with oxygen absorbers in a cool, dry place.

Rehydration:

4 Tbs Powder
1 cup Water
Mix powder with water and stir. Add more or less for consistency and flavor.

Tips:

Customize your vegetable broth powder by adding different herbs and spices according to your preference. Also great as a base for soups or for seasoning rice and pasta dishes.

Cherry Electrolyte Drink

Enhance the water for your hike with electrolytes found in natural juices, providing 1,071 mg Potassium, 710 mg Sodium, and 47 mg Magnesium.

Tbs:	10	Servings:	2	Serving Size:	5 Tbs + 2 cups (480 g)	Calories:	175
Prep Time:	15 min	Freeze-Dry Time:	25-35 hrs			Shelf-Life:	15-20 yrs

Ingredients: (Makes 5½ cups liquid)
4 cups Unsweetened Coconut Water
1 cup 100% Pure Tart Cherry Juice
½ cup 100% Pure Lemon Juice
½ tsp Redmond Real Salt or Himalayan Salt
½ tsp Pure Cane Sugar (optional - adds 5 calories)

3 cups mixture needed for tray size Small
4 cups mixture needed for tray size Medium

5 cups mixture needed for tray size Large
10 cups mixture needed for tray size X-Large

Directions:
Purchase liquids and/or run fruits through a juicer. The salt must be pure with no additives. Stir all ingredients together until blended. Place your empty tray in the freezer and pour your liquids onto your tray. Pre-freeze until solid. Freeze-dry on normal settings for 25-35 hours or until completely dry and crumbly. Pulverize into a fine powder using a grinder or blender. Store the electrolyte powder in airtight containers or mylar bags with oxygen absorbers in a cool, dry place.

Rehydration:
5 Tbs Powder
16 oz (2 cups) Water
Mix powder with water and shake until dissolved.

Tips: For enhanced results rehydrate your drink mix powder with Sparkling Water. If you already have the powders, an individual serving is 2 Tbs Coconut Water Pwd + 2 Tbs Cherry Juice Pwd + 1 Tbs Lemon Juice Pwd + ¼ tsp Redmond Real Salt + ¼ tsp Cane Sugar added to 16 oz of Water.

Electrolyte Boost

Add this electrolyte mix to a 24 oz bottle of water to get a boost of minerals. Provides 1,042 mg Potassium, 1,140 mg Sodium, and 45 mg Magnesium. Use juice to get the boost with a sweeter flavor.

Tbs:	36	Servings:	96	Serving Size:	1⅛ tsp + 3 cups (720 g)	Calories:	4
Prep Time:	10 min	Freeze-Dry Time:	n/a			Shelf-Life:	20-25 yrs

Bulk Powder Ingredients:
1 cup Redmond Real Salt or Himalayan Salt
½ cup Pure Cane Sugar
½ cup Pure Potassium Chloride Powder
¼ cup Pure Magnesium Glycinate Powder

Directions:
Measure out dry ingredients and mix. Pulverize into a fine powder using a grinder or blender. Store the electrolyte powder in airtight containers or mylar bags with oxygen absorbers in a cool, dry place.

Rehydration:
1⅛ tsp Powder (rounded teaspoon)
24 oz Water or Juice
Mix powder with water and shake until dissolved. This amount can be doubled.

Tips:
For one individual 24 oz Bottle of Water or Juice add ½ tsp Redmond Real Salt, ¼ tsp Pure Cane Sugar, ¼ tsp Pure Potassium Chloride Powder, and ⅛ tsp Pure Magnesium Glycinate Powder

APPENDIX THREE: WORKSHEETS

The provided worksheets are designed to assist you with preparations before and reminders during your backpacking trips. These sheets contain informational sections, prompts, record-keeping spaces, and to-do lists, all aimed at ensuring your meal planning, supply sourcing, and ultimately your expedition, goes seamlessly. You have the option to print out these pages and store them in a three-ring binder for convenient organization.

Scan the QR code for a printable PDF
or visit: BPPDF.2MHE.COM.

Backpacking Worksheets

Food Worksheets

FD Kitchen Worksheets

Record Keeping Worksheets

IMPORTANT BACKPACKING PRINCIPLES

Research & plan for your adventure! Here are a few things to keep in mind.

Backpackers need:
- [ ] Food
- [ ] Water
- [ ] Shelter
- [ ] Warmth
- [ ] Light
- [ ] Safety

Backpacking food should be:
- [ ] Nutritious
- [ ] Lightweight
- [ ] Packable
- [ ] Shelf-stable
- [ ] Ready-to-eat
- [ ] Easy Clean-up

Backpacker Care:
- [ ] Get Enough Sleep
- [ ] Consume Nutritious Foods
- [ ] Stay Hydrated
- [ ] Keep Fit and Limber
- [ ] Dress for the Weather
- [ ] Protect Yourself
- [ ] Be Sanitary
- [ ] Learn Extra Skills

Backpacking Principles:
- [ ] Understand the Environment
- [ ] Carefully Plan the Trip
- [ ] Menu Plan for Nutrients
- [ ] Prepare & Pack Supplies
- [ ] Map Routes & Exit Routes
- [ ] Locate Supply Points
- [ ] Know Your Water Sources
- [ ] Leave Trip Info With a Friend

Backpacker Paperwork:
- [ ] Driver's License or ID
- [ ] Permits or Passport, if needed
- [ ] Insurance Plan Information
- [ ] Allergy Information
- [ ] List of Medications
- [ ] Emergency Contact List
- [ ] Credit Card, Cash
- [ ] Wallet, Keys

Backpacking Tips:
- [ ] Physically Train for Long Hikes
- [ ] Find a Backpack that Fits Right
- [ ] Select the Best Gear for You
- [ ] Pack Meals with lots of Calories
- [ ] Select Hikes Suited to your Abilities
- [ ] Always Hike with a Buddy
- [ ] Preserve Surroundings
- [ ] Embrace Nature

Leave No Trace Principles:
- [ ] Plan Ahead And Prepare
- [ ] Travel & Camp On Durable Surfaces
- [ ] Respect Wildlife
- [ ] Leave What You Find
- [ ] Minimize Campfire Impacts
- [ ] Dispose of Waste Properly
- [ ] Be Considerate Of Other Visitors

Mistakes to Avoid:
- [ ] Improper Footwear
- [ ] Not Practicing with Your Pack
- [ ] Carrying Too Much or Too Little Gear
- [ ] Running Out of Water or Food
- [ ] Ignoring the Weather or Wildlife
- [ ] Leaving Behind Damage or Garbage
- [ ] Not Enough Trip Research

BACKPACKING SUPPLIES CHECKLIST

When choosing from the suggested supplies, be mindful of your pack's weight; only pack what you'll use. Not every backpacker will need every item.

Tools
- [ ] Backpack and Pack Cover
- [ ] Multi-tool
- [ ] Knife
- [ ] Paracord, Carabiners
- [ ] Duct Tape
- [ ] Notebook & Pen

Navigation
- [ ] Physical Maps
- [ ] Compass/GPS
- [ ] Binoculars
- [ ] Two-Way Radio
- [ ] Cell Phone & Solar Charger
- [ ] Camera

Protection
- [ ] Sunscreen, Aloe
- [ ] Sunglasses
- [ ] Pepper Spray
- [ ] Lip Balm
- [ ] Whistle
- [ ] Signaling Mirror

Hydration
- [ ] Water Bottles
- [ ] Hydration Bladders
- [ ] Water Filter
- [ ] Measuring Cup
- [ ] Collapsible Bucket
- [ ] Back up Water Purification

Nutrition
- [ ] Calorie-Dense Meals
- [ ] Extra Day's Supply of Food
- [ ] Energy Food (bars, chews)
- [ ] Energy Beverages
- [ ] Trail Mix and Snacks
- [ ] Food Canister or Hang Bag

Kitchen
- [ ] Stove Kit
- [ ] Cooking Fuel
- [ ] Cookset
- [ ] Dishes
- [ ] Utensils
- [ ] Collapsible Cup

Clothes-Warm Weather
- [ ] Wicking T-shirt
- [ ] Wicking Underwear
- [ ] Quick-drying Pants or Shorts
- [ ] Sun-shielding Hat/Bandana
- [ ] Long-sleeve Shirt for Sun

Clothes-Cool Weather
- [ ] Wicking long-sleeve T-shirt
- [ ] Wicking Long Underwear
- [ ] Pants
- [ ] Gloves, Hat
- [ ] Fleece Jacket

Footwear
- [ ] Boots or Hiking Shoes
- [ ] Synthetic or Wool Socks
- [ ] Sandals
- [ ] Gaiters
- [ ] Other - Raingear

Shelter
- [ ] Tent/Tarp
- [ ] Reflective Blanket
- [ ] Sleeping Bag and Pad
- [ ] Stuffable Pillowcase

Fire
- [ ] Lighter
- [ ] Matches
- [ ] Fire Starter
- [ ] Waterproof Container

Light
- [ ] Flashlight
- [ ] Headlamp
- [ ] Batteries
- [ ] Lantern

Hygiene
- [ ] Biodegradable Hand Soap
- [ ] Quick-dry Towel
- [ ] Insect Repellent
- [ ] Toiletry & Dental Items
- [ ] Condoms
- [ ] Ziplock bags

Sanitation
- [ ] Biodegradable Dish Soap
- [ ] Dish Sponge
- [ ] Toilet Paper, in small rolls
- [ ] Sanitation Trowel
- [ ] Wag Bags
- [ ] Sealable Garbage Bags

Emergency
- [ ] First Aid Kit
- [ ] Travel Sewing Kit
- [ ] Field Guides
- [ ] Paperwork in sealed bag
- [ ] Cash/Credit
- [ ] Exit Routes

FIRST AID KIT CHECKLIST

Get your basic First Aid Kit ready for the trail

- [ ] Disposable Gloves (2 pairs)
- [ ] Scissors, compact
- [ ] Tweezers
- [ ] Thermometer
- [ ] Safety Pins
- [ ] Waterproof Adhesive Bandages
- [ ] Triangular Bandages (sling)
- [ ] Elastic Bandages
- [ ] Adhesive Tape
- [ ] Moleskin, Cotton Balls, & Q-Tips
- [ ] Sterile Gauze Pads, Steri-strips
- [ ] Antiseptic Wipes
- [ ] Antiseptic Spray/Solution

- [ ] Alcohol-based Hand Sanitizer
- [ ] CPR Mask
- [ ] Instant Cold Packs
- [ ] Burn Shield/Burn Cream
- [ ] Antiseptic Ointment
- [ ] Pain Relievers
- [ ] Antihistamines
- [ ] Antidiarrheal Medication
- [ ] Charcoal Tablets
- [ ] Malaria Kit, if needed
- [ ] Snakebite Kit, if needed
- [ ] Personal Medications
- [ ] First Aid Manual

TOILETRY & DENTAL ITEMS

Grab these items to make hygiene more comfortable on the trail!

- [ ] Eco-friendly Concentrated Soap
- [ ] Travel Solid Deodorant
- [ ] Nail Clippers
- [ ] Nail File
- [ ] Travel Hairbrush & Hair Ties
- [ ] Travel Razor
- [ ] Glasses/Contact Supplies
- [ ] Feminine Hygiene Products

- [ ] Pack of Facial Tissue
- [ ] Toothbrush
- [ ] Biodegradeable Toothpaste
- [ ] Floss or Flosser
- [ ] Pick or Toolset
- [ ] Mouthwash
- [ ] Lozenges
- [ ] Sugar-free Gum

TRAIL LOG

Date:	Location:	
Start Time:	End Time:	Total Time:

Names of Backpacking Companions	Trail Nick Name

Trail Name:	**Parking Available:** ☐ Yes ☐ No $
Distance:	**Park Fees:** ☐ No ☐ Yes: $
Type: ☐ Loop ☐ Out & Back ☐ One Way	**Permits Needed:** ☐ No ☐ Yes:
Difficulty: ☐ Easy ☐ Intermediate ☐ Hard	**Extra Regulations:** ☐ No ☐ Yes:

Season: ☐ Spring ☐ Summer ☐ Fall ☐ Winter **Temperature:** ☐ Nice ☐ Hot ☐ Cool ☐ Cold

Expected Weather: ☐ Sunny ☐ Partly Cloudy ☐ Cloudy ☐ Windy ☐ Rain ☐ Snow ☐ Storms

Plants & Animals Observed:

Challenges Experienced:

Favorite Memories:

MEAL PLANNING INFORMATION

The following worksheets will help you create complete meal plans which will provide nutrition for the days you go backpacking.

The Calories Lists

Using the information from all the recipes and foods from this book we compiled lists of calories to help you quickly and easily select foods for your daily diet.

Calculate

With our worksheet it's simple to calculate the calories needed. You will multiply your body weight by your activity level to get the calories needed for the day. This can then be broken down per meal by multiplying by the percentage. We have a chart of examples to get you started.

Understanding Our Meal Plans & Grocery Lists

Our meal plans are designed with convenience and efficiency in mind. Each meal has a set of recipes that are created to yield larger quantities, typically serving a minimum of four people at 2 servings each. This approach allows you maximize the benefits of freeze-drying by preparing meals in bulk and ensuring you have a stockpile of ready-to-eat meals for your future adventures. Select an example meal plan, print off a grocery list and individual blank worksheets, and determine your caloric needs.

For example, someone weighing 150 lbs going on a 1 hour hike needs about 750 calories for breakfast. When French Toast Sticks are chosen for breakfast a serving has 204 calories. The recipe has 10 servings, which means you can have 2 servings and you can also provide 2 servings for 4 other people. Keep in mind that the grocery list accounts for the entire recipe, not just the portion consumed in the meal. This approach is cost-effective and time-saving, as it reduces the frequency of both cooking and grocery shopping. This supply can be especially useful for busy days, unexpected guests, or emergency situations.

Blank meal plans

We've included a blank daily worksheet and a blank 3-day worksheet that can be used to design your own delicious meal plans. Visit BPPDF.2MHE.COM or use the Printable Worksheets QR Code to print off as many blank worksheets as you need. To fill out a worksheet you will need the food name and the calories (kcal) for the number of servings you plan to eat. Once you have it filled in, simply add up the kcal to make sure you have enough calories for each day.

More Meal Plans!

To get your hands on the printable pages of these and even more meal plans, scan the QR code or visit BPMP.2MHE.COM.

Calories of a Serving of the Recipes

Breakfast

123	Blueberry Lemon Granola
127	Cornmeal Muffin Bites
171	Spinach Sunrise Skillet
174	Savory Sausage Scramble
177	Banana Pancakes
187	Hearty Pancakes
204	French Toast Sticks
217	Cheesy Grits
218	Chocolate Muffin Bites
219	Choco-Raspberry Chia Pudding
225	Blueberry Vanilla Chia Pudding
230	Breakfast Brunch
232	Pumpkin Pie Oatmeal
239	Berries and Cream Oatmeal
245	Denver Delight Quiche
248	Apple Pie Oatmeal
271	Mango Coconut Chia Pudding
275	Ham Brunch
298	Hearty Breakfast Casserole
305	Classic Ham and Egg Quiche
315	Cinnamon Roll Bites

Lunch

130	Veggie Shepherd's Pie
163	Turkey Sweet Potato Skillet
195	Basil Chicken Stir Fry
206	Vegetarian Quinoa Casserole
206	Fiesta Chicken
232	Egg Roll in a Bowl
241	Beef Bulgogi
250	Mexican Enchilada Casserole
255	Sweet and Sour Pork
278	Zucchini Parmesan
285	Vegetarian Chili
300	Chicken, Rice, Broccoli Casserole
332	Lazy Lasagna
337	Tuna Noodle Casserole
360	Chicken Salad
365	Hamburger Mac
377	Vegetable Quesadilla Strips
434	Chicken Quesadilla Strips
461	Easy Grilled Cheese Bites
470	Beef Quesadilla Strips
489	Sloppy Joe Casserole

Dinner

126	Chickpea Curry
158	Rice and Vegetable Medley
167	Herbed Mushroom Risotto
176	Beef & Barley Stew
184	Beef Stew
190	Fried Rice
202	Beef Stroganoff

Dinner (cont.)

213	Chicken Korma
219	Beef Vegetable Stew
226	Loaded Veggie Goulash
242	Yellow Chicken Curry
243	Lemon Herb Chicken
269	Pork Carnitas
319	Classic Chili
327	Steak Strips & Vegetables
350	Pad Thai
359	Spicy Pork Chili
380	Cheesy Macaroni
385	Chicken Alfredo Pasta
388	Pork Lo Mein
407	Meat Lovers Chili

Soups

49	Tomato Soup
106	Pumpkin Soup
107	Vegetable Medley Soup
119	Vegetable Barley Soup
120	Beef Noodle Soup
125	Creamy Tomato Basil Soup
129	Chicken Noodle Soup
131	Spicy Shrimp & Corn Chowder
136	Italian Wedding Soup
137	Spicy Chicken Tortilla Soup
141	Potato Leek Soup
151	Thai Coconut Curry Soup
153	Minestrone Soup
160	Creamy Mushroom Soup
163	Broccoli Cheddar Soup
173	Creamy Salmon & Dill Soup
187	Lentil Soup
195	Seafood Chowder
225	Tuscan White Bean Soup
227	Lentil, Sausage & Potato Soup
354	Southwest Black Bean Soup

Snacks

43	Cauliflower Nibbles
44	Salsa
49	Vegetable Crisps
58	Apple Pie Trail Mix
64	Sweet Potato Cubes
72	Pineapple Applesauce
74	Blueberry Applesauce
80	Pear Sauce
84	Berry S'mores Trail Mix
84	Fruit Crisps
89	Garden Herb Trail Mix
89	Nutty Nanners Trail Mix
98	Choco-Raspberry Trail Mix
100	Mixed Fruit Medley

Snacks (cont.)

106	Tropical Bliss Trail Mix
106	Cheese Crisps
108	Peachy Keen Trail Mix
117	Ranch Dip
118	Berry Nutty Trail Mix
138	Spicy Fiesta Trail Mix
160	Strawberry Yogurt Drops

Treats

90	Marshmallows
91	Oil-Free Brownie Bites
100	Mini Ice Cream Cones
110	Taffy Puffs
110-150	Mini Cookies
116	Drizzled Banana Crisps
116	Lemon Burst Cookies
120	Colorful Candy Orbs
130	Popped Caramel Spheres
130	Tropical Smoothie Cubes
131	Berry Smoothie Cubes
138	Strawberry Pudding
150	Ice Cream Sandwich Sticks
171	Simple Cherry Cobbler
184	Quick Peach Cobbler
187	Creamy Ice Cream
192	Zucchini Cake Bites
197	S'mores Bites
204	Lemon Tea Bread Bites
223	Butterscotch Pudding
334	Creamsicle Cubes

Drinks

3	Cold Brew Coffee
4	Electrolyte Boost
5	Spiced Cold Brew Coffee
5	Vanilla Cold Brew Coffee
15	Mocha Cold Brew Coffee
20	Vegetable Broth
45	Bone Broth
50-70	Vegetable Juices
50-80	Greens Juices
80-150	Dairy Milk
90	Carrot Juice
90-110	Fruit Juices
90-120	Citrus Juices
110	Rice Milk
130	Pineapple Juice
130	Oat Milk
175	Cherry Electrolyte Drink
180	Chocolate Milk
240	Strawberry Milk
150-200	Protein Shakes
160-300	Smoothies

Calories of a Serving of Individual Foods

Fruits pg 70

17	Lemons
20	Limes
26	Rhubarb
30	Plums
32	Cranberries
40	Tangerines
42	Kiwi, Golden
46	Watermelon
47	Mandarins
49	Strawberries
50	Peaches
51	Apricots
52	Grapefruit
60	Cantaloupe
62	Blackberries
62	Grapes
62	Nectarines
64	Honeydew
64	Raspberries
75	Oranges
82	Pineapple
84	Blueberries
87	Cherries
99	Mangos
101	Pears
104	Apples
105	Bananas
117	Pomegranate
159	Coconut Meat
160	Avocados

Vegetables pg 73

4	Peppers, Hot
5	Garlic
5	Scallions
6	Celery
7	Spinach
7	Swiss Chard
8	Cucumber
8	Kale
10	Bok Choy
10	Lettuce
11	Eggplant
15	Mushrooms
16	Tomatoes
18	Okra
18	Squash, Yellow
19	Radish
20	Asparagus
21	Squash, Zucchini
22	Cabbage

Vegetables (cont.)

25	Carrots
27	Cauliflower
27	Leeks
27	Peas, Snap/Snow
28	Brussel Sprouts
29	Beets
31	Broccoli
31	Green Beans
34	Turnips
39	Peppers, Sweet
42	Squash, Spaghetti
44	Onions
45	Mixed Vegetables
49	Pumpkin
52	Rutabaga
62	Peas, Green
75	Parsnips
82	Squash, Butternut
88	Corn
158	Yams
162	Sweet Potatoes
164	Potatoes

Meat & Seafood pg 80

58	Chicken
60	Scallops
61	Ham
67	Turkey
70	Roast Beef
77	Haddock
78	Eggs
85	Shrimp
89	Cod
100	Crab
105	Bass
109	Snapper
110	Tilapia
110	Tuna
111	Anchovies
120	Turkey Bacon
120	Lobster
122	Catfish
130	Clams
134	Herring
140	Carp
150	Mussels
160	Ground Beef
160	Stew Meat
160	Bacon
160	Pork Loin/Roast
160	Oysters

Meat & Seafood (cont.)

162	Trout
175	Salmon
177	Sardines
180	Steak
190	Ham
190	Roasted Poultry
200	Beef Patties
220	Kabobs/Beef Strips
220	Ground Poultry
220	Poultry Slices or Strips
223	Mackerel
227	Beef Filets
255	Beef Pot Roast
324	Meatballs
328	Pork Chops

Dairy pg 78

15	Whipped Cream
39	Ricotta Cheese
51	Cream Cheese
57	Sour Cream
60	Almond Milk
80	Skim Milk
80	Feta Cheese
84	Cottage Cheese
90	Mozzarella Cheese
100	Sweet Cream
100	1% Milk
100	Swiss Cheese
100	Brie Cheese
110	Rice Milk
110	Colby Cheese
110	Parmesan Cheese
120	Cheddar Cheese
122	2% Milk
139	Kefir
150	Whole Milk
154	Plain Yogurt
160	1% Chocolate Milk
208	Vanilla Yogurt
243	Blueberry Yogurt
243	Strawberry Yogurt
250	Strawberry Ice Cream
270	Vanilla Ice Cream
270	Butter Pecan Ice Cream
270	Pecan Praline Ice Cream
285	Chocolate Ice Cream
300	Mint Chocolate Chip Ice Cream
320	Cookie Dough Ice Cream
330	Cookies & Cream Ice Cream
450	Coconut Milk

Legumes & Grains pg 84		**Condiment Packets**		**Seeds & Nuts**	
10	Sprouts	0	Pepper Packet, 0.1 g	159	Pistachios, 1 oz, 1/4 cup
80	Tofu	0	Salt Packet, 0.6 g	160	Almonds, 1 oz or 24 nuts
90	Edamame	0	Mustard Packet, 7 g	160	Pepitas, 1 oz, 1/4 cup
110	Quinoa	0	Dill Relish Packet, 9 g	160	Cashews, 1 oz
110	Seitan	0	Vinegar Packet, 9 g	180	Pine Nuts, 1 oz, 3 Tbs
140	Oats	6	Soy Sauce Packet, 8 g	180	Sunflower Kernels, 1 oz, 1/4 cup
150	Tempeh	7	Hot Sauce Packet, 7 g	180	Peanuts, 1 oz or 40 nuts
160	Buckwheat	10	Ketchup Packet, 9 g	184	Brazil Nuts, 1 oz
170	Wheat Berries	15	Sweet Relish Packet, 9 g	190	Walnuts, 1 oz, 1/4 cup
176	Couscous	26	Honey Packet, 9 g	190	Pecans, 1 oz, 1/4 cup
193	Barley	35	Jelly Packet, 14 g	200	Macadamia Nuts, 1 oz, 1/4 cup
210	Rice	52	Ranch Packet, 12 g		**Store Snacks**
210	Pasta	78	Vegetable Oil Packet, 9 g	70	Club Crackers, ½ oz or 4 crackers
230	Lentils	90	Mayonnaise Packet, 12 g	70	Turkey Jerky, 1 oz
230	Peas, dry	120	Avocado Oil, 1 Tbs, 15 g	80	Beef Jerky, 1 oz
240	Beans, dry	210	Peanut Butter Packet, 32 g	100	Meat Stick, 1 oz
270	Chickpeas	220	Almond Butter Packet, 32 g	190	Peanut Butter Crackers, 39 g
				190	Cheese Sandwich Crackers, 39 g

Determine Calories Needed

Select Your Activity Level for the Day:

Low Activity/Rest Day	15
Moderate Activity/1 hr hike	20
High Activity/2 hr hike w pack	25
Extreme Activity/6 hr hike w pack	30

When to Eat Your Calories:

While backpacking, it is recommended to consume your calories as follows:

25%	Breakfast
15%	Lunch
25%	Dinner
35%	Snacks

Quickly Calculate the Calories Needed for Your Day:

Body Weight in pounds multiplied by Activity Level equals Calories Needed Daily. Break it down further into meals by multiplying by the percentage.

Weight (lbs)	**Activity Level**	**Calories Needed**	
			x 0.25 **Breakfast** =
			x 0.15 **Lunch** =
	x	=	x 0.25 **Dinner** =
			x 0.35 **Snacks** =

Examples:

Weight	Activity		Calories	Breakfast	Lunch	Dinner	Snacks
50 lbs	x	15	750	188	112	188	262
	x	20	1,000	250	150	250	350
	x	25	1,250	313	187	313	437
	x	30	1,500	375	225	375	525
75 lbs	x	15	1,125	281	169	281	394
	x	20	1,500	375	225	375	525
	x	25	1,875	469	281	469	656
	x	30	2,250	562	338	562	788
100 lbs	x	15	1,500	375	225	375	525
	x	20	2,000	500	300	500	700
	x	25	2,500	625	375	625	875
	x	30	3,000	750	450	750	1,050
125 lbs	x	15	1,875	469	281	469	656
	x	20	2,500	625	375	625	875
	x	25	3,125	781	469	781	1,094
	x	30	3,750	938	562	938	1,312
150 lbs	x	15	2,250	562	338	562	788
	x	20	3,000	750	450	750	1,050
	x	25	3,750	938	562	938	1,312
	x	30	4,500	1,125	675	1,125	1,575
175 lbs	x	15	2,625	656	394	656	919
	x	20	3,500	875	525	875	1,225
	x	25	4,375	1,094	656	1,094	1,531
	x	30	5,250	1,312	788	1,312	1,838
200 lbs	x	15	3,000	750	450	750	1,050
	x	20	4,000	1,000	600	1,000	1,400
	x	25	5,000	1,250	750	1,250	1,750
	x	30	6,000	1,500	900	1,500	2,100
225 lbs	x	15	3,375	844	506	844	1,181
	x	20	4,500	1,125	675	1,125	1,575
	x	25	5,625	1,406	844	1,406	1,969
	x	30	6,750	1,688	1,012	1,688	2,362
250 lbs	x	15	3,750	938	562	938	1,312
	x	20	5,000	1,250	750	1,250	1,750
	x	25	6,250	1,562	938	1,562	2,188
	x	30	7,500	1,875	1,125	1,875	2,625
275 lbs	x	15	4,125	1,031	619	1,031	1,444
	x	20	5,500	1,375	825	1,375	1,925
	x	25	6,875	1,719	1,031	1,719	2,406
	x	30	8,250	2,062	1,238	2,062	2,888

*Meal Plan for:*_____ *date:*_____

Easily calculate the calories needed for your day by multiplying your body weight in pounds by your expected activity level. Determine per meal by multiplying the daily calories by the percentage.

Low Activity/Rest Day	15
Moderate Activity/1 hr hike	20
High Activity/2 hr hike w pack	25
Extreme Activity/6 hr hike w pack	30

Weight (lbs)	Activity Level	Daily Calories Needed
	x	=

x 0.25 Breakfast =	
x 0.15 Lunch =	
x 0.25 Dinner =	
x 0.35 Snacks =	

	Food	Servings	kcal
Breakfast 25%			
Lunch 15%			
Dinner 25%			
Additions 35%			

Daily Total kcal:

Meal Plan 1

Easily calculate the calories needed for your day by multiplying your body weight in pounds by your expected activity level. Determine per meal by multiplying the daily calories by the percentage.

Low Activity/Rest Day	15
Moderate Activity/1 hr hike	20
High Activity/2 hr hike w pack	25
Extreme Activity/6 hr hike w pack	30

Weight (lbs)	Activity Level	Daily Calories Needed
		1500

x 0.25	Breakfast =		375
x 0.15	Lunch =		225
x 0.25	Dinner =		375
x 0.35	Snacks =		525

	Food	Servings	kcal
Breakfast 25% (357)	Ham Brunch (pg 93)	½	137
	Berries & Cream Oatmeal (pg 94)	½	119
	Freeze-dried Pears (pg 72)	1	101
Lunch 15% (245)	Egg Roll in a Bowl (pg 106)	½	116
	Freeze-dried White Rice (pg 86)	½	105
	Vegetable Crisps (pg 140)	½	24
Dinner 25% (312)	Mexican Enchilada Casserole (pg 101)	1	250
	Freeze-dried Spaghetti Squash (pg 77)	1	42
	Freeze-dried Asparagus (pg 73)	1	20
Additions 35% (626)	Spicy Fiesta Trail Mix (pg 133)	1	138
	Chocolate Muffin Bites (pg 99)	½	109
	Freeze-dried Plums (pg 72)	1	30
	Pecans (pg 169)	½	95
	Colorful Candy Orbs (pg 141)	½	50
	S'mores Bites (pg 142)	½	98
	Cheese Crisps (pg 140)	1	106

Daily Total kcal: (1541)

Grocery List for Meal Plan 1

Dry Goods	**Dairy**	**Canned/Carton Goods**
6 slices Bread	8 cups 2% Milk	3 cans Enchilada Sauce
6 Corn Tortillas	4 cups shredded Cheddar Cheese	2 cans Black Beans
8 cups Old-Fashioned Rolled Oats	1 lb Pepper Jack Cheese	2 cans Corn
4 cups Teddy Grahams	1 lb Monterey Jack Cheese	½ cup Applesauce
1 cup Pecans	14 large Eggs	
1 cup Spicy Peanuts		
½ cup Pepitas Seeds		
½ cup Sunflower Seeds		

Pantry Staples	**Produce**	**Freeze-dried Stock**
2 cups Flour	2 cup Mixed Berries	(Process a batch if you need them)
2 cup Granulated Sugar	2 medium 5" Sweet Potatoes	Freeze-dried Pears
¾ cup Cocoa Powder	2 medium 2" Beets	Freeze-dried Plums
2½ tsp Baking Powder	2 small 2" Turnips	Freeze-dried Corn
1½ tsp Black Pepper	3 small 1" x 5" Carrots	Freeze-dried Asparagus
4 tsp Salt	2 cups grated Carrots	Freeze-dried Spaghetti Squash
2 tsp Vanilla Extract	3 small 1" x 5" Parsnips	Freeze-dried White Rice
½ cup Soy Sauce	1 small Onion	Freeze-dried Mini Marshmallows
½ tsp Mustard	1 large Onion	
	1 large sweet Onion	
	8 Green Onions	
	8 cloves Garlic	
	2 Tbs fresh grated Ginger	
	3 cups Spinach	
	7 cups thinly sliced Cabbage	

Butcher/Deli Case		**Other**
1 lb Ham		50 oz Party Bag of Skittles
4 lbs Ground Beef		2 cup M&M's Candies

This grocery list will make multiple servings of each recipe and feeds about 4 people for 1 day.

Meal Plan 2

Easily calculate the calories needed for your day by multiplying your body weight in pounds by your expected activity level. Determine per meal by multiplying the daily calories by the percentage.

Low Activity/Rest Day	15
Moderate Activity/1 hr hike	20
High Activity/2 hr hike w pack	25
Extreme Activity/6 hr hike w pack	30

Weight (lbs)	Activity Level	Daily Calories Needed
		2000

x 0.25	Breakfast =	500
x 0.15	Lunch =	300
x 0.25	Dinner =	500
x 0.35	Snacks =	700

	Food	servings	kcal
Breakfast 25% (498)	Hearty Breakfast Casserole (pg 94)	1	298
	Strawberry Pudding (pg 148)	1	138
	Freeze-dried Grapes (pg 71)	1	62
Lunch 15% (382)	Chicken, Rice, & Broccoli Casserole (pg 102)	1	300
	Butternut Squash Crisps (pg 77)	1	82
Dinner 25% (469)	Tuscan White Bean Soup (pg 125)	1½	337
	Club Crackers (pg 169)	1	70
	Freeze-dried Peas (pg 76)	1	62
Additions 35% (684)	Garden Herb Trail Mix (pg 134)	1	89
	Zucchini Cake Bites (pg 145)	½	96
	Freeze-dried Blueberries (pg 70)	1	84
	Sunflower Kernels (pg 169)	1	180
	Tropical Mango Smoothie Cubes (pg 149)	½	65
	Mini Ice Cream Cones (pg 143)	1	100
	Turkey Jerky (pg 169)	1	70

Daily Total kcal: (2033)

Grocery List for Meal Plan 2

Dry Goods	**Dairy**	**Canned/Carton Goods**
3 cups Sunflower Kernels 1 box Club Crackers	4 cup 2% Milk 3 cups Shredded Cheddar Cheese 1 cup Coconut Yogurt 23 large Eggs	7 cups Chicken Broth 1 can 10.75 oz Cream of Chicken Soup 3 cans (15 oz each) Cannellini Beans 1 cup Applesauce, unsweetened 2 cans Pineapple Chunks 1 pint Coconut Water ½ cup Green Olives

Pantry Staples	**Produce**	**Freeze-dried Stock**
3 cups Flour 4 cup Granulated Sugar 2 tsp Baking Powder 1 tsp Baking Soda 1 cup Brown Sugar 4 Tbs Cornstarch 2 tsp Vanilla Extract 1½ tsp Cinnamon 1 tsp Ground Ginger 5 tsp Salt 1¼ tsp Black Pepper ¼ tsp Red Pepper Flakes ¼ tsp Italian Seasoning ½ tsp Dried Oregano 1 tsp Dried Thyme 2 Bay Leaves	4½ cups Diced Mango 2 large Banana 4 cups (1 lb) Strawberries 2 large Carrots 1 large Celery Stalk 1 large Bell Pepper 1 cup Spinach 2 cups chopped Kale 2 cups Broccoli 2 med Zucchini 1 large Onion 4 Green Onions 4 cloves Garlic	(Process a batch if you need them) Freeze-dried Grapes Freeze-dried Butternut Squash Chips Freeze-dried Green Peas Freeze-dried Blueberries Freeze-dried Corn Freeze-dried Asparagus Freeze-dried White Rice

Butcher/Deli Case		**Other**
1 lb Chicken Sausage 2 lbs Cooked Chicken		12 oz Frozen Hashbrowns 1 box Mini Ice Cream Cones 4 Turkey Jerky

This grocery list will make multiple servings of each recipe and feeds about 4 people for 1 day.

Meal Plan 3

Easily calculate the calories needed for your day by multiplying your body weight in pounds by your expected activity level. Determine per meal by multiplying the daily calories by the percentage.

Low Activity/Rest Day	15
Moderate Activity/1 hr hike	20
High Activity/2 hr hike w pack	25
Extreme Activity/6 hr hike w pack	30

Weight (lbs)	Activity Level	Daily Calories Needed
		2500

x 0.25	Breakfast =	625
x 0.15	Lunch =	375
x 0.25	Dinner =	625
x 0.35	Snacks =	875

	Food	Servings	kcal
Breakfast 25% (623)	Classic Ham and Egg Quiche (pg 92)	1	305
	Mango Coconut Chia Seed Pudding (pg 100)	1	271
	Freeze-dried Mandarin Oranges (pg 72)	1	47
Lunch 15% (380)	Tuna Noodle Casserole (pg 102)	1	337
	Cauliflower Nibbles (pg 138)	1	43
Dinner 25% (617)	Chicken Korma (pg 111)	1½	319
	Freeze-dried White Rice (pg 86)	1	210
	Freeze-dried Corn (pg 74)	1	88
Additions 35% (898)	Tropical Bliss Trail Mix (pg 132)	1	106
	Lemon Tea Bread Bites (pg 144)	½	102
	Freeze-dried Apples (pg 70)	1	104
	Cashews (pg 169)	1	160
	Popped Caramel Spheres (pg 141)	½	65
	Simple Cherry Cobbler (pg 147)	1	171
	Cheese Crackers (pg 169)	1	190

Daily Total kcal: (2518)

Grocery List for Meal Plan 3

Dry Goods
1 premade Pie Crust
1 lb Egg Noodles
1 cup Chia Seeds
2½ cup Cashews
½ cup Flaked Coconut

Dairy
4 cup 2% Milk
3½ cup Almond Milk
1½ cup shredded Cheddar Cheese
2 cups Plain Yogurt
12 large Eggs

Canned/Carton Goods
4 cans (13.5 oz ea) Coconut Milk
2 cans Cream of Mushroom Soup
4 cans Tuna
2 cups Chicken Broth
1 cup Applesauce, unsweetened

Pantry Staples
5 cups All-Purpose Flour
2¼ cup Granulated Sugar
2 tsp Baking Soda
1 tsp Baking Powder
½ tsp Cinnamon Powder
2½ Tbs Salt
2 tsp Black Pepper
1 tsp Onion Powder
1 tsp Turmeric Powder
2 tsp Ground Cumin
2 tsp Ground Coriander
1 tsp Thyme
3 Tbs Vanilla Extract
¼ tsp Almond Extract
¾ cup Lemon Juice
½ cup Maple Syrup
¼ cup Korma Curry Sauce
¼ cup Soy Sauce

Produce
4 cups chopped Mango
4 cups Sweet Cherries
2 Lemons
2 cups Peas, frozen
3 large heads Cauliflower (6 lbs)
2 med Onion
6 cloves Garlic
2 Tbs grated Ginger

Freeze-dried Stock
(Process a batch if you need them)
Freeze-dried Mandarin Oranges
Freeze-dried Apples
Freeze-dried Corn
Freeze-dried Mango pieces
Freeze-dried Pineapple
Freeze-dried White Rice

Butcher/Deli Case
¾ lb Ham
3 lbs Chicken Breasts

Other
34 oz Party Bag of Caramel M&M's
4 packages Cheese Crackers

This grocery list will make multiple servings of each recipe and feeds about 4 people for 1 day.

Meal Plan 4

Easily calculate the calories needed for your day by multiplying your body weight in pounds by your expected activity level. Determine per meal by multiplying the daily calories by the percentage.

Low Activity/Rest Day	15
Moderate Activity/1 hr hike	20
High Activity/2 hr hike w pack	25
Extreme Activity/6 hr hike w pack	30

Weight (lbs)	Activity Level	Daily Calories Needed
		3000

x 0.25	Breakfast =	750
x 0.15	Lunch =	450
x 0.25	Dinner =	750
x 0.35	Snacks =	1050

	Food	Servings	kcal
Breakfast 25% (760)	Savory Sausage Scramble (pg 91)	2	348
	Apple Pie Oatmeal (pg 95)	1	248
	Freeze-dried Pineapple (pg 72)	2	164
Lunch 15% (458)	Fiesta Chicken (pg 106)	1	360
	Freeze-dried Penne Pasta (pg 86)	1	70
	Freeze-dried Zucchini Chips (pg 78)	2	
Dinner 25% (790)	Beef Stroganoff (pg 111)	3	638
	Freeze-dried Mashed Potatoes (pg 76)	1	254
	Freeze-dried Asparagus (pg 73)	1	
Additions 35% (997)	Berry Nutty Trail Mix (pg 132)	2	236
	Oil-free Brownie Bites (pg 145)	1	91
	Strawberry Yogurt Drops (pg 136)	1	160
	Almonds (pg 169)	1	160
	Mixed Fruit Medley (pg 139)	1	100
	Ice Cream Sandwich Sticks (pg 142)	1	150
	Meat Stick (pg 169)	1	100

Daily Total kcal: (3005)

Grocery List for Meal Plan 4

Dry Goods	Dairy	Canned/Carton Goods
8 cups Old-Fashioned Rolled Oats 24 oz Egg Noodles 3 cup Almonds ½ cup Dark Chocolate Chips	2 cups 2% Milk 2 cusp Sour Cream 64 oz Strawberry Greek Yogurt 18 large Eggs	1 can (15 ounces) Black Beans 1 can (15 ounces) Corn 1 can (14.5 ounces) diced Tomatoes 4 cups Beef Broth 1 cup Unsweetened Applesauce

Pantry Staples	Produce	Freeze-dried Stock
1 cup All-Purpose Flour 1 cup Granulated Sugar 1 cup Brown Sugar ½ teaspoon Baking Powder 3 Tbs Arrowroot flour ½ cup Unsweetened Cocoa Powder 2 tsp Cinnamon ½ tsp Nutmeg 2½ Tbs Salt 2 tsp Black Pepper 1 Tbs Chili powder 1 tsp Paprika 1 tsp ground Cumin ½ tsp dried Oregano ¼ cup Dijon Mustard 1 teaspoon Vanilla Extract	2 lb Mushrooms 1 med Bell Pepper 2 large Bell Peppers 1 med Jalapeño Pepper ¼ cup Cilantro 7 cloves Garlic 3 med Onion 1 large Onion 4 large Apples 5 medium Mangoes 2 lbs Strawberries 5 Mandarin Oranges 1½ lbs Blueberries 2 lbs Seedless Grapes 6 Golden Kiwi 1 large Pineapple	(Process a batch if you need them) Freeze-dried Pineapple Freeze-dried Zucchini Chips Freeze-dried Asparagus Freeze-dried Mashed Potatoes Freeze-dried Penne Pasta Freeze-dried Strawberry Slices Freeze-dried Blueberries

Butcher/Deli Case		Other
1 lb Chicken Sausage 2 lbs Chicken Breasts 2 lb Beef Sirloin		1 Box Ice Cream Sandwiches 4 Meat Sticks

This grocery list will make multiple servings of each recipe and feeds about 4 people for 1 day.

Meal Plan 5

Easily calculate the calories needed for your day by multiplying your body weight in pounds by your expected activity level. Determine per meal by multiplying the daily calories by the percentage.

Low Activity/Rest Day	15
Moderate Activity/1 hr hike	20
High Activity/2 hr hike w pack	25
Extreme Activity/6 hr hike w pack	30

Weight (lbs)	Activity Level	Daily Calories Needed
		3500

x 0.25	Breakfast =	875
x 0.15	Lunch =	525
x 0.25	Dinner =	875
x 0.35	Snacks =	1225

	Food	Servings	kcal
Breakfast 25% **860**	Spinach Sunrise Skillet (pg 91)	3	342
	Chocolate Raspberry Chia Seed Pudding (pg 100)	2	438
	Freeze-dried Tangerines (pg 73)	2	80
Lunch 15% **508**	Chicken Salad (pg 104)	1	360
	Club Crackers (pg 169)	1	70
	Freeze-dried Sweet Peppers (pg 76)	2	78
Dinner 25% **827**	Classic Chili (pg 114)	2	638
	Cornmeal Muffin Bites (pg 98)	1	127
	Freeze-dried Peas (pg 76)	1	62
Additions 35% **1306**	Berry S'mores Trail Mix (pg 132)	2	168
	Mini Cookies (pg 146)	1	150
	Freeze-dried Pineapple (pg 72)	1	82
	Pistachios (pg 169)	2	318
	Creamsicle cubes (pg 150)	1	334
	Quick Peach Cobbler (pg 147)	1	184
	Turkey Jerky (pg 169)	1	70

Daily Total kcal: 3501

Grocery List for Meal Plan 5

Dry Goods
½ cup Cornmeal
1 cup Chia Seeds
1½ cup Golden Grahams Cereal
½ cup Milk Chocolate Chips
2 cup Raw Cashews
2 cups Pistachios
1 box Club Crackers

Dairy
16 oz Cream Cheese
7 cups Almond Milk
1 cup Buttermilk
1 cup 2% Milk
28 large Eggs

Canned/Carton Goods
1 cup Dill Pickle Relish
1 can (15 oz) Kidney Beans
1 can (15 oz) Black Beans
2 cups Beef Broth
1 can (6 oz) Tomato Paste
1 can (14 oz) diced Tomatoes
½ cup Applesauce

Pantry Staples
2¾ cups Flour
1¼ cup + 2 Tbs Sugar
½ cup Cocoa Powder
1 tablespoon Baking Powder
1 Tbs Baking Soda
1 tsp Cinnamon
3 Tbs Salt½ tsp Salt
2½ tsp Black Pepper
2 Tbs Chili Powder
1 Tbs Ground Cumin
½ tsp Dried Oregano
1 tsp Paprika
½ cup Maple Syrup

Produce
6 large stalks Celery
6 cups Fresh Spinach
3 large Bell Pepper
1 med Red Bell Pepper
1 large Red Onion
1 med Onion
12 Green Onions
2 cloves Garlic
14 Medjool Dates
4 cups Raspberries
2 med Bananas, ripe
8 Oranges
8 medium Peaches

Freeze-dried Stock
(Process a batch if you need them)
Freeze-dried Tangerines
Freeze-dried Sweet Peppers
Freeze-dried Green Peas
Freeze-dried Pineapple
Freeze-dried Mixed Berries
(strawberries, blueberries, raspberries)
Freeze-dried Mini Marshmallows

Butcher/Deli Case
8 cups cooked Chicken Breast
2 lb Ground Beef

Other
1 box Mini Cookies (or homemade)
4 Turkey Jerky

This grocery list will make multiple servings of each recipe and feeds about 4 people for 1 day.

Meal Plan 6

Easily calculate the calories needed for your day by multiplying your body weight in pounds by your expected activity level. Determine per meal by multiplying the daily calories by the percentage.

Low Activity/Rest Day	15
Moderate Activity/1 hr hike	20
High Activity/2 hr hike w pack	25
Extreme Activity/6 hr hike w pack	30

Weight (lbs)	Activity Level	Daily Calories Needed
		4000

x 0.25	Breakfast =	1000
x 0.15	Lunch =	600
x 0.25	Dinner =	1000
x 0.35	Snacks =	1400

	Food	Servings	kcal
Breakfast 25% **1032**	Hearty Breakfast Casserole (pg 94)	2	596
	Blueberry Vanilla Chia Seed Pudding (pg 100)	1	385
	Freeze-dried Apricots (pg 70)	1	51
Lunch 15% **650**	Cheesy Macaroni (pg 117)	1½	570
	Tomato Soup (pg 121)	1	49
	Freeze-dried Broccoli (pg 74)	1	31
Dinner 25% **1046**	Pork Carnitas (pg 119)	2	538
	Freeze-dried White Rice (pg 86)	2	420
	Freeze-dried Corn (pg 74)	1	88
Additions 35% **1284**	Apple Pie Trail Mix (pg 133)	2	116
	Lemon Burst Cookies (pg 146)	2	408
	Drizzled Banana Crisps (pg 144)	2	232
	Pepitas (pg 169)	2	320
	Taffy Puffs (pg 141)	1	110
	Mini Ice Cream Cones (pg 143)	2	200
	Peanut Butter Crackers (pg 169)	1	190

Daily Total kcal: 4012

Grocery List for Meal Plan 6

Dry Goods	Dairy	Canned/Carton Goods
1 cup Chia Seeds	2 cups 2% Milk	½ cup Green Olives
½ cup Walnuts	6 cups Almond Milk	10 cups diced Tomatoes
2 cups Pepitas	5 cups shredded Cheddar Cheese	3 cups Vegetable Broth
2 lbs Macaroni Pasta	8 oz Cream Cheese	2 cup Chicken Broth
40 Mini Nilla Wafers (or 16 regular)	1 cup Sour Cream	⅔ cup Orange Juice
6 oz Chocolate Chips	1 cup Greek Yogurt	
	17 large Eggs	

Pantry Staples	Produce	Freeze-dried Stock
3 cups All-purpose Flour	4 med Onions	(Process a batch if you need them)
2 cups Granulated Sugar	4 Green Onions	Freeze-dried Apricots
1 tsp Baking Powder	10 cloves Garlic	Freeze-dried Broccoli
½ tsp Baking Soda	1 large Bell Pepper	Freeze-dried Corn
8 tsp Salt	1 cup Spinach	Freeze-dried White Rice
3 tsp Black Pepper	4 cups Blueberries	Freeze-dried Apple pieces
2 Tbs Ground Cumin	6 Bananas	
1 tsp Mustard Powder	2 Lemons	
3 Tbs Vanilla Extract	2 Tbs Fresh Lemon Juice	
½ cup Maple Syrup		

Butcher/Deli Case		Other
1 lb Chicken Sausage		12 oz Frozen Hashbrowns
4 lbs Pork Shoulder		2 lb bag of Salt Water Taffy
		1 box Mini ice Cream Cones
		4 pkgs Peanut Butter Crackers

This grocery list will make multiple servings of each recipe and feeds about 4 people for 1 day.

Meal Plan 7

Easily calculate the calories needed for your day by multiplying your body weight in pounds by your expected activity level. Determine per meal by multiplying the daily calories by the percentage.

Low Activity/Rest Day	15
Moderate Activity/1 hr hike	20
High Activity/2 hr hike w pack	25
Extreme Activity/6 hr hike w pack	30

Weight (lbs)	Activity Level	Daily Calories Needed
		4500

x 0.25	Breakfast =	1125
x 0.15	Lunch =	675
x 0.25	Dinner =	1125
x 0.35	Snacks =	1575

	Food	Servings	kcal
Breakfast 25% **1119**	Denver Delight (pg 92)	2	490
	Pumpkin Pie Oatmeal (pg 95)	2½	580
	Freeze-dried Strawberries (pg 73)	1	49
Lunch 15% **671**	Southwest Black Bean Soup (pg 131)	1½	531
	Club Crackers (pg 169)	1	70
	Freeze-dried Cauliflower (pg 74)	1	70
Dinner 25% **1079**	Chicken Alfredo Pasta (pg 113)	2½	962
	Sweet Potato Cubes (pg 138)	1	90
	Freeze-dried Snap Peas (pg 76)	1	27
Additions 35% **1661**	Peachy Keen Trail Mix (pg 134)	2	216
	French Toast Sticks (pg 96)	1	204
	Freeze-dried Nectarines (pg 72)	2	124
	Macadamia Nuts (pg 169)	2	400
	Mixed-Berry Smoothie Cubes (pg 149)	2	262
	Strawberry Ice Cream Bites (pg 79)	1½	375
	Beef Jerky (pg 169)	1	80

Daily Total kcal: 4530

Grocery List for Meal Plan 7

Dry Goods	Dairy	Canned/Carton Goods
1 premade Pie Crust 8 cups Old-Fashioned Rolled Oats 16 oz Fettuccine Pasta 1 box Club Crackers 1 cup Pecan Halves 2 cups Macadamia Nuts ½ cup White Chocolate Chips	7 cups 2% Milk 1 cup Half & Half 1 cup Shredded Cheddar Cheese 2 cups Parmesan Cheese 2 cups Sour Cream 1 cup of Greek Yogurt 18 large Eggs	2 cans Pumpkin Puree 2 qts Vegetable Broth 4 cans (15 oz each) Black Beans 2 cans Corn

Pantry Staples	Produce	Freeze-dried Stock
1 cup Brown Sugar 3 tsp Cinnamon ½ tsp Nutmeg 6½ tsp Salt 4 tsp Black Pepper 2 tsp Chili Powder 2 Tbs Onion powder 2 Tbs Garlic powder 2 tsp Ground Cumin 1 tsp Smoked Paprika 2 tsp Vanilla Extract	4 oz Mushrooms 8 large 5" Sweet Potatoes 1 large Bell Pepper 2 large Red Bell Pepper 3 large Onions 10 cloves Garlic 2 cups Baby Spinach 2 cups Kale 2 cups Blueberries 2 large Banana 2 cups Blackberries 2 cups Strawberries	(Process a batch if you need them) Freeze-dried Strawberries Freeze-dried Cauliflower Freeze-dried Snap Peas Freeze-dried Nectarines Freeze-dried Peach pieces

Butcher/Deli Case		Other
½ lb Ham 2 lb Chicken Breast		32 slices Bread (1 lb loaf) 1 quart Strawberry Ice Cream 4 Beef Jerky

This grocery list will make multiple servings of each recipe and feeds about 4 people for 1 day.

Meal Plan 8

Easily calculate the calories needed for your day by multiplying your body weight in pounds by your expected activity level. Determine per meal by multiplying the daily calories by the percentage.

Low Activity/Rest Day	15
Moderate Activity/1 hr hike	20
High Activity/2 hr hike w pack	25
Extreme Activity/6 hr hike w pack	30

Weight (lbs)	Activity Level	Daily Calories Needed
		5000

x 0.25	Breakfast =	1250
x 0.15	Lunch =	750
x 0.25	Dinner =	1250
x 0.35	Snacks =	1750

	Food	Servings	kcal
Breakfast 25% (1260)	Savory Sausage Scramble (pg 91)	4	968
	Blueberry Lemon Granola (pg 96)	2	246
	Freeze-dried Watermelon (pg 73)	1	46
Lunch 15% (736)	Sweet & Sour Pork (pg 109)	2	510
	Freeze-dried White Rice (pg 86)	1	210
	Freeze-dried Cucumber Chips (pg 75)	2	16
Dinner 25% (1241)	Lazy Lasagna (pg 110)	3	996
	Lentil Soup (pg 123)	1	227
	Freeze-dried Okra (pg 76)	1	18
Additions 35% (1789)	Nutty Nanners Trail Mix (pg 134)	2	320
	Cinnamon Roll Bites (pg 98)	1	315
	Freeze-dried Cherries (pg 70)	2	174
	Pine Nuts (pg 169)	2	360
	Almond Butter Packet (pg 169)	1	220
	Ice Cream Sandwich Sticks (pg 142)	2	300
	Meat Stick (pg 169)	1	100

Daily Total kcal: (5026)

Grocery List for Meal Plan 8

Dry Goods	**Dairy**	**Canned/Carton Goods**
2 cups Rolled Oats	1 cup Milk	2 cans, 10 oz ea, Pineapple
12 oz Macaroni Noodles	4 cups shredded Cheddar Cheese	2 cans, 4 oz each, Mushrooms
3 cups Lentils	3 cups Cottage Cheese	4 cans Tomato Sauce
1 cup Walnuts	1 cup Butter	2 qts Vegetable Broth
2 cups Pine Nuts	20 large Eggs	1 cup Applesauce

Pantry Staples	**Produce**	**Freeze-dried Stock**
4⅔ cups All-Purpose Flour	6 cups Blueberries	(Process a batch if you need them)
1 cup Granulated Sugar	1 lb Mushrooms	Freeze-dried Watermelon
2 cups Brown Sugar	3 med Green Bell Pepper	Freeze-dried Cherries
3½ Tbs Ground Cinnamon	3 large Carrots	Freeze-dried Okra
2½ Tbs Salt	3 large Celery Stalks	Freeze-dried Cucumber Chips
3 tsp Black Pepper	4 med Onions	Freeze-dried White Rice
1 tsp Cumin	1 large Onion	Freeze-dried Banana Slices
1 tsp Turmeric	5 cloves Garlic	
1 cup Ketchup		
1 pkg Yeast (2¼ tsp)		
4 Tbs Lemon Juice		
2 Tbs Maple Syrup		

Butcher/Deli Case		**Other**
1 lb Chicken Sausage		1 box Ice Cream Sandwiches
2 lb Pork Steak		4 Almond Butter Packets
1 lb Hamburger		4 Meat Sticks

This grocery list will make multiple servings of each recipe and feeds about 4 people for 1 day.

REHYDRATION INFORMATION

Rehydration is not always necessary.

If you prefer a crispy snack, enjoy it directly from the packaging or container. For soup preparation, incorporate the freeze-dried ingredients into the pot and adjust the water quantity accordingly. Dry fruits and vegetables are ideal for pulverizing into a powder and mixing into soups, sauces, or smoothies. Certain foods need less water for rehydration. Begin with a smaller amount (HALF) and gradually increase as needed.

Rehydration General Rule of Thumb:

 +

1 cup Freeze-dried Food

*½ - 1 cup Water** (start with ½ cup)

*Add a small amount of water gradually, stir or turn items, and add the rest as needed.

Meals 5-20+ min	Combine cold or hot water, stir, let it rest, then cook for best flavor. . Alternatively, break it up in an oven-safe dish, add hot water, cover, and bake in the oven like a casserole.
Cooked Meats 5-60 min	Transfer the food to a dish and add enough hot water to cover it. Excess water can cause ingredients cooked with meats to become mushy.
Fruits & Vegetables 1-10 min	Allow to soak in water until proper consistency. Or arrange food on a tray and lightly spray with cold water. Turn or stir to ensure both sides are coated. Let it absorb, then spray more as necessary.
Raw Meats 30 min - 3+ hrs	Place raw meat in a dish, add cold water or broth, and refrigerate overnight. Pat dry with paper towel and cook thoroughly.
Eggs 2-5 min	Mix 2 tablespoons of egg powder with 2 tablespoons of cold water. Stir and let it sit for a few minutes before using as you would a raw egg.
Powders 2-5 min	Gradually add small amounts of cold water and stir. Typically, the ratio is about 50:50 water to powder, regardless of the type of powder.
Cheeses 5-15 min	Soak large pieces of cheese in water. Wrap cheese slices in damp paper towels and let them sit. Spritz shredded cheese with cold water. Other cheeses are best used dry or incorporated into recipes.
Desserts 5-10 min	Place the treat and a moist paper towel inside a Ziploc bag and let it sit. Alternatively, wrap the treat in a moist paper towel. Or simply enjoy it crunchy!

Note: Some foods will take considerably longer to rehydrate than others in the same category.

REHYDRATION CALCULATIONS

Here is an easy way to calculate the amount of water needed for rehydration.

1. Prior to freeze-drying, use a kitchen scale to determine initial weight in grams.
2. Repeat the weight-check method until completely dry.
3. After freeze-drying is complete, weigh the portion again to obtain its final weight.
4. Calculate the weight of water by subtracting the final weight from the initial weight.
5. To determine the total water needed for rehydration, multiply the weight of water removed by the chosen unit of measurement.

Each gram of water removed is equal to:

0.00423 cups
0.0667 Tablespoons
0.2347 teaspoons
0.03527 ounces

Determine Water Needed for Rehydration

Portion weight (in grams)		Total Water Removed (g)	Multiply By Chosen Unit	Total Water Needed
Prior to FD	**After FD**			
_____ g	_____ g	_____ g	x 0.00423 cup	_____ c
_____ g	_____ g	_____ g	x 0.06667 Tbs	_____ T
_____ g	_____ g	_____ g	x 0.23471 tsp	_____ t
_____ g	_____ g	_____ g	x 0.03527 oz	_____ oz

Example

Portion weight (in grams)		Total Water Removed (g)	Multiply By Chosen Unit	Total Water Needed
Prior to FD	**After FD**			
200 g	*80* g	*120* g	x 0.00423 cup	*0.51* cup

CONVERSIONS

Use these handy conversions to make life in the kitchen a little easier.

1 CUP =
16 tablespoons,
8 ounces
240 ml

1/2 CUP =
8 tablespoons
120 ml

1 PINT =
2 cups,
16 ounces
480 ml

1 GALLON =
4 quarts,
8 pints,
16 cups,
128 ounces
3.8 liters

1 QUART =
2 pints,
4 cups,
32 ounces,
950 ml

1 teaspoon = 5 ml
1 tablespoon = 3 teaspoons = 15 ml
2 tablespoons = 1 ounce = 30 ml
4 tablespoons = 1/4 cup = 60 ml
5 tablespoons + 1 teaspoon = 80 ml

oz	grams	lbs
1/2	14	
3/4	21	
1	28	
2	57	1/8
3	85	
4	113	1/4
5	142	
6	170	
7	198	
8	227	1/2
9	255	
10	284	
11	312	
12	340	3/4
13	369	
14	397	
15	425	
16	454	1
24	680	1.5
32	907	2
40	1134	2.5
48	1361	3
56	1588	3.5
64	1814	4
72	2041	4.5
80	2268	5

FOODS YOU CANNOT FREEZE-DRY

Foods rich in oil or fat, as well as those high in sugar, are not suitable for freeze-drying. However, incorporating small quantities of these ingredients into prepared dishes typically yield satisfactory results.

It's advisable to consume meals or products containing oils within 1 to 5 years, as fats tend to become rancid with prolonged storage.

Freeze-Dryer NO's

High Fat:

- Oils
- Butter
- Mayonnaise
- Nuts/Nut Butters
- Peanut Butter
- Pure Chocolate

High Sugar:

- Honey
- Syrup
- Soda
- Jam
- Jelly
- Preserves

Other:

- Alcohol
- Bones
- Oreos
- Vinegar
- Fruit Snacks
- Candy Canes

GREAT FOODS TO FREEZE-DRY

Fruits

- Apples
- Apricots
- Avocado
- Bananas
- Blackberries
- Blueberries
- Cantaloupe
- Cherries
- Coconut
- Cranberry
- Grapefruit
- Grapes
- Honeydew
- Kiwi, Golden
- Lemons
- Limes
- Mandarins
- Mangos
- Nectarines
- Oranges
- Peaches
- Pears
- Pineapple
- Plums
- Pomegranate
- Raspberries
- Rhubarb
- Strawberries
- Tangerines
- Watermelon

Vegetables

- Asparagus
- Beets
- Bok Choy
- Broccoli
- Brussel Sprouts
- Cabbage
- Carrots
- Cauliflower
- Celery
- Corn
- Cucumber
- Eggplant
- Garlic
- Green Beans
- Kale
- Leeks
- Lettuce
- Mushrooms
- Okra
- Onions
- Parsnips
- Peas, Green/Snap
- Peppers, Hot/Sweet
- Potatoes
- Pumpkin
- Radish
- Rutabaga
- Scallions
- Spinach
- Squash, Summer
- Squash, Winter
- Sweet potatoes
- Swiss Chard
- Tomatoes
- Turnips
- Yams

Dairy

- Cheese Curds
- Condensed Milk
- Cottage Cheese
- Cream Cheese
- Half & Half
- Hard Cheeses
- Ice Cream
- Milk Cow/Goat
- Soft Cheeses
- Sour Cream
- Whipped Cream
- Yogurt*/Kefir*
  *change dry temp to 90°F

Eggs

- Cooked
- Raw (Pre-freeze Solid)
- Scrambled
- Skillets
- Casseroles
- Quiche

Meats

Beef - Lean
- Deli Meats
- Ground/Patties
- Filets/Steaks
- Kabobs/Meatballs
- Roast/Shredded
- Stew Meat/Strips

Pork - Lean
- Bacon
- Chops
- Deli Meats
- Ham
- Loin
- Shredded Roast

Poultry
- Deli Meats
- Ground/Chopped
- Roast/Shredded
- Slices/Strips
- Turkey Bacon
- Game Fowl

Seafood

White Fish
- Bass
- Catfish
- Cod
- Haddock
- Snapper
- Tilapia

Oily Fish
- Carp
- Herring
- Mackerel
- Salmon
- Trout
- Tuna

Shellfish
- Clam
- Crab
- Lobster
- Oyster
- Scallops
- Shrimp

Legumes

- Beans, dry
- Peas, dry
- Sprouts

- Chickpeas
- Soybeans
- Tempeh

- Lentils
- Split Peas
- Tofu

Grains

- Barley
- Oats/Oatmeal
- Rice

- Bread/Sweetbread
- Pasta/Couscous
- Rye

- Buckwheat
- Quinoa
- Wheat/Seitan

Meals

- Beef stroganoff
- Breakfast Skillet
- Casseroles
- Chicken parmesan
- Chili
- Chow mein
- Creole
- Fajitas

- Goulash
- Gumbo
- Hamburger patties
- Hash browns
- Lasagna
- Macaroni & Cheese
- Mashed potatoes
- Meatballs/Meat Loaf

- Pasta
- Pizza Casserole
- Roast Turkey Dinner
- Roast Beef Dinner
- Soups
- Spaghetti
- Stews
- Tuna Salad

Herbs*

- Basil
- Chives
- Cilantro
- Dill Weed
- Fennel
- Ginger
- Horseradish
- Marjoram
- Oregano
- Parsley
- Peppermint
- Rosemary
- Sage
- Spearmint
- Stevia
- Tarragon
- Thyme
- Turmeric

*change dry temp to 90°F

Drinks

- Broth
- Coconut Water
- Coffee
- Cow/Goat Milk
- Eggnog
- Fruit Juices
- Greens Juices
- Hot Cocoa
- Oat/Rice Milk
- Protein Shakes
- Smoothies
- Vegetable Juices

Snacks

- Applesauce
- Breads
- Croutons
- Diluted Sauces
- French Onion Dip
- Guacamole
- Nacho Cheese
- Pizza
- Ranch Dip
- Refried Beans
- Salsa
- Sweet Breads

Desserts

- Cake
- Cheesecake
- Cookies
- Ice Cream
- Ice Cream Sandwiches
- Jell-O
- Marshmallows
- Mousse
- Pie
- Pudding
- Shortcake
- Twinkies

Candies#

Use Whole
- Candy Corn
- Caramel Apple Pops
- Caramel M&M's
- Gummy Bears

Cut into Pieces
- Airheads (⅓)
- Bit 'O Honey (⅓)
- Caramels (½)
- Jolly Ranchers (⅓)

- Gummy Worms
- Junior Mints
- Lemonheads
- Life Saver Gummies

- Laffy Taffy (¼)
- Milk Duds (½)
- Mini Milky Way (½)
- Salt Water Taffy (¼)

- Mamba
- Peach Rings
- Skittles
- Stuffed Puffs

- Mini Snickers (½)
- Starburst (¼)
- Tootsie Chews (½)
- Twix (¼)

#use Candy mode

GETTING STARTED CHECKLIST

Approve & Inspect Items in Your Order

- ☐ Inspect for Damage (HR: 801-386-8960)
- ☐ Harvest Right Freeze-dryer
- ☐ Shelving unit (inside the appliance)
- ☐ 6' power cord (black)
- ☐ Drain line tubing (clear)
- ☐ Vacuum pump
- ☐ Vacuum hose (black)
- ☐ Vacuum pump oil (unless oil-free)
- ☐ Oil filter (unless oil-free)
- ☐ Impulse sealer
- ☐ Stainless steel trays (3, 4, 5, 6, or 7)
- ☐ Package of Mylar bags
- ☐ Package of oxygen absorbers (OA)
- ☐ Harvest Right owner's manual
- ☐ Harvest Right Guide to Freeze-drying
- ☐ Additional Accessories

Positioning your Machine

- ☐ Carefully Move into position
- ☐ Environment is Clean & Dry
- ☐ Room Temperature is Cool (45°F - 75°F)
- ☐ Adequate Ventilation on both sides
- ☐ Table, Cart, or Countertop
- ☐ Surface is stable and level

Tasks while you Wait

- ☐ Read the Harvest Right Owner's Manual.
- ☐ Open the door and ensure the shelving unit is connected and positioned correctly.
- ☐ Inspect the rubber gasket & acrylic door and wipe with warm water and a cotton cloth.
- ☐ Attach the drain hose to the fitting on the side of the appliance.
- ☐ Allow the vinyl hose to fall into a 5-gallon bucket while hanging loosely.
- ☐ Add the ⅜" Y fittings to your tubing by cutting the line & pushing the ends onto the fitting.
- ☐ Attach the power cord, but do not plug it in until the 24 hours have passed.
- ☐ Position the pump by placing it on the right side or below the freeze-dryer.
- ☐ Add the included oil to your pump up to just above the centerline.
- ☐ Attach vacuum hose to fitting on right side & attach the other end to the pump.
- ☐ Plug the pump into the receptacle on the back of the freeze-dryer.
- ☐ Flip the vacuum pump switch to the ON position. (It won't turn on.)
- ☐ Place fans to blow directly on the vacuum pump and on the left side of the appliance.
- ☐ Find locations for your equipment: impulse sealer, food funnel, FoodSaver®, etc.
- ☐ Find a good storage place for your packaging materials: Mylar bags and oxygen absorbers.
- ☐ Store your accessories: silicone mats, molds, parchment, dividers, corner stackers, etc.

After the 24 hours

- ☐ Plug freeze-dryer into prepared outlet
- ☐ Close drain valve on side of freeze-dryer
- ☐ Close door in two turns & check seal
- ☐ Flip power switch to ON position
- ☐ Test the Freeze function (40 min)
- ☐ Test the Vacuum function (30 min)
- ☐ Set up the Interface (10 min)
- ☐ Complete the Bread Run (24 hours)

FREEZE-DRYING STEPS

Putting Food IN to your Freeze-Dryer

1. Prepare food to a thickness of ½" - ¾" or cut it into pieces.

2. Pre-freeze the food for 24-48 hours to enhance appliance efficiency & prevent messes.

3. Inspect the Oil in the Pump, ensuring it is clear and at a level between half-full and maximum.

4. Connect the freeze-dryer to power, turn the Switch on, position the Gasket, close the Door, verify the Seal, and securely latch the Handle.

5. Access the Customize Screen to adjust Temperature and Time settings if necessary.

6. Initiate the pre-cooling process by pressing Start, allowing the chamber to cool for a minimum of 15-90 minutes.

7. Direct a fan towards the left side of the freeze-dryer.

8. Once prompted (after at least 15 minutes), close the Drain Valve.

9. Weigh the trays, then insert them into the freeze-dryer, ensuring the Door is closed, the Seal is checked, and the Handle is fully latched.

10. Press Continue and wait for 24-60+ hours for the freeze-drying cycle to complete. Begin preparing the next batch of food during the waiting period.

Taking Food OUT of your Freeze-Dryer

1. Once the three phases are finished, the Extra Dry Time phase begins. You have the option to cancel at any point to inspect the food. Set the Extra Dry Time to 24 hours; there is no risk of overdrying.

2. Ensure the drain hose is positioned in an empty bucket, press Cancel, gradually open the Drain Valve, and wait 5 minutes for the pressure to release.

3. Open the Door, take out the food, and check for any cold or soft spots. Weigh each tray.

4. Place the trays back inside. Set the More Dry Time to at least 4 hours and monitor the weight after 2 hours. Repeat as necessary.

5. Once the weight remains unchanged, indicating full dryness, package the food accordingly.

6. Transfer the food from the trays directly into appropriate storage containers, such as a 7-mil Mylar bag heat-sealed with an Oxygen Absorber (OA) or a canning jar vacuum-sealed with an OA.

7. Add the required amount of Oxygen Absorber (100cc per quart, 300cc per gallon) to remove excess oxygen, then seal the Mylar bag or canning jar.

8. Defrost the Chamber by opening the door and selecting No Defrost (ends the cycle) or by selecting the Defrost option.

9. Clean the components of the freeze-dryer using a soft cloth and warm water, and sterilize with isopropyl alcohol or Everclear.

10. Direct a fan into the chamber to aid in drying, then proceed with the next batch.

CAPACITY

Tray Maximum Amounts

Harvest Right HOME	Max Weight	Max Liquid	Machine Maximums	
Small, 3 tray	2.3 lbs	3.3 cups	7 lbs	10 cups
Medium, 4 tray	2.5 lbs	4.2 cups	10 lbs	16.8 cups
Large, 5 tray	3.2 lbs	5.9 cups	16 lbs	29.5 cups
X-Large, 6 tray	5.8 lbs	10.5 cups	35 lbs	62.4 cups

Harvest Right PRO	Max Weight	Max Liquid	Machine Maximums	
SmallPRO, 4 tray	2.5 lbs	3.7 cups	10 lbs	15 cups
MediumPRO, 5 tray	3 lbs	4.7 cups	15 lbs	23.4 cups
LargePRO, 6 tray	4.5 lbs	6.4 cups	27 lbs	38.3 cups
X-LargePRO, 7 tray	7.1 lbs	11.1 cups	50 lbs	78 cups

StayFresh	Max Weight	Max Liquid	Machine Maximums	
Medium, 4 tray	4.5 lbs	5.5 cups	18 lbs	22 cups
Medium, 7 tray	2.5 lbs	5.5 cups	18 lbs	38.5 cups
Mega, 6 tray	8.3 lbs	10 cups	50 lbs	60 cups

Blue Alpine	Max Weight	Max Liquid	Machine Maximums	
Medium, 5 tray	3 lbs	4 cups	15 lbs	20 cups
Large, 5 tray	5 lbs	8.1 cups	25 lbs	40.5 cups

Prep4Life	Max Weight	Max Liquid	Machine Maximums	
The Cube, 4 tray	3.5 lbs	5.7 cups	14 lbs	23 cups

3-tray FREEZE-DRYER BATCH LOGS PAGE#

Keep track of how the foods process in your freeze-dryer.

Batch #		Start Cooling	Trays In	Trays Out	Run Time	Extra Dry	Total
		am pm	am pm	am pm	hrs	hrs	hrs
Start Date:		Customize Temp	Time	Check Time:	am pm	am pm	am pm
End Date:		Freeze					Subtract Dry from Wet for Water Loss
		Dry		mTorr:			
Tray Contents Description:	Examples: Raw, Cooked, Thickness, Liquid, Spread	Pre-Frozen	Wet grams	Check 1 grams	Check 2 grams	Dry grams	
1		Y / N					
2		Y / N					
3		Y / N					
Notes			Chamber Cleaned: Y / N	Oil Changed: Y / N	Maint. Needed: Y / N		

Batch #		Start Cooling	Trays In	Trays Out	Run Time	Extra Dry	Total
		am pm	am pm	am pm	hrs	hrs	hrs
Start Date:		Customize Temp	Time	Check Time:	am pm	am pm	am pm
End Date:		Freeze					Subtract Dry from Wet for Water Loss
		Dry		mTorr:			
Tray Contents Description:	Examples: Raw, Cooked, Thickness, Liquid, Spread	Pre-Frozen	Wet grams	Check 1 grams	Check 2 grams	Dry grams	
1		Y / N					
2		Y / N					
3		Y / N					
Notes			Chamber Cleaned: Y / N	Oil Changed: Y / N	Maint. Needed: Y / N		

Batch #		Start Cooling	Trays In	Trays Out	Run Time	Extra Dry	Total
		am pm	am pm	am pm	hrs	hrs	hrs
Start Date:		Customize Temp	Time	Check Time:	am pm	am pm	am pm
End Date:		Freeze					Subtract Dry from Wet for Water Loss
		Dry		mTorr:			
Tray Contents Description:	Examples: Raw, Cooked, Thickness, Liquid, Spread	Pre-Frozen	Wet grams	Check 1 grams	Check 2 grams	Dry grams	
1		Y / N					
2		Y / N					
3		Y / N					
Notes			Chamber Cleaned: Y / N	Oil Changed: Y / N	Maint. Needed: Y / N		

4-tray FREEZE-DRYER BATCH LOGS PAGE#

Keep track of how the foods process in your freeze-dryer.

Batch #		Start Cooling	Trays In	Trays Out	Run Time	Extra Dry	Total
		am pm	am pm	am pm	hrs	hrs	hrs
Start Date:		Customize	Temp	Time	Check Time:	am pm	am pm	am pm	
End Date:		Freeze Dry			mTorr:				Subtract Dry from Wet for Water Loss
Tray Contents Description:	Examples: Raw, Cooked, Thickness, Liquid, Spread		Pre-Frozen	Wet grams	Check 1 grams	Check 2 grams	Dry grams	
1			Y / N					
2			Y / N					
3			Y / N					
4			Y / N					
Notes			Chamber Cleaned: Y / N	Oil Changed: Y / N	Maint. Needed: Y / N		

Batch #		Start Cooling	Trays In	Trays Out	Run Time	Extra Dry	Total
		am pm	am pm	am pm	hrs	hrs	hrs
Start Date:		Customize	Temp	Time	Check Time:	am pm	am pm	am pm	
End Date:		Freeze Dry			mTorr:				Subtract Dry from Wet for Water Loss
Tray Contents Description:	Examples: Raw, Cooked, Thickness, Liquid, Spread		Pre-Frozen	Wet grams	Check 1 grams	Check 2 grams	Dry grams	
1			Y / N					
2			Y / N					
3			Y / N					
4			Y / N					
Notes			Chamber Cleaned: Y / N	Oil Changed: Y / N	Maint. Needed: Y / N		

Batch #		Start Cooling	Trays In	Trays Out	Run Time	Extra Dry	Total
		am pm	am pm	am pm	hrs	hrs	hrs
Start Date:		Customize	Temp	Time	Check Time:	am pm	am pm	am pm	
End Date:		Freeze Dry			mTorr:				Subtract Dry from Wet for Water Loss
Tray Contents Description:	Examples: Raw, Cooked, Thickness, Liquid, Spread		Pre-Frozen	Wet grams	Check 1 grams	Check 2 grams	Dry grams	
1			Y / N					
2			Y / N					
3			Y / N					
4			Y / N					
Notes			Chamber Cleaned: Y / N	Oil Changed: Y / N	Maint. Needed: Y / N		

5-tray FREEZE-DRYER BATCH LOGS PAGE#

Keep track of how the foods process in your freeze-dryer.

Batch #		Start Cooling	Trays In	Trays Out	Run Time	Extra Dry	Total
		am pm	am pm	am pm	hrs	hrs	hrs
Start Date:		Customize Temp Time		Check Time:	am pm	am pm	am pm	
End Date:		Freeze						Subtract Dry from Wet for Water Loss
		Dry		mTorr:				
Tray Contents Description:	Examples: Raw, Cooked, Thickness, Liquid, Spread	Pre-Frozen	Wet grams	Check 1 grams	Check 2 grams	Dry grams	
1		Y / N					
2		Y / N					
3		Y / N					
4		Y / N					
5		Y / N					
Notes			Chamber Cleaned: Y / N	Oil Changed: Y / N	Maint. Needed: Y / N		

Batch #		Start Cooling	Trays In	Trays Out	Run Time	Extra Dry	Total
		am pm	am pm	am pm	hrs	hrs	hrs
Start Date:		Customize Temp Time		Check Time:	am pm	am pm	am pm	
End Date:		Freeze						Subtract Dry from Wet for Water Loss
		Dry		mTorr:				
Tray Contents Description:	Examples: Raw, Cooked, Thickness, Liquid, Spread	Pre-Frozen	Wet grams	Check 1 grams	Check 2 grams	Dry grams	
1		Y / N					
2		Y / N					
3		Y / N					
4		Y / N					
5		Y / N					
Notes			Chamber Cleaned: Y / N	Oil Changed: Y / N	Maint. Needed: Y / N		

Batch #		Start Cooling	Trays In	Trays Out	Run Time	Extra Dry	Total
		am pm	am pm	am pm	hrs	hrs	hrs
Start Date:		Customize Temp Time		Check Time:	am pm	am pm	am pm	
End Date:		Freeze						Subtract Dry from Wet for Water Loss
		Dry		mTorr:				
Tray Contents Description:	Examples: Raw, Cooked, Thickness, Liquid, Spread	Pre-Frozen	Wet grams	Check 1 grams	Check 2 grams	Dry grams	
1		Y / N					
2		Y / N					
3		Y / N					
4		Y / N					
5		Y / N					
Notes			Chamber Cleaned: Y / N	Oil Changed: Y / N	Maint. Needed: Y / N		

6-tray   FREEZE-DRYER BATCH LOGS   PAGE#

Keep track of how the foods process in your freeze-dryer.

Batch #		Start Cooling	Trays In	Trays Out	Run Time	Extra Dry	Total
		am pm	am pm	am pm	hrs	hrs	hrs
Start Date:		Customize	Temp	Time	Check Time:	am pm	am pm	am pm	
End Date:		Freeze / Dry			mTorr:				Subtract Dry from Wet for Water Loss
Tray Contents Description:	Examples: Raw, Cooked, Thickness, Liquid, Spread		Pre-Frozen	Wet grams	Check 1 grams	Check 2 grams	Dry grams	
1			Y / N					
2			Y / N					
3			Y / N					
4			Y / N					
5			Y / N					
6			Y / N					
Notes				Chamber Cleaned: Y / N	Oil Changed: Y / N	Maint. Needed: Y / N	

Batch #		Start Cooling	Trays In	Trays Out	Run Time	Extra Dry	Total
		am pm	am pm	am pm	hrs	hrs	hrs
Start Date:		Customize	Temp	Time	Check Time:	am pm	am pm	am pm	
End Date:		Freeze / Dry			mTorr:				Subtract Dry from Wet for Water Loss
Tray Contents Description:	Examples: Raw, Cooked, Thickness, Liquid, Spread		Pre-Frozen	Wet grams	Check 1 grams	Check 2 grams	Dry grams	
1			Y / N					
2			Y / N					
3			Y / N					
4			Y / N					
5			Y / N					
6			Y / N					
Notes				Chamber Cleaned: Y / N	Oil Changed: Y / N	Maint. Needed: Y / N	

Batch #		Start Cooling	Trays In	Trays Out	Run Time	Extra Dry	Total
		am pm	am pm	am pm	hrs	hrs	hrs
Start Date:		Customize	Temp	Time	Check Time:	am pm	am pm	am pm	
End Date:		Freeze / Dry			mTorr:				Subtract Dry from Wet for Water Loss
Tray Contents Description:	Examples: Raw, Cooked, Thickness, Liquid, Spread		Pre-Frozen	Wet grams	Check 1 grams	Check 2 grams	Dry grams	
1			Y / N					
2			Y / N					
3			Y / N					
4			Y / N					
5			Y / N					
6			Y / N					
Notes				Chamber Cleaned: Y / N	Oil Changed: Y / N	Maint. Needed: Y / N	

7-tray   FREEZE-DRYER BATCH LOGS   PAGE#

Keep track of how the foods process in your freeze-dryer.

Batch #		Start Cooling	Trays In	Trays Out	Run Time		Extra Dry		Total	
		am pm	am pm	am pm		hrs		hrs		hrs
Start Date:		Customize	Temp	Time	Check Time:	am pm		am pm	am pm	Subtract Dry from Wet for Water Loss
End Date:		Freeze								
		Dry			mTorr:					
Tray Contents Description:	Examples: Raw, Cooked, Thickness, Liquid, Spread			Pre-Frozen	Wet grams	Check 1 grams		Check 2 grams	Dry grams	
1				Y / N						
2				Y / N						
3				Y / N						
4				Y / N						
5				Y / N						
6				Y / N						
7				Y / N						
Notes					Chamber Cleaned: Y / N		Oil Changed: Y / N		Maint. Needed: Y / N	

Batch #		Start Cooling	Trays In	Trays Out	Run Time		Extra Dry		Total	
		am pm	am pm	am pm		hrs		hrs		hrs
Start Date:		Customize	Temp	Time	Check Time:	am pm		am pm	am pm	Subtract Dry from Wet for Water Loss
End Date:		Freeze								
		Dry			mTorr:					
Tray Contents Description:	Examples: Raw, Cooked, Thickness, Liquid, Spread			Pre-Frozen	Wet grams	Check 1 grams		Check 2 grams	Dry grams	
1				Y / N						
2				Y / N						
3				Y / N						
4				Y / N						
5				Y / N						
6				Y / N						
7				Y / N						
Notes					Chamber Cleaned: Y / N		Oil Changed: Y / N		Maint. Needed: Y / N	

Batch #		Start Cooling	Trays In	Trays Out	Run Time		Extra Dry		Total	
		am pm	am pm	am pm		hrs		hrs		hrs
Start Date:		Customize	Temp	Time	Check Time:	am pm		am pm	am pm	Subtract Dry from Wet for Water Loss
End Date:		Freeze								
		Dry			mTorr:					
Tray Contents Description:	Examples: Raw, Cooked, Thickness, Liquid, Spread			Pre-Frozen	Wet grams	Check 1 grams		Check 2 grams	Dry grams	
1				Y / N						
2				Y / N						
3				Y / N						
4				Y / N						
5				Y / N						
6				Y / N						
7				Y / N						
Notes					Chamber Cleaned: Y / N		Oil Changed: Y / N		Maint. Needed: Y / N	

TROUBLESHOOTING

Harvest Right™ Customer Service: 1-801-386-8960

We recommend Harvest Right freeze-dryers! We have had wonderful experiences with them. Their customer service is excellent. They are dedicated to helping you ensure the proper functioning of your freeze-dryer. Even if your machine is beyond its warranty period, they will offer the guidance and parts needed for any repairs. For easy access to HarvestRight's website, utilize our affiliate shortcut: FDHR.2MHE.COM or scan the QR Code provided.

The Freeze-dryer Problem Diagnosis Guide

This marks your initial step in seeking help with any concerns regarding your Harvest Right freeze-dryer. Once on the site, head to the upper right corner and click on "Customer Support." Then, scroll down to select a category that best fits your issue among options like Set Up & Basics, Vacuum Error, Refrigeration Issues, Drying Issues, Touchscreen Issues, Power Issues, and Software Versions. Following this, the Diagnosis Guide will lead you through troubleshooting steps tailored to your problem. There's a plethora of valuable assistance available for various concerns, along with customer support articles to explore. If you're unable to resolve the issue using the guide, you can submit a support ticket for personalized assistance, directly from the same page.

Blue Alpine Customer Service: 1-208-607-1722

They have a contact form to send to them directly from their website. They also offer an email: contact@bluealpinefreezedryers.com. To get 1% off your order enter the following in the discount code box at checkout: MICROHOMESTEADINGEDUCATIONCOM

StayFresh Customer Service: 1-424-420-7534

Facebook Groups & Pages

Think about becoming a member of freeze-drying Facebook communities to engage with individuals who share similar interests, discover recipe ideas, receive helpful tips, and find assistance with machine-related problems. These groups typically boast a considerable number of experienced members, providing a swift avenue for acquiring valuable information.

"Food Preservation with freeze-drying" is a Facebook group hosted by Micro-Homesteading Education. To join, scan the QR Code provided or utilize the shortcut FDFB.2MHE.COM.

Contact Us:

Email: freeze-drying@micro-homesteading-education.com
Website: www.micro-homesteading-education.com
Facebook Group: www.facebook.com/groups/foodpreservationwithfreezedrying

MAINTENANCE LOG

Keep track of your freeze-dryer maintenance and repair expenses.

Date	Part/Service	Cost	Notes

IMPORTANT INFORMATION
ABOUT MY FREEZE-DRYER

Chosen Name

Size Option

Model Number

Serial Number

Purchase Date

Order Number

Software

Updates

Vacuum Pump

Oil Change Info

Preferred Oil

Customer Service

NOTES

Links Reference Page

Printable Backpacking Worksheets
BPPDF.2MHE.COM

Website: www.Micro-Homesteading-Education.com
Shortcut: GO.2MHE.COM

Access Additional Meal Plans
BPMP.2MHE.COM

Recommended Accessories and Equipment
FDR.2MHE.COM

Facebook Group: Food Preservation with Freeze Drying
FDFB.2MHE.COM

Leave a review on Amazon:
BPR.2MHE.COM

Harvest Right™: FDHR.2MHE.COM 801-386-8960

- Software Update: https://harvestright.com/software-update/
- The Owners Manual: https://harvestright.com/wp-content/uploads/2020/08/Owners-Manual-072020-DIGITAL.pdf

Be one of the first to read the newest manuscript from Micro-Homesteading Education even before it's published! All we hope for is honest feedback in a review on Amazon once it is live.
Become one of our Advanced Readers today by sending an email to
contact@micro-homesteading-education.com.

GLOSSARY

A **Abrasive:** Harsh or corrosive.
Accelerate: To speed up a process.
Accumulate: Increase gradually.
Additive: A substance added to food to increase its storage life.
Airtight: Impermeable to air.
Allergens: A common substance that has the ability to induce an allergy.
Alpine Zone: Also known as 'above the treeline'. The high-elevation areas where trees are unable to grow.
Altitude: Elevation above sea level.
Ambient temperature: Average temperature of an environment.
AMC: Appalachian Mountain Club. Mainly known as the organization in charge of the hut system in the White Mountains.
Aqua Blazing: Taking a waterway instead of the Trail.
Artificial: Not natural. Man-made.
AT: Appalachian Trail
ATC: Appalachian Trail Conservancy. Non-profit organization in charge of protecting and maintaining the Trail.
Automated: Operates without needing adjustment or instructions.
Awol: 'The A.T. Guide'. The only map a thru-hiker needs.

B **Bacteria:** Single-celled microorganisms which can cause disease.
Balds: Barren areas on many mountain tops. Their existence is mostly a mystery.
Base Weight: Total Pack Weight - Consumables (food, water, etc) = Base Weight
Batch: The quantity prepared during one operation.
Bear Bag: Hung in a tree to prevent attracting any bears. Usually contains food, trash, toiletries - anything with a strong odor.
Best if used by date: Recommended date to eat food before it loses its nutrients.
Biner: Short for 'carabiner' - the metal loop with a spring loaded opening generally used for ropes.
Bivy: Short for 'bivouac sack' - a mini tent-like shelter.
Bladder: Or 'water reservoir'. Smaller collapsible water container.
Blanch: Process of steaming food to remove its skin. Typically 3-5 minutes in boiling water.
Blaze: Used to mark the Trail. Typically a 2 x 6 inch strip of paint on a tree located near eye level.
Blue Blaze: The blaze that leads to a water source.
Bluff: Steep cliff.
Boil: Cook in boiling water.
Botulism: Acute food poisoning caused by bacteria.
Bounce Box: Box of supplies you ship or 'bounce' forward to pick up in your next trail town.
Bushwhacking: Hiking off trail. Done for the adventure of it or because you are lost.

C **Cache:** Hiding place. Typically where you or a trail angel would stash food and other goodies.
Cairn: Pile of rocks or stones to mark the trail. Used instead of a blaze if there are no trees.
Camel Up: Drinking as much water as possible at a water source to prevent from carrying it.
Canning: Preserving food in jars by the use of heat.
Cathole: Hole in the ground dugout for human waste. Ideally at least 6 inches deep and at least 200 feet away from a water source.
Climate: Average weather condition of a place.
Commercial: Products designed for large markets.
Compress: Reduce in volume or size.
Consistency: Firmness or density of a substance.
Consume: To eat or use a substance.
Contaminated: Soiled from exposure to bacteria.
Contour Lines: Lines used on a topographical map to display variations in elevation.
Conversion: To change from one measurement to another.
Coolant: Fluid used to cool the temperature in a machine.
Cowboy Camping: Camping underneath the stars without a tent.
Cowboy Coffee: Mixing water with unfiltered coffee grounds.
Crampons: Metal frame used on boots for traction in snowy and icy conditions.
Cuben Fiber: High-performance fabric, also known as "Dyneema", used as an ultralight material for some tents and bags.
Cycle: Interval of time from the beginning of a process to the end.

D **Debris:** Waste materials such as lint, dirt, or dust.
Decay: Gradually decrease in quality.
Decibels: Unit for expressing sound.
DEET: Ingredient used in insect repellents - also known as 'diethyltoluamide'
Default: Pre-set setting that runs automatically.
Defrost: The process of melting ice.
Dehydrate: Remove water from food.
Deplete: To lessen, finish or empty a substance.
Desiccant: A substance that absorbs moisture from the surrounding environment. Not for use with freeze-dried foods.
Deteriorate: Decrease in quality.

Discoloration: Losing original coloration.
Distribute: To lay out a substance or weight evenly over a surface.
Double Blaze: Two blazes aligned vertically to signal a sharp turn in the Trail.
Drain line: Thin plastic tube used to drain water out of a machine.
Dromedary Bag: Large collapsible water container.
Droppin' Trout: Taking down your pants. Shouted as a warning to other hikers in a shelter that you are about to change clothes.
Dry cycle: Interval of time in which drying takes place.

E **Edible:** Safe to eat.

F **False Summit:** Sense of approaching the summit and then realize it is only a small plateau.
FKT: 'Fastest Known Time'. The speed record held for completing the Appalachian Trail either 'supported' or 'unsupported'.
Flip-flop: Thought of as hiking the Trail in two separate 'halves' instead of one continuous stretch.
Food grade: A material that is safe for the storage of food products.
Footprint: Separate 'floor' of your tent used as a groundcloth or additional protective barrier.
Freeze cycle: Interval of time in which freezing takes place.
Freeze-drying: The process of removing water from food through freezing, heating, and sublimation.
Freezer burn: The loss of moisture from frozen foods, leaving the food shriveled.

G **Gaitors:** Leggings used to protect your shins and ankles from thick brush or prevent water from draining into your feet.
Gap: Low spot on a ridge line in between mountains.
Gas: Vaporous state of a liquid or solid.
Gasket: A rubber seal used to make a joint airtight.
GORP: "Granola, Oats, Raisins and Peanuts" or "Good Ole Raisins and Peanuts". Also called 'Trail Mix'.
Green Tunnel: The Appalachian Trail. Referring to the heavily wooded green forests that the Trail snakes through.
Guylines: Chord or rope used to tie down the tent or tarp.

H **Hiker Box:** Box of freebies. Generally leftover food or gear from previous hikers located in hostels or shelters.
Hiker Trash: Tongue-and-cheek term for thru-hikers. After a week on the Trail, we have been (proudly?) known to resemble vagrants.
Hostel: Trail town lodging. Like a hotel with bunk beds.
Humidity: Degree of moisture in the atmosphere.
Huts: Large cabins mostly associated with being in the White Mountains and organized by the ATC.
HYOH: 'Hike Your Own Hike' expression.

I **Impulse sealer:** A machine used to seal plastic using heat.

K **Kindling:** Small firewood used to ignite a fire.
Knob: Small mountain or rounded hill.

L **Lean-to:** Simple shelter structure comprised of a roof angled at a 45 degrees. Generally only has 3 walls.
Life-sustaining shelf-life: The time until a food product is not safe to consume.
Lightweight: Less than average weight.
Liquid: Fluid state of a product.
Logbook: Every shelter has a register. Used as a record for safety of last known location. Also used to communicate with other hikers.
Lubricant: Substance used to oil components to prevent friction.

M **Mercury:** A liquid, heavy metallic element.
Microorganisms: Organisms invisible to the naked eye.
Minerals: Elements found on earth and in food essential for bodily health and growth.
Moisture: Small quantities of condensed liquid, typically water.
Molecules: A tiny particle of a substance composed of one or more atoms.
MTorr (T): A very small pressure unit used to measure vacuum pressure.
Mylar bags: Food-grade plastic bags used to store dry food.

N **NERO:** "Near Zero" day. Hiking only a mile or less.
NOBO: Northbound hiker. Georgia to Maine.
Nutrition content: The number of healthy vitamins and minerals contained in food.

O **O-rings:** Rubber rings used to seal fittings, making them airtight.
Outlet: Receptacle for an electronic plug.
Oxidize: To introduce oxygen.
Oxygen Absorbers: A sealed sachet that contains iron fillings used to absorb oxygen from sealed containers. Used for freeze-drying.

P **Pocket Rocket:** Trademarked named for an MSR stove. Has become a generic term for a small foldable canister stove top.
Postholing: Process of stepping in snow and leaving a hole.
Pre-freezing: To freeze foods 24-48 hours before freezing them to a lower temperature in the freeze-dryer.
Predetermined: A direction or decision made before the process begins.
Preservation: The act of prolonging the life of food.
Pressure: The force exerted on a surface.

Privy: Bathroom at a shelter. Most of the time a simple wooden outhouse with a composting toilet hole.

Proteins: A molecule made up of amino acids, enzymes, and antibodies.

PUDs: 'Pointless Ups and Downs'. Referring to the rolling nature of the trail.

R **Reconstitute:** To restore food to its original condition by adding water.

Rehydrate: To add moisture back into a product.

Residual: The small amount of a substance that remains after most of it has been removed.

Retains: Holds in a substance.

Ridge-runner: Somewhat like an informal Park Ranger. Generally a volunteer interested in promoting respect for the Trail.

Roast: Cook by exposing to surrounding heat, as in an oven.

S **Sauté:** Fry food in a small amount of fat, water, or other liquid.

Scramble: Type of 'hands and knees' hiking in steep or rocky sections where walking is not an option. See Mihousac Notch.

Sealer: A piece of machinery used to seal containers through a vacuum or heat.

Section Hiker: Someone who hikes the Appalachian Trial in sections over a longer period of time than a continuous thru-hike.

Serving size: Recommended portion of food for a meal.

Shelf-life: Period of time in which a product can be stored and remain edible.

Shelter: Simple wooden structures scattered every 10-20 miles along the entire Trail. Most hold around 8-12 hikers.

Silica Gel: A type of desiccant that is used to remove moisture from packaged items. Not for use with freeze-dried foods.

Silicone: A flexible water and heat-resistant substance that is used to create molds.

Slack Packing: Not carrying gear for the day, Getting dropped at Trailhead A in the morning & picked up at Trailhead B in the afternoon.

SOBO: Southbound hiker. Maine to Georgia.

Solid: The hard state of a substance.

Spoil: To lose all valuable nutrients and quality.

Stealth Camping: Camping in a site that has not been used as a campsite before.

Sublimation: The process of water passing directly from a solid to a vapor state, bypassing the liquid state.

Substitution: To replace one product with another similar product.

Suction: The act of removing a substance, such as air, from a container.

Switch Back: Used to zig-zag and lengthen the trail for a more moderate incline instead of hiking straight up a very steep incline.

T **Tare:** To adjust the scale to make the weight of the container 0.

Thru Hiker: One who hikes the Trail in one continuous run or within a year time frame.

Torr (t): A unit of pressure measured in millimeters of mercury.

Townie: 'Dayhikers', 'Bathers' or people from town.

Trail Angel: Giver of Trail Magic. A volunteer who helps hikers with a place to stay, a shuttle to the trail head, free food, anything.

Trail Magic: Given by Trail Angels. The goodies a Trail Angel offers out of goodwill.

Trail Name: Name a hiker goes by on the Trail. A sort of 'alter-ego'. Almost all hikers go by a trail name.

Trailhead: Where a section of trail begins. Usually at a road crossing.

Treeing a Bear: Act of surprising a bear and it sliding down a tree.

Triple Crown: Three major USA hiking trails: The Appalachian Trail, The Pacific Crest Trail, The Continental Divide Trail. One who completes all three is known as a 'Triple Crowner'.

Triple point: The temperature and pressure at which water can be a solid, liquid, or gas.

U **UL:** 'Ultralight'. A minimalist backpacking mentality.

V **Vacuum pump:** A machine that creates a low-pressure environment by removing air.

Valve: Mechanical device which stops or starts the flow of liquid or air.

Ventilation: Circulation of air.

Versatile: Something that can be used in many ways.

Vestibule: Porch of a tent.

Vitamins: Organic compounds that are beneficial for growth and nutrition.

Volume: Measurement of liquid content.

W **Warp:** Curving or bending of a straight surface.

Webwalking: Taking the lead for the group and walking through all of the fresh spider webs.

White Blaze: The iconic blaze that marks the Appalachian Trail.

Wicking: The process of absorbing or moving liquid by capillary action.

Widowmaker: Dead tree waiting to fall and make a widow out of the unsuspecting hiker's wife.

Work For Stay: Instead of paying for a room, at select hostels and huts, many hikers choose to work or volunteer for a few hours.

Y **Yellow Blazing:** Driving to the next trail head and essentially skipping a chunk of hiking. Opposite of 'purist'.

Z **ZERO Day:** Lazy and luxurious days of hiking zero miles.

REFERENCES

Text References

Allcot, D. (2015, May 13). 10 items to have in your emergency Bag. Lotsa Helping Hands.
https://lotsahelpinghands.com/blog/emergency-bag/

Altai. (2021, September 4). What you need to pack for a week-long camping trip. Altai Gear.
https://altaigear.com/what-you-need-to-pack-for-a-week-long-camping-trip/

American Red Cross. (2018). Survival kit supplies. Redcross.
https://www.redcross.org/get-help/how-to-prepare-for-emergencies/survival-kit-supplies.html

Andrea. (2018, December 17). Hiking risks and the mistakes hikers make. Embracing the Wind. https://embracingthewind.com/hiking-risks/

Aqua-Calc. (2020). Online Food Calculator. Food Volume to Weight Conversions. Aqua-Calc.com.
https://www.aqua-calc.com/calculate/food-volume-to-weight

Asorson, E. (n.d.). 5-Day ultralight backpacking meal plan. Erik the Blacks' Backpacking Blog.
https://blackwoodspress.com/blog/16547/ultralight-backpacking-meal-plan/

B, A. (2020, June 23). 12 Tips for better sleep while backpacking. Exploring Wild. https://exploringwild.com/sleep-better-while-backpacking/

Backpacker. (2020, September 10). The essential rules of backpacking nutrition. Backpacker.
https://www.backpacker.com/skills/the-essential-rules-of-performance-nutrition/

Borg, C. (2021, June 16). Hiking for beginners on a budget. Outforia. https://outforia.com/hiking-for-beginners-on-a-budget/

Bryant, C. (2008, January 7). How to find water in the wild. MapQuest Travel.
https://www.mapquest.com/travel/survival/wilderness/how-to-find-water.htm

Cabotaje, A. (2020, August 17). 8 wilderness survival tips. Right as Rain.
https://rightasrain.uwmedicine.org/life/leisure/wilderness-survival-tips

Cage, C. (2021, May 25). How much water to carry: backpacker's guide to hydration. Greenbelly Meals.
https://www.greenbelly.co/pages/how-much-water-should-i-carry-backpacking

Camotrek. (2020, May 17). 14 hiking hazards you should be aware of. Camotrek. https://camotrek.com/blogs/news/hiking-hazards/

Carter, K. (2016, September 28). These benefits of hiking will make you want to hit the trails. Shape.
https://www.shape.com/fitness/cardio/benefits-hiking-will-make-you-want-hit-trails

Collins, D. (2014, September 10). Protect your food - keep wildlife wild. CleverHiker.
https://www.cleverhiker.com/essential-trail-skills/episode-8-protect-your-food-keep-wildlife-wild

Collins, D. (2017, March 5). Top 12 beginner backpacking blunders. CleverHiker.
https://www.cleverhiker.com/blog/top-12-beginner-backpacking-blunders?rq=blunders

Collins, D. (2019, May 24). 21 tips for backpacking on a budget. CleverHiker.
https://www.cleverhiker.com/blog/21-tips-for-backpacking-on-a-budget

Cortazu. (2020, September 4). Solo backpacking tips for beginners. Cortazu.
https://cortazu.com/blogs/news/solo-backpacking-tips-for-beginners

Fernandez, B. (2020, November 11). How to pack food for a backpacking trip: 8 essential tips. Go Backpacking.
https://gobackpacking.com/pack-food-tips/

Fuller, K. (n.d.). Key tips for backpacking meals and food dehydration. The Outbound.
https://www.theoutbound.com/c0f42eece220a3b8a064930978792ad9/key-tips-for-backpacking-meals-and-food-dehydration

Gerber, K. (2020, March 11). Resupply 101 options & tips for food drops on your long-distance hike. Katie Gerber.
http://katiegerber.com/resupply-options-long-distance-hike/

Greenbelly Meals. (n.d.). The Backpacker's Dictionary | 75 hiking Words and terms.
https://www.greenbelly.co/pages/appalachian-trail-backpacking-terms

Hernandez, J. (n.d.). Hiking, the truth about environmentally safe and healthy hiking. Environment.
https://www.environment.co.za/food-health-and-the-environment/environmentally-safe-healthy-hiking.html

House, M. (2023, March 29). Finding water on the trail. Mountain House.
https://mountainhouse.com/blogs/backpacking-hiking/finding-water-on-the-trail

Howard, R. (2016, February 9). Freeze-dried food versus dehydrated food: what's the difference? Harvest Right.
https://harvestright.com/blog/2016/freeze-dried-food-versus-dehydrated-food-whats-the-difference/

Hunter, J. (2019, January 15). The only 4 things you need to survive in the wild. Primal Survivor.
https://www.primalsurvivor.net/how-to-survive-in-the-wild-without-any-supplies/

Jackson, J. (2017, March 23). 6 ways to keep bears away from camp. Outside Online.
https://www.outsideonline.com/outdoor-gear/camping/6-ways-keep-animals-raiding-your-camp-food/

James, J. (2020, November 22). Long-term camping gear list. Survival Freedom.
https://survivalfreedom.com/long-term-camping-gear-list-14-must-have-items/

Jern, M. (2021, March 25). 7 simple ways to go zero-waste and reduce environmental impact while hiking. Tapp Water.
https://tappwater.co/en/zero-waste-hiking-water/

Kates, J. (2020, December 3). Benefits of hiking: physical, mental and beyond. Ace Fitness.
https://www.acefitness.org/resources/everyone/blog/7736/benefits-of-hiking-physical-mental-and-beyond/

Krasomil, N. (2022a, February 19). 2022 optimal setup. The Packable Life.
https://www.thepackablelife.com/hiking/gear/ultralight-backpacking-gear

Krasomil, N. (2022b, October 27). Backpacking food: meal plan tips & ideas for your next hike. The Packable Life.
https://www.thepackablelife.com/hiking/tips/backpacking-food

Krezevska, T. (2015, June 1). Backpacking food storage ideas. Trail Recipes. https://www.trail.recipes/food-planning/backpacking-food-storage-ideas/

LankaXpress. (n.d.). Weather Forecast April 2. https://www.lankaxpress.com/weather-forecast-april-2/

Long, S. (2021, June 19). 10 best backpacking cookware sets in 2022. 99 Boulders. https://www.99boulders.com/best-backpacking-cookware

McKay, B., & McKay, K. (2021, May 16). 9 ways to start a fire without matches. The Art of Manliness. https://www.artofmanliness.com/skills/outdoor-survival/9-ways-to-start-a-fire-without-matches/

McNamara, C. (2023, July 18). Best backpacking gear of 2022. GearLab. https://www.outdoorgearlab.com/topics/camping-and-hiking/best-backpacking-gear

Megan. (2022, August 6). Homemade Electrolyte Powder (easy natural DIY sports drink!). Eat Beautiful. https://eatbeautiful.net/homemade-electrolyte-powder-easy-natural-diy-sports-drink/

Mertins, B. (2018, January 8). How to survive in the wild with nothing. Nature Mentoring. https://nature-mentor.com/how-to-survive-in-the-wild-with-nothing/

Micro-Homesteading Education. (2023). The Only Beginner Freeze Drying Book You'll Ever Need. Book by Micro-Homesteading Education. https://www.micro-homesteading-education.com

MSR Gear. (2020, September 22). How much backpacking stove fuel should I carry? The Summit Register. https://www.msrgear.com/blog/stoves-101-how-much-fuel-should-i-carry/

Nutritionix. (2019). Nutritionix. The Calculators. Nutritionix.com. https://www.nutritionix.com/

NutritionValue. (2019). Nutritional Values For Common Foods And Products. Nutritionvalue.org. https://www.nutritionvalue.org/

Outdoor Herbivore. (2012, January 15). How to cook when backpacking. Outdoor Herbivore. https://blog.outdoorherbivore.com/camp-tips/how to-cook-when-backpacking/

Perera, T. (2022, January 28). Why it's important to stay hydrated while hiking. Nerdy Naut. https://www.nerdynaut.com/why-its-important-to-stay-hydrated-while-hiking

Perry, C. (2023, June 13). How Much Water You Should Drink A Day, According To Experts. Forbes Health. https://www.forbes.com/health/body/how-much-water-you-should-drink-per-day/#footnote_2

PreparedBC. (2020, July 17). Building an emergency kit? think "camping at home". [Video]. YouTube. https://www.youtube.com/watch?v=oPV9MH7xLq4

Rei Co-op. (n.d.-a). Food storage and handling for campers and backpackers. Rei Co-Op. https://www.rei.com/learn/expert-advice/food-handling-storage.html

Rei Co-op. (n.d.-b). Meal planning for backpacking. Rei Co-Op. https://www.rei.com/learn/expert-advice/planning-menu.html

Rei Co-op. (2019, February 5). Backpacking gear list: what to bring on a backpacking trip. Rei Co-Op. https://www.rei.com/learn/expert-advice/backpacking-checklist.html

Richards, A. (2021, February 23). Zero-waste hiking. Outdoors Magic. https://outdoorsmagic.com/article/zero-waste-hiking/

Robbins, L. (2017, May 1). Everything you need to know about water when hiking. Monkeys and Mountains. https://monkeysandmountains.com/drinking-water-when-hiking/

Rogers, K. (2021, December 1). You get lost in the wilderness. Do you know how to survive? CNN. https://edition.cnn.com/travel/article/wilderness-how-to-survive-wellness/index.html

Seitz, D. (2020, February 5). How to find drinkable water in the wild. Popular Science. https://www.popsci.com/story/diy/find-drinkable-water-wild/

Shrader, M. B. (2021, June 17). How to Make a Homemade Electrolyte Drink. Mary's Nest. https://marysnest.com/how-to-make-a-homemade-electrolyte-drink/

Smith, D. (2022, January 11). How to eat your favorite town food on the trail. Backpacking Light. https://backpackinglight.com/freeze-drying-techniques/

The Wandering Queen. (n.d.). Backpacking for Beginners. https://www.thewanderingqueen.com/backpacking-for-beginners/

Very Well Fit. https://www.facebook.com/verywell. (2018). Know more. Be healthier. Verywell Fit. https://www.verywellfit.com/

W, A. (2020, April 10). How much weight should you carry backpacking. Exploration Solo. https://explorationsolo.com/how-much-weight-should-you-carry-backpacking/

Weigh School - Weights, Food & Nutrition. (n.d.). Weigh School. https://weighschool.com/

Werner, P. (2015, July 31). How to pack a lot of backpacking food into a small space. Section Hiker. https://sectionhiker.com/how-to-pack-a-lot-of-backpacking-food-into-a-small-space/

Wonderland Guides. (2015, October 19). Tips for re-hydrating dried foods in the backcountry. Wonderland Guides. https://www.wonderlandguides.com/backcountry-cooking/dehydrating-food/tips-for-re-hydrating-dried-foods-in-the-backcountry

Woods, S. D. (2020, March 16). The best items to stock for any emergency, according to survivalists. The Strategist. https://nymag.com/strategist/article/best-emergency-kit-items.html

World Health Organization. (2020, April 29). Healthy diet. World Health Organisation. https://www.who.int/news-room/fact-sheets/detail/healthy-die

Image References

Cleanwaste. (n.d.). Wag Bag [Photograph]. Retrieved from https://www.nrs.com/cleanwaste-wag-bags/pvf9

Nepalidevu. (2021, July 11). *Mountain hiking* [Image]. Pixabay. https://pixabay.com/photos/mount-everest-mountains-trekking-6395759/

Gareth Hubbard. (2020, June 3). *Vegetables on wooden table* [Image]. Unsplash. https://unsplash.com/photos/qPcSUERqBAc

Gold, D. (2017, June 30). *Vegetable mix* [Image]. Unsplash. https://unsplash.com/photos/4_jhDO54BYg

Gonullu, M. (2020, December 10). *Impulse sealer* [Image]. Pexels. https://www.pexels.com/photo/bag-sealer-near-piles-of-cardboard-boxes-in-storehouse-6152271/

Grabowska, K. (2020, April 14). *Spice spoons* [Image]. Pexels.
> https://www.pexels.com/photo/composition-of-spoonfuls-with-various-spices-4199098/

Jens Johnsson. (2016, March 28). *Scooping water using a green cup* [Image]. Pexels.
> https://www.pexels.com/photo/person-scooping-water-using-green-cup-66090/

Kal Visuals. (2018, August 2). *Maps* [Image]. Unsplash. https://unsplash.com/photos/3sVhudiAl84

Lumen. (2015, July 6). *Camping pots* [Image]. Pixabay. https://pixabay.com/photos/fire-campfire-tent-camp-warehouse-832842/

Lukas Robertson. (2017, January 16). *Hiking backpacks in a truck bed* [Image]. Unsplash. https://unsplash.com/photos/9qJb_wCFCrM

Maminounou. (2023, May 16). *Mountain lions* [Image]. Pixabay. https://pixabay.com/photos/puma-picture-animals-cougar-7997999/

Riya26. (2020, July 28). *Night camping* [Image]. Pixabay. https://pixabay.com/photos/tent-camping-hills-man-silhouette-5441144/

Schoefolt, P. (2022, February 20). *Sleeping bear* [Image]. Pexels.
> https://www.pexels.com/photo/a-brown-bear-sleeping-on-the-grass-11245582/

Shopify Partners. (n.d.-a). *Building a campfire* [Image]. Burst.
> https://burst.shopify.com/photos/building-a-fire-in-front-of-tent?q=building+campfire

Shopify Partners. (n.d.-b). *Camping pocket survival kit* [Image]. Burst.
> https://burst.shopify.com/photos/camping-pocket-survival-kit-flatlay?q=survival+pack

Shopify Partners. (n.d.-c). *Kitchen tools* [Image]. Burst. https://burst.shopify.com/photos/kitchen-ready-for-cooking?q=kitchen+tools

Shopify Partners. (n.d.-d). *Row of camping tents* [Image]. Burst. https://burst.shopify.com/photos/row-of-camping-tents?q=camping+gear

Shutov, M. (2018, November 25). *Trail mix* [Image]. Unsplash. https://unsplash.com/photos/pUa1On18Jno

Stevepb. (2015, August 28). *First aid kit* [Image]. Pixabay. https://pixabay.com/photos/first-aid-kit-first-aid-kit-medical-908591/

Van Sant, E. (2018, February 1). *Hiking boots* [Image]. Unsplash. https://unsplash.com/photos/n8V1Zht4U54

Young Lee, S. (n.d.). *Cooking on gas* [Image]. Burst. https://burst.shopify.com/photos/cooking-on-gas?q=camping+gear

OpenAI. (2024). ChatGPT (March DALL·E) [Images]. https://chat.openai.com. First aid case, Recipes include Egg Roll in a Bowl, Blueberry Lemon Granola, Beef Bulgogi, Pork Carnitas, Pork Lo Mein, Spicy Pork Chili, Lemon Herb Chicken, Beef Vegetable Soup, Vegetable Barley Soup, Chicken Noodle Soup, Creamy Salmon & Dill Soup, Spicy Shrimp & Corn Chowder, Thai Coconut Curry Soup, Southwest Black Bean Soup, Cauliflower Bites, and Mixed Fruit Medley. Other items are Salsa, Marshmallows, Creamy Ice Cream, Oil-Free Brownie Bites, Cold Brew Coffee, Fruit Juices, Vegetable Juices, Greens Juices, Citrus Juices, Carrot Juice, Prune Juice, Pineapple Juice, Tomato Juice, Milk, Chocolate Milk, Strawberry Milk, Oat Milk, Rice Milk, Bone Broth, Vegetable Broth, Coconut Water, and Smoothies.

Canva. (2024). Canva for Teams [Images]. https://www.canva.com/. Hot water pouring into a Mylar bag of freeze-dried food, campfire with Mylar bags, 9 containers of chopped food, kitchen scale, kcal green square, microfiber cloth, solar battery charger and phone, Tarp tent between two trees, Food sealer with pistacio nuts in bags, Beef Chili Label, Contour map, Hiker at supply point, Happy Blue Water Droplet, Arm with Muscles, Orange temt, Two empty canning jars, Beef Jerky, Open Metal Cans of Vegetables, Chopper, 45F to 75F, Two camping stoves, Oil pouring out of a jug, Drawing of taking notes, Spinach Sunrise Skillet, Savory Sausage Scramble, Classic Ham and Egg Quiche, Hearty Breakfast Casserole, Banana Pancakes, Cornmeal Muffin Bites, Chocolate Muffin Bites, Chocolate Raspberry Chia Seed Pudding, Vegetarian Quinoa Casserole, Hamburger Mac, Chicken Salad, Loaded Veggie Shepherd's Pie, Grilled Cheese, Chicken Korma, Beef Stroganoff, Pad Thai, Chicken Alfredo Pasta, Herbed Mushroom Risotto, Meat Lovers Chili, Beef & Barley Stew, Cheesy Macaroni, Fried Rice, Beef Stew, Tomato Soup, Lentil, Sausage & Potato Soup, Lentil Soup, Seafood Chowder, Spicy Chicken Tortilla Soup, Broccoli Cheddar Soup, Tuscan White Bean Soup, Minestrone Soup, Tomato Basil Soup, Creamy Mushroom Soup, Cheese, Pear Sauce, Ranch Dip, Yogurt Drops, Ice Cream Sandwiches Mini Cookies, Lemon Burst Cookies, Mini Ice Cream Cones, Cardamom Cold Brew Coffee, Spiced Cold Brew Coffee, Vanilla Cold Brew Coffee, Mocha Cold Brew Coffee, and Electrolyte Drink.

Contracted Images:

Front Cover: Images from Roman Dolgikh from Unsplash, design by: ritasriharningsih from 99Designs and Christina Jewell of MHE.

Dobson, Rebecca. Denver Delight Quiche, Cinnamon Roll Bites, Grilled Cheese Bites, Sloppy Joe Casserole, Classic Chili, Vegetable Medley Protein Soup, Potato Leek Soup, Pumpkin Soup, Blueberry Applesauce, Pineapple Sauce, Butterscotch Pudding, and Strawberry Pudding.

Harston, Nancy. Breakfast Brunch, Ham Brunch, Berries and Cream Oatmeal, Apple Pie Oatmeal, Blueberry Vanilla Pudding, Mango Coconut Pudding, Hearty Pancakes, Mexican Enchilada Casserole, Chicken and Rice Casserole, Tuna Noodle Casserole, Basil Chicken Stir Fry, Ground Turkey Sweet Potato Skillet, Chicken Quesadilla Strips, Beef Quesadilla Strips, Vegetable Quesadilla Strips, Vegetarian Chili, Sweet and Sour Pork, Zucchini Parmesan, Lazy Lasagna, Beef Bulgogi, Rice and Vegetable Medley, Steak Strips and Vegetables, Beef Noodle Soup, Sweet Potato Cubes, Quick 'n' Easy Peach Cobbler, Lemon Tea Bread Bites, and Zucchini Cake Bites.

Jewell, Christina. Author bio picture, freeze-dryer with shelves taken out, removing silicone gasket on freeze-dryer, Bear hang, bags of freeze-dried food in Mylar bags, and a woman in the woods holding freeze-dried chicken salad. Meals going into the freeze-dryer, meals coming out of the freeze-dryer, and a backpack in the woods with Mylar bags and a personal camp stove. A chopper cutting onion, a chopper cutting mushroom, and chicken noodle soup going in the freeze-dryer. Hot water pouring into a Mylar bag of freeze-dried food, Mylar bags on a camping table with a personal stove, Italian Wedding Soup, Drizzled Banana Crisps, Creamsicle Cubes, Tropical Mango Smoothie Cubes, Mixed-Berry Smoothie Cubes.

Prickett, Katilyn. Oil change on pump, freeze-dried fruit medley, empty chamber with ice, empty chamber, roller berry tool, tray scoop, trays with silicone mats and parchment, drawer of MRE pouches and oxygen absorbers, tray lids, trays with stackers, pantry with totes and freeze-dryer, FoodSaver with attachment and freeze-dried eggs, freeze-dried skittles, freeze-dried carmel m&ms, and freeze-dried taffy.

AUTHOR BIO

The authors of this book are passionate advocates of self-sustainability and micro-homesteading. With over 35 years of combined experience in horticulture, gardening, animal husbandry, and food preservation, they bring a wealth of knowledge to help readers achieve food stability and self-sustainability without feeling overwhelmed.

Micro-Homesteading Education believes in the power of small steps and starting where you are. Their mission is to share information and practical tips on growing nutritious food, raising healthy animals, creating a micro-homestead, and preserving the harvest. They understand the joy that comes from seeing plants thrive and pantries filled with homemade, mouth-watering meals.

Katilyn Prickett & Christina Jewell

With a deep commitment to sharing their knowledge, Micro-Homesteading Education takes extra care to provide information suitable for beginners while maintaining a thorough approach. Their goal is to support readers in learning various homesteading skills by breaking down complex topics into manageable steps.

Join Micro-Homesteading Education on this educational and inspiring journey, where you'll learn simple yet effective ways to grow, raise, and preserve your food. Discover the satisfaction of cultivating your resources and creating a more sustainable lifestyle for yourself and your family. ♥

Contact Us:

Email: contact@micro-homesteading-education.com
Website: www.micro-homesteading-education.com

Facebook Groups & Pages

www.facebook.com/microhomesteadingeducationcom
www.facebook.com/groups/foodpreservationwithfreezedrying

Scan the QR code or visit the shortcut to
Facebook Group: FDFB.2MHE.COM.